The Music of Tōru Takemitsu

Tōru Takemitsu (1930–96) was the best known Japanese composer of his
generation, bringing aspects of Eastern and Western traditions together, yet he
remained something of an elusive figure. The composer's own commentaries
about his music, poetic and philosophical in tone, have tended to deepen the
mystery and much writing on Takemitsu to date has adopted a similar attitude,
leaving many questions about his compositional methods unanswered. This book
is the first complete study of the composer's work to appear in English. It is also
the first book in this language to offer an in-depth analysis of his music.
Takemitsu's works are increasingly popular with Western audiences and Peter
Burt attempts for the first time to shed light on the hitherto rather secretive world
of his working methods, as well as place him in context as heir to the rich tradition
of Japanese composition in the twentieth century.

PETER BURT is Vice-Chairman of the Takemitsu Society in the United Kingdom
and editor of the Takemitsu Society Newsletter. He is currently editing a special
commemorative issue of *Contemporary Music Review* devoted to Tōru Takemitsu.

Music in the Twentieth Century

GENERAL EDITOR   Arnold Whittall

This series offers a wide perspective on music and musical life in the twentieth century. Books included range from historical and biographical studies concentrating particularly on the context and circumstances in which composers were writing, to analytical and critical studies concerned with the nature of musical language and questions of compositional process. The importance given to context will also be reflected in studies dealing with, for example, the patronage, publishing, and promotion of new music, and in accounts of the musical life of particular countries.

Recently published titles

The Music of Conlon Nancarrow
Kyle Gann
0 521 46534 6

The Stravinsky Legacy
Jonathan Cross
0 521 56365 8

Experimental Music: Cage and Beyond
Michael Nyman
0 521 65297 9
0 521 65383 5

The BBC and Ultra-Modern Music, 1922–1936
Jennifer Doctor
0 521 66117 X

The Music of Harrison Birtwistle
Robert Adlington
0 521 63082 7

Four Musical Minimalists: La Monte Young, Terry Riley, Steve Reich, Philip Glass
Keith Potter
0 521 48250 X

Fauré and French Musical Aesthetics
Carlo Caballero
0 521 78107 8

The Music of Tōru Takemitsu
Peter Burt
0 521 78220 1

The Music of
Tōru Takemitsu

Peter Burt

DATE DUE

CAMBRIDGE
UNIVERSITY PRESS

CAMBRIDGE UNIVERSITY PRESS
Cambridge, New York, Melbourne, Madrid, Cape Town, Singapore, São Paulo

Cambridge University Press
The Edinburgh Building, Cambridge CB2 2RU, UK

Published in the United States of America by Cambridge University Press, New York

www.cambridge.org
Information on this title: www.cambridge.org/9780521782203

First published 2001
Reprinted 2003
This digitally printed first paperback version 2006

A catalogue record for this publication is available from the British Library

Library of Congress Cataloguing in Publication data

Burt, Peter, 1955–
The music of Tōru Takemitsu / Peter Burt.
    p.   cm. – (Music in the twentieth century)
Includes bibliographical references (p.   ) and index.
ISBN 0 521 78220 1
1. Takemitsu, Tōru – Criticism and interpretation.   I. Title.   II. Series.
ML410.T134 B87   2001
780′.92–dc21   00-045505

ISBN-13 978-0-521-78220-3 hardback
ISBN-10 0-521-78220-1 hardback

ISBN-13 978-0-521-02695-6 paperback
ISBN-10 0-521-02695-4 paperback

for Sumine

Contents

Acknowledgements

So many have helped me in some way or another over the course of the seven years that I have been working on Takemitsu's music that there are bound to be some omissions in the list of names that follow. In particular in Japan, where fabulous largesse seems to be a cultural norm, I have received such generous assistance from so many people that I am certain to have forgotten to mention one or two here, and I apologise in advance to anyone who feels they have been left out.

Although wholly rewritten, this book has its origins in my doctoral thesis, and in the first place thanks are therefore due to my supervisor, Peter Manning, and other members of the music department staff at Durham University who assisted me in various ways – in particular my benefactor Michael Spitzer, who offered magnanimous hospitality whenever I needed to seek shelter in Durham during my two years of exile in London. Thanks are also due to Professor Manning for his assistance in procuring me two valuable scholarships – from the Japan Foundation Endowment Committee, and the Gen Foundation – and of course to the staff of those institutions themselves for enabling me to make the two trips to Japan without which my knowledge of Takemitsu would have remained vague and incomplete indeed.

In Japan, my sincere appreciation is due to the former Principal of Kunitachi College of Music, Dr Bin Ebisawa, as well as staff members Cornelia Colyer and Hitoshi Matsushita, the librarian, for providing me with such a royal welcome during the disorientating early days of my first visit. I would also particularly like to thank the fellow researchers in my chosen field who have been so generous in sharing with me the fruits of their knowledge: Yōko Narazaki, Noriko Ohtake and above all Mitsuko Ono, a sort of walking encyclopaedia on Takemitsu who has been of invaluable help in correcting my many factual errors. Further gratitude is due especially to the flautist Hideyo Takakawa for introducing me to his teacher Mr Hiroshi Koizumi, and to him in turn for first introducing me to the composer's widow Mrs Asaka Takemitsu and daughter Maki. I would also like to thank the composer Mr Jōji Yuasa for granting me the time to interview him about his early years with Takemitsu in the *Jikken Kōbō*, and Fr. Joaquim Benitez of Elisabeth University, Hiroshima, who kindly agreed to meet me in London and look over my thesis three years ago. Takebumi

Itagaki, Kiyonori Sokabe, Masato Hōjō and Yūji Numano have also all been of invaluable assistance, and above all, perhaps, I must express my deepest gratitude to Ms Sumine Hayashibara and her mother Kiku on the one hand, and Ms Emiko Kitazawa and her mother Etsuko on the other, without whose offers of hospitality on, respectively, my first and second visits to Japan I would have been unable to come here at all.

I must also mention here my friend Junko Kobayashi, Chairman of the Takemitsu Society in London, who has been so helpful in checking over Japanese proper nouns with me; as well as Sally Groves of Schott's and her Tōkyō counterpart, Nanako Ikefuji, for lending me scores of Takemitsu's music. And finally, I must thank the music books' Editor of Cambridge University Press, Penny Souster, for having sufficient faith in the potential of my thesis to undertake a book on Takemitsu. I hope what follows will in some small measure repay the trust she has invested in me.

Tōkyō, July 2000

The author gratefully acknowledges the permission of the following publishers to quote copyright materials in the music examples:

Examples 31, 34 from *Sacrifice* and 43–6 from *The Dorian Horizon* ©1967 by Ongaku no Tomo Sha Corp.; used by permission

Examples 53–5 from *Asterism* (Edition Peters No. 6630064, ©1969 by C F Peters Corporation, New York), 56, 57 from *November Steps* (Edition Peters No. 66299, ©1967 by C F Peters Corporation, New York) and 57–62, 64 from *Green* (Edition Peters No. 66300, ©1969 by C F Peters Corporation, New York) reproduced by kind permission of Peters Edition Limited, London

Examples 47 (Webern), 83(v), 105(i) and 118(ii) copyright Universal Edition AG (Wien); reproduced by permission of Alfred A. Kalmus Ltd

Examples 9–11, 13, 18, 19, 21–7, 37–9, 47 (Takemitsu), 48, 50–2, 65–7, 69, 70, 72–4, 76–80, 81(i), 83(iv), 84(i), 85(i), 86(i), 89, 90, 91(i–iii), 120(i), 129, 134 reproduced by permission of Editions Salabert, Paris/United Music Publishers Ltd

Examples 82(i–ii), 83(ii) reproduced by permission of Editions Alphonse Leduc, Paris/United Music Publishers Ltd

Examples 82(iii), 83(i, iii), 84(ii), 85(ii), 86(ii–iii) reproduced by permission of Editions Durand S.A. Paris/United Music Publishers Ltd

Examples 1–3, 5, 6, 16, 17, 40–2, 81(ii–iii), 87, 91(iv–xii), 92–9, 101, 105(ii), 106–12, 114–15, 117, 118(i), 119, 120(ii–v), 122–3, 125–6, 128, 130–3 reproduced by permission of Schott & Co., Ltd

Note on conventions

Throughout this book, Japanese personal names are rendered according to the Western rather than Japanese convention, in which the family name follows the given name (Tōru Takemitsu, *not* Takemitsu Tōru). Transliteration of Japanese words follows the Hepburn system, and in the interests of consistency – albeit at the risk of appearing pretentious – this has been applied even to words generally given in English without diacritical marks (Tōkyō, Ōsaka, etc.).

Introduction

The title of this book is 'The *Music* of Tōru Takemitsu', and despite the many other fascinating issues, biographical and artistic, that it is tempting to explore in an examination of this many-faceted genius – composer, festival organiser, writer on aesthetics, author of detective novels, celebrity chef on Japanese TV – it is with Takemitsu's legacy as a composer that the following chapters are predominantly concerned. In fact, the book's scope is even narrower still, for although Takemitsu, as the worklist at the end of this volume will show, produced a vast amount of music for film, theatre, television and radio as well as a number of other pieces of more 'populist' character, such works lie beyond the remit of the present study, which for the most part deals only with the composer's 'classical' scores for the concert platform. Right from the start, however, it should be emphasised that such an approach focuses on only a small area of Takemitsu's versatile creativity, and it should always be borne in mind that these other areas of activity were an ever-present backdrop to his 'mainstream' work, interacting fruitfully with the latter in ways which it has been possible to hint at in the following pages, but – regretfully – not examine in more detail.

The bulk of this work, then – chapters 2 to 11 – is concerned with descriptions of Takemitsu's music for the concert room, examining the principal scores in roughly chronological sequence, and including a certain amount of biographical information to set them in context. Though this section is continuous, the reader will probably soon realise that the arrangement of these chapters reflects an implicit, provisional division of the composer's career into three 'periods', dealt with respectively in chapters 2–4, 5–8 and 9–11 of the book. Although rather schematic and certainly no watertight compartmentalisation, this periodisation is nevertheless one which, in its broad outlines at least, would appear to find support amongst other writers on the subject. Certainly the suggested transition from 'second' to 'third' period represented, as we shall see, a change of style so dramatic that it has been hard for commentators to miss it: Yōko Narazaki, for instance, who divides the composer's music into two periods, speaks of a 'change from an "avant-garde" to a "conservative" style'[1] around the end of the 1970s; Jun-ichi Konuma, more robustly, of a substitution of 'eroticism' for 'stoicism' in the composer's *Quatrain* of 1975.[2]

On this basis, it is true, it might be argued that a bipartite scheme, hinging on the incontrovertible fact of this obvious stylistic conversion, constitutes an adequate working description of the composer's development, and that further sub-division would be hair-splitting and superfluous. Nevertheless, I feel that there is a second, if less spectacular, distinction to be made between the *juvenilia* from the first decade of Takemitsu's composing career (from 1950 onwards), and the works which succeeded them from around the turn of the 1960s. The 'journeyman' works from the period prior to this point are of interest insomuch as they reflect, in their purest form, the stylistic imprints of those American and European composers by whom Takemitsu was initially most profoundly influenced in his rather isolated situation in post-war Japan. By contrast, the works from around 1960 onwards reveal a very rapid assimilation of all the preoccupations Takemitsu became aware of as his knowledge of the domestic and international music scene enlarged dramatically – not only those of the modernist avant-garde, but also, and most importantly, of John Cage and, through his influence, of traditional Japanese music. The change wrought upon the musical language of the 'first period' by these powerful outside influences has not escaped the attention of other writers on the subject: Yukiko Sawabe, for instance, certainly agrees on the appearance of at least two new elements in Takemitsu's music around 1960, 'traditional Japanese instruments and the discovery of "nature" in music, a discovery in which the composer was encouraged by his encounter with John Cage'.[3] Broadly speaking, too, the rather simplistic-sounding picture of the composer's career as a 'beginning–middle–end' triptych that emerges from the addition of this second transitional point is not without support from other commentators. Although he locates the two turning points in 1957 and 1973/4, for instance, Kenjiro Miyamoto's tripartite scheme is in other respects more or less identical with my own;[4] while both Takashi Funayama[5] and Miyuki Shiraishi,[6] speak, less specifically, of 'early, middle and late periods' in the composer's work.

The approach adopted towards Takemitsu's music in the course of these central chapters is, the reader will soon realise, primarily an analytical one. This to a certain extent reflects the perceptual biases and academic training of the author, and in particular the origins of this book in my own doctoral thesis, rather than any intrinsic advantages such a method might have when applied to Takemitsu's music. In fact, the latter is emphatically *not* carefully put together for the benefit of future academics to take apart again, and analytic approaches towards it therefore have a tendency to take the researcher up what eventually proves to be a blind alley. Takemitsu's own writing about music, significantly, rarely gives away any technical information about his musical construction or contains music-type examples, concerning itself instead with abstract philosophical problems expressed in a flowery and poetic language, and many commentators – particularly in Japan – have followed his example in dealing with the music on this level, rather than venturing into the murkier waters of his actual compositional method. One has the feeling, therefore, that one is going against the grain of the composer's own preferred concept of appropriate descriptive language by attempting to submit his music to dissection with the precision tools of Western analysis, and is perhaps justly rewarded with a certain ultimate impenetrability.

Nevertheless, as I have explained elsewhere,[7] I do not believe that one should for this reason be deterred from making the effort to understand Takemitsu's music on a more technical level. Such an enterprise, I would suggest, is well worth undertaking, for two reasons in particular. First, despite its shortcomings, it is able to uncover a good deal of the still rather secretive goings-on behind the surface of Takemitsu's music, as the following pages will reveal. And secondly, by its very impotence to explain the whole of Takemitsu's creative thinking, it illustrates the extent to which the construction of his music is governed by decisions of a more 'irrational' nature, which even the most inventive of scholars is powerless to account for. Mapping out the area which *is* tractable to analysis, in other words, at the same time gives the measure of that vaster territory which is *not*.

Why this should be so, why Takemitsu's music should ultimately resist analytical explanation, is a question to which I attempt to give some answers in my twelfth and final chapter, which steps outside the bounds of the remit I claimed for this book at the beginning of this introduction to examine some of the more abstract and philosophical issues surrounding his work: offering an assessment of his status as a composer, an examination of some of his aesthetic views (to the extent that I understand them), and an evaluation of some of the more frequent criticisms to which he has been subject. The other place where my subject matter transgresses beyond the bounds of my own self-imposed limitations is at the very beginning of the book. To understand fully the nature of Takemitsu's achievement, it is necessary to see him not only in relation to the international Western music scene, but also in relation to the aesthetic preoccupations of the composers who preceded him in the decades since Western music was first introduced to Japan. As, however, this is a history for the most part almost entirely unfamiliar to Westerners, it has been considered imperative to give a brief overview of the subject in the opening chapter. It is with this pre-history, then – the story of the arrival of Western music in Japan and the development of Japanese composition that succeeded it – that *The Music of Tōru Takemitsu* begins.

1 Pre-history: how Western music came to Japan

Popular culture has ensured that at least one or two key elements in the story of Japan's unique and often turbulent relationship with the Western world have become familiar to a wider audience. Stephen Sondheim's 1975 musical *Pacific Overtures*, for instance, charts the course of events subsequent to that momentous day in the nineteenth century when Japan was finally rudely awakened from its quarter-millennium of feudal stability by a dramatic intervention of modernity. The day in question was 8 July 1853, when Commodore Matthew Calbraith Perry of the United States Navy sailed into Uraga harbour with his powerfully armed ironclad steamboats, the *kurofune* ('black ships'); and to understand the boldness and historical significance of Perry's adventure, one has to travel back in time a quarter of a millennium further still, to 1603. For it was in that year that Ieyasu Tokugawa finally acceded to an office familiar to Westerners, once again, from populist sources, in this case James Clavell's 1975 novel and its subsequent film and television versions: the title of military dictator of all Japan, or *Shōgun*.

Having attained this sovereign position at great cost by finally subjugating the powerful regional warlords (*daimyō*), the Tokugawa family was understandably anxious to preserve the fragile centralised power it had established. In particular, wary of the colonial ambitions of the foreign nationals then resident in Japan – and of any alliance between these and their *daimyō* subordinates – they embarked on a campaign of draconian measures to protect their country from the perceived alien menace. Japanese Christians were martyred, foreign nationals repatriated, and the Japanese themselves forbidden to travel abroad, until by 1641 no contact with the outside world remained except for a small community of Dutch traders confined to their island ghetto of Deshima in Nagasaki harbour. Japan, allowing its subjects no egress and outsiders no ingress, had succeeded within a few decades in turning itself into a self-contained 'hermit kingdom', and henceforth would enforce the most stringent measures to ensure that – right up to the arrival of Perry's ships over two hundred years later – this exclusion policy would remain virtually inviolate.

'Virtually' inviolate, but not entirely so; despite the dire penalties risked by those who sought to transgress against the exclusion order, from the eighteenth century onwards various seafarers – Russian, American, British, French and Dutch – all made efforts to persuade the Japanese to reopen their country to foreign commerce. Furthermore, while the Japanese could not travel to the outside world, or make contact with its inhabitants, the educated classes, at least, could read about what was happening there – at first secretly, as various items of information were smuggled in through approved Dutch and Chinese traders, and then more openly, after the *Shōgun* Yoshimune (1716–45) rescinded the ban on the importation of foreign books (provided they contained no reference to Christian teaching) in 1720. As a result of this new development, there eventually came into existence the group known as the *rangakusha* or 'Dutch Scholars', whose painstaking efforts to translate works written in that language, starting from scratch, finally bore fruit when the first European work to be published in Japan, an anatomy textbook, appeared in 1774. Significantly, besides medicine, the other area of Western expertise about which the Japanese were especially curious was military science – and with good reason. In the following century Takashima Shūhan (1798–1866), who had learned about Western ordnance from textbooks, was to warn the governor of Nagasaki after the British success in the Anglo-Chinese war that Japan was no more capable of resistance than China, and that the latter's defensive measures had been 'like child's play'.[1] In the eyes of modernisers such as Shūhan, Japan's need to acquire mastery of this particular branch of Western learning was no longer simply a matter of scholarly curiosity, but of his country's very survival as an independent nation in the face of the predatory desires of an industrialised West.

This gradual dissemination of Western ideas was one of a number of factors by means of which the formerly impregnable edifice of the exclusionist administration was brought increasingly under attack over the course of the years. Other weapons in the armoury of the reforming *Zeitgeist* included the revitalisation of traditional *shintō* beliefs and the beginnings of research into national history – both of which developments tended to call into question the legitimacy of the *Shōgun*'s primacy over the Emperor, who had been reduced to the role of a mere puppet since the Tokugawa ascendancy. But the force which was to act as perhaps the most eloquent advocate for the abandonment of isolationism was operating on a rather more mundane level than any of the above: that of everyday economic transactions. The period of the Tokugawa Shōgunate saw the emergence of a mercantile class in the cities, and of coin rather than rice as the favoured medium of exchange through which they conducted their business. The ruling military élite (*samurai*) of Japan's traditional feudal hier-

archy contracted huge debts to this newly emergent bourgeoisie, which
they then attempted to displace on to their already overstretched peasant
subjects. As a result, the agricultural economy started to crumble, to be
'replaced by a mercantile economy which Japan was unable to support
without calling on the outside world'.[2] Even without the additional per-
suasive capacities of Commodore Perry's superior firepower, therefore,
capitulation to the American demand for trading opportunities, when at
last it came, was by then a matter of stark economic necessity.

After the gunboats, the diplomacy: as follow-up to his first audacious
violation of the exclusion order in 1853, Perry returned with an augmented force in February of the following year, and on this occasion made
the long-awaited breakthrough. An agreement concluded on 31 March
allowed him the use of the twin ports of Shimoda and Hakodate for
limited trade, and provided for consular representation for his country.
This success of Perry's soon prompted others to follow his example:
similar treaties were signed with the British in October of the same year,
and with the Russians and Dutch in February and November of the following year respectively. Thereafter events moved inexorably to bring about
the eventual downfall of the *ancien régime*, although the force that was
finally responsible for toppling the ruling military dictatorship, or *bakufu*,
perhaps came from a somewhat unexpected quarter. For ultimately it was
forces loyal to the Emperor which brought about the resignation of the last
Shōgun in 1867 and, after a brief civil war, the formation of a provisional
government and restoration of the Emperor to what was considered his
rightful place at the head of the political structure (the so-called '*Meiji
Restoration*'). There thus arose the somewhat paradoxical situation that
the foundations of what eventually proved to be the first Western-style
government in Japan were prepared by precisely those forces in society
which had initially viewed the *bakufu*'s accommodation with foreigners as
a betrayal, and whose battle-cry had once been '*Sonno jōi!*' – 'Revere the
Emperor and expel the barbarians!'

The conflicting ideologies which rendered this situation so paradoxical –
the 'modernising' spirit of the new administration, in opposition to a sometimes aggressive nostalgia for traditional Japanese certainties on the part of
those who had helped bring it to power – afford one of the first glimpses of a
clash of values that has had a central role in determining Japan's subsequent
cultural development right up to the present day. The historian Arnold
Toynbee (1889–1975), who took an especial interest in this aspect of Japan's
cultural history, once coined a handy pair of expressions to describe these
kinds of opposing responses that may be 'evoked in a society which has been
thrown on the defensive by the impact of an alien force in superior

strength'.[3] The attitude of the progressives and 'modernisers', on the one hand, he characterised as the 'Herodian'[4] position; that of 'the man who acts on the principle that the most effective way to guard against the danger of the unknown is to master its secret, and, when he finds himself in the predicament of being confronted by a more highly skilled and better armed opponent . . . responds by discarding his traditional art of war and learning to fight his enemy with the enemy's own tactics and own weapons'.[5] On the other hand, in opposition to this receptive, mimetic attitude, Toynbee posited the idea of 'Zealotism': the stance taken by 'the man who takes refuge from the unknown in the familiar, and when he joins battle with a stranger who practises superior tactics and enjoys formidable new-fangled weapons . . . responds by practising his own traditional art of war with abnormally scrupulous exactitude'.[6]

For Toynbee, the course of action ultimately chosen by the nineteenth-century Japanese in response to their dramatic exposure to Western technological prowess constituted the 'Herodian' reaction *par excellence*: for him, the Japanese were 'of all the non-Western peoples that the modern West has challenged . . . perhaps the least unsuccessful exponents of "Herodianism" in the world so far'.[7] Though at first sight this might appear to be a sweepingly imperious, 'etic' pronouncement on the situation, it is nevertheless one that would appear to be given a certain 'emic' validation when one considers certain reactions on the part of the Japanese themselves – such as the remarks of Takashima Shūhan quoted a few paragraphs previously, or the craze for wholesale Europeanisation that followed in the wake of the *Meiji* restoration, when the desire of the Japanese ruling classes to remodel themselves on the lines of their newly found trading partners went far beyond the minimum necessary to acquire an adequate military competence. But side by side with such sycophantic imitation by a small élite there co-existed amongst the population at large other, drastically less welcoming responses to the Western intrusion – of such a nature to suggest that, as one leading authority on Japanese culture expressed it, Western culture was 'accepted as a necessity but its donors were disliked'.[8] And at this point one becomes aware that the image conjured by Toynbee, of a wholehearted subjugation to the 'Herodian' ideal, might require a certain qualification, to say the least. In fact, the truth of the matter would appear to be rather that the atavistic reaction described by Toynbee as 'Zealotism' on no account perished with Perry, and has indeed never really gone away since. To an extent it can be highly profitable, indeed, to regard much of the subsequent cultural history of Japan as ideologically motivated by the dialectical opposition between the twin forces of progressive cosmopolitanism and regressive nationalism: an oscillation, as the Takemitsu scholar Alain Poirier expresses it, 'between expressions of a nationalism, betraying itself sometimes in the form of violent protectionism, and of a willingness to be open towards the Occident'.[9]

This 'oscillation' described by Poirier, however, constitutes only one mode of expression – what might be called the 'diachronic' – of the underlying opposition, betraying itself above all in the form of horizontal, historical fluctuations of power between two polar positions, of which the most dramatic in recent times have probably been the disastrous resurgence of political nationalism before and during the Second World War, and the extreme receptivity towards Americanisation in the Occupation years that succeeded it. But at the same time this fundamental tension also expresses itself vertically, as it were 'synchronically', as a kind of basic and ongoing schism in the Japanese psyche, what has been described as 'a kind of double structure or perhaps parallelism of lifestyle and intellectual attitude of the modern Japanese'.[10] In this compromise between 'modern' imperatives and 'traditional' instincts, experience tends to be compartmentalised, with Western behavioural codes operating in certain areas – for example, in most areas of 'public', corporate life – but with other, predominantly private domains reserved as sites wherein citizens tend 'consciously or unconsciously to maintain the traditions passed on from generation to generation'.[11] In both of the above manifestations, this interplay of forces – not necessarily a destructive one – has played a crucial role in shaping both the historical development and everyday orientation of Japanese culture during the modern period. And – as we shall very shortly discover – this has been as much the case with the composition of Western-style music in Japan, as with any other form of cultural activity. Horizontally, throughout the historical period that has elapsed since this European art form was first transplanted to Japanese soil, we shall observe fluctuations between imitation of the West and declarations of nationalistic independence; vertically, taking a 'slice of time' through any particular moment in that history, we shall observe time and again in the work of individual composers the same preoccupation with establishing their own equilibrium between these recurrent, inimical forces – the centrifugal force of adopting a Western idiom, the centripetal one of defining, by contrast, a uniquely 'Japanese' identity. Indeed – as Miyamoto has correctly observed – this opposition between an imported foreign culture and their own, and the manner of dealing with both, was long conceived as the 'central problem' facing Western-style Japanese composers.[12]

The channels of transmission through which this Western music first came to be re-established in Japan are essentially three in number. First, there was the reintroduction of Christian devotional music – silent since the early years of the seventeenth century, but gradually being heard once again following the reopening of the ports in the 1850s, and especially after the ban on Christianity was abrogated in 1873. Secondly, there was the incorporation of musical study into the school curricula, of which more must be said shortly. But the most assiduous cultivation of Western music of all initially occurred as a by-product of reform in that sphere in which the spur towards modernisation was most keenly felt: the creation of a modern fighting force. Military drill on the Western model naturally required Western-style martial music, and there thus came into being first of all the simple fife-and-drum bands known as *kotekikai*, and then – after September 1869, when the Satsuma clan were loaned instruments and given instruction by the Irish-born bandmaster John William Fenton (1828– ?) – full-blown military bands on the Western model. Fenton's band acquired its own instruments from England in 1870 and later became the official band of the Japanese navy, its directorship passing in 1879 to the Prussian musician Franz Eckert (1852–1916); while the army was to establish its own band in 1872, at first under the leadership of Kenzō Nishi, and then subsequently – and in interesting contrast to the naval band – under the direction of two French bandmasters: Gustave Charles Dagron, who presided until 1884, and his successor Charles Edouard Gabriel Leroux (1850–1926).

The importance of these developments for the wider dissemination of Western music resides in the fact that, besides their proper function within the armed forces, these bands also performed roles which demanded that they appear in a more public situation. One such function was the provision of ceremonial music for diplomatic occasions, out of which expediency grew the creation of what still remains Japan's national anthem to this day, *Kimi ga yo* – possibly one of the earliest examples of 'Western-style' composition to involve at least a partial Japanese input. But in addition, and more importantly still, the military bands played a vital role in the reception of Western music in Japan by giving public recitals of it, to such an extent that 'until about 1879 . . . musical activity was organised around the military band, and it was the band that pioneered the way in what today we would call the public concert'.[13]

It was during the 1880s that, alongside these military band concerts, public recitals also began to be given by Japan's first generation of music school students. As already suggested, the institution of a public education system on Western lines was the third and, ultimately, probably the most decisive factor in the promulgation of Western music in Japan. For, in their earnest efforts to imitate wholesale the pedagogic practices of the West, the

Ministry of Education had stipulated in its regulations of 1872 that singing practice should form part of the school curriculum at elementary level, and instrumental tuition at middle-school level. This was in spite of the fact that at the time the facilities for putting such Utopian ideals into practice were totally lacking – 'an act symptomatic of the progressiveness of the authorities, who had received the baptism of the new spirit of the Reformation'.[14]

Much of the responsibility for turning such ambitious schemes into reality was entrusted to an aristocratic Ministry official called Shūji Izawa (1851–1917), who on the orders of the Ministry was sent to the United States in 1875 to examine American pedagogic methods, and to study music under the Director of the Boston Music School, Luther Whiting Mason (1828–96). In October 1879, shortly after Izawa's return to Japan, a 'Music Study Committee' (*Ongaku Torishirabe Gakari* – effectively a small music college) was set up at Izawa's recommendation, and in the same month he set forth his ideals for musical education in his 'Plan for the Study of Music'. If the reception history of Western-style music in *Meiji*-era Japan has up till now read rather like one of uncritical, if not necessarily sympathetic, assimilation, then this document of Izawa's supplies us with one of our first glimpses of a counter-tendency. But at the same time, Izawa was clearly too much of a realist to lapse into mere reaffirmation of traditionalist certainties. Instead – and fascinatingly – by describing 'three general theories', he sets out his argument for the future direction of Japanese musical studies in almost classical dialectic fashion. First comes the 'thesis', to the effect that since 'Western music has been brought to almost the highest peak of perfection as a result of several thousand years of study since the time of the Greek philosopher Pythagoras', it would be better to cultivate such music exclusively and abandon the 'inadequate Eastern music' entirely. Next comes an 'antithetical' proposition: since every country has its own proper culture, it would be absurd to try to import a foreign music, and therefore the best policy would be to bestow the utmost care on the cultivation of one's own musical heritage. So far, it is easy to discern in these two opposing arguments fairly conventional statements of classic 'Herodian' and 'Zealotist' positions respectively. But it is at this point that Izawa adds something new, something that we have so far not directly encountered at any point in our discussion of this topic. As a third possible option – and it is clearly the one which Izawa himself favours – he suggests a 'synthesis' of the above antithetic alternatives: the possibility of 'taking a middle course between the two views, and by blending Eastern and Western music establish[ing] a new kind of music which is suitable for the Japan of today'.[15] And it is here that one catches sight, for the first time, of a yearning that was to prove something of an *idée fixe* for so many Japanese musicians throughout the hundred-plus years that have subsequently elapsed: the desire for a resolution, on a musical level at least, of that 'double structure' in the Japanese psyche already referred to, the quest for some sort of synthesis of Japanese and European musics in a higher unity.

In Izawa's own case, however, the means he considered adequate for the realisation of this ambitious project seem, with hindsight, almost embarrassingly naïve. *Shōgaku Shōka-Shū*, the collection of primary-school songs which embodied Izawa's theories, and of which the first set eventually appeared in November 1881, was compiled from three sources of material, each of which reflects one of the 'three general principles' referred to in the text of the 'Plan for the Study of Music' mentioned above. Thus the conservative, 'Zealotist' approach is reflected in the incorporation of 'Works employing materials from *gagaku* and popular song';[16] a progressive, forward-looking attitude finds expression in the inclusion of 'Newly composed works'; while the third, synthetic option is represented by what are described as 'Famous Western tunes supplied with Japanese lyrics'. It is with the last of these in particular, however, that the inadequacy of Izawa's rather amateurish approach becomes especially apparent. Essentially this attempt at reconciling the two cultures reflected his belief that it was only in their advanced forms that Eastern and Western musics diverged, their basic elements – such as those found in children's songs – apparently being 'strikingly similar'. But the one enduring achievement of the manner in which this philosophy was put into practice seems to have been to sow in Japanese minds such confusing ideas – prevalent to this day – as, for example, that *Auld Lang Syne* is actually a traditional Japanese folksong called *Hotaru no Hikari*. Moreover, while it had been Izawa's original intention that traditional Japanese and Western music should be studied alongside one another, as the years passed the former option was gradually abandoned, to be revived again only after the Second World War. Thus his idealistic vision of an accommodation between Eastern and Western traditions began to fade, and Japanese musical education began to devote its energies, for the most part, towards an unequivocal pursuit of excellence in the 'European' tradition.

Most of these energies were, of course, directed towards the acquisition of performance skills, but it was nevertheless a comparatively short time before the first efforts at Western-style composition by academically trained Japanese musicians began to manifest themselves. Unusually – given the course of subsequent history – the credit for producing the first instrumental work of this kind goes to a woman composer, Nobu[ko]

Kōda (1870–1946), whose *Violin Sonata* appeared in 1897;[17] while in the sphere of 'serious' vocal music, the title of pioneer is conventionally accorded to Rentarō Taki (1879–1903), many of whose songs, such as *Kōjō no Tsuki* or *Hana*, are still well known to most Japanese today, and, despite the obvious diatonicism of their material, often mistakenly thought of as 'traditional' in origin. Additionally, in his final years before his premature death from tuberculosis, Taki contributed some of the earliest specimens of solo piano music to the Japanese repertory – a *Menuetto* in B minor in 1900, and the interesting *Urami* ('Regret') of 1903.

Taki's brief career also included a period of foreign study at the Leipzig Conservatoire: a form of finishing which was obviously considered highly desirable for any musician wishing to be taken seriously at this period, when all but one of the teachers at the Tōkyō Music School (which the 'Music Study Committee' had become in 1887) were of German extraction, and Japanese musicians tended 'to think of the German traditions as the only ones'.[18] Thus we find Taki's example emulated a few years later by the colourful figure whom Japan still reveres as the first great patriarch in its canon of domestic composers, Kōsaku Yamada (1886–1965). After graduating as a singer from the Tōkyō Music School in 1908, Yamada moved to Berlin to study for four years at the Hochschule with Max Bruch and Karl Leopold Wolf, where in 1912 he produced Japan's first ever home-grown symphony, *Kachidoki to Heiwa* ('Victory and Peace'), followed in 1913 by a late Romantic-style tone poem, *Mandara no Hana* ('Flower of the Mandala'). It was in order to perform such ambitious works as these that in 1915, after his return to Japan, he organised the first Japanese symphony orchestra; a second orchestra which he founded in 1924 – after the financial collapse of the former – was eventually to develop into the present-day orchestra of the NHK.[19] Yamada was also closely involved with the struggle to establish opera in Japan, forming his own troupe, the *Nihon Gakugeki Kyōkai* ('Japanese Music Drama Association'), in 1920; and in addition to such activities, he somehow found time to produce an estimated 1,500 or so instrumental, vocal and operatic scores, throughout which the influence of his Germanic training is evident – perhaps, indeed, is reflected in the very fact of his choosing to bequeath the world such a monumental legacy. Yet even here, in the case of this most thoroughly Occidentally trained of early Japanese composers, one catches sight in later years of a counteracting assertion of national difference. It surfaces, for instance, in the composer's search for a manner in which a style of vocal music conceived to suit the contours of German speech might be adapted to reflect adequately the very different intonational patterns of Japanese – a quest which oddly parallels the efforts of European composers such as

Bartók, for instance, to rid their vocal music of the inappropriate accents of the Austro-German hegemony. And it also emerges clearly, of course, in the picturesque titles bestowed on the instrumental pieces, or the texts and subject matter chosen for his songs and operas – for example, in his most successful work, *Kurofune* ('Black Ships', 1940), which is loosely based on the famous relationship between the Japanese girl Okichi-san and the American Consul, and which Eta Harich-Schneider has neatly described as 'a Puccini opera from the Eastern standpoint'.[20]

The example of Taki and Yamada established the foundations of a recognisable 'school' of German-style composition in Japan, and in the footsteps of these two pioneers there followed a whole generation of 'Germanic' composers, with a particular interest in vocal music: Ryutarō Hirota (1892–1952), Shinpei Nakahama (1887–1952), Nagayo Moto'ori (1885–1945) and Kiyoshi Nobutoki (1887–1965). One notes in the manner in which this particular style was propagated a very Japanese form of cultivation: an initial mimesis of another culture is then faithfully reproduced as composers working in the same style form themselves into groups, or as their method is transmitted by the conservative, Confucian method from revered teacher to reverent pupil. A similar pattern emerged, for example, a generation later, after Saburo Moroi (1903–77) returned from his period of study in Berlin (1934–36) with Leo Schrattenholz to found what he described as his 'analysis school' of composers rigorously trained on the Germanic model: Yoshiro Irino (1921–80), Minao Shibata (1916–96), and his own son Makoto Moroi (1930–).

However, the one exception to the German monopoly on instruction at the Tōkyō Music School – the French conductor Noël Péri – points to the early establishment of a tentative alternative to the Germanic model: one that subsequently would exert considerable appeal for Japanese composers, precisely because so many *fin-de-siècle* French artists had themselves been turning their sights towards 'the East' in the hope of discovering an alternative to the oppressive weight of their own cultural history. One thinks here, for example, of Van Gogh's reinterpretations of Hiroshige woodcuts, or (most pertinently for our present purposes) of Debussy's epiphanic exposure to Asiatic music at the 1889 Paris Exposition and his choice of a Hokusai engraving to embellish the score of *La Mer*. It was not long, therefore, before some Japanese composers turned to this alternative tradition to further their studies – the pioneer being Tomojirō Ikenouchi (1906–91), the first Japanese to enter the Paris Conservatoire, where he studied composition under Paul Henri Büsser (1873–1972) from 1927 to 1936. Ikenouchi's pupils were to include several distinguished figures in Japanese music, such as Saburō Takata (1913–), Akio Yashiro (1929–76),

Toshirō Mayuzumi (1929–97) and Akira Miyoshi (1933–); while the shadow of French influence was also to fall heavily upon such composers as Meiro Sugawara (1897–1988) and Kunihiko Hashimoto (1904–48).

Of course, the fascination exerted on these composers by 'impressionistic' music in particular was in no small measure due to the fact that, precisely for the reasons outlined at the beginning of the previous paragraph, it reflected back at them, from a European perspective, many of the preoccupations of their own indigenous musical culture. The modally based, 'non-functional' harmonic idiom was eminently adaptable for use with the scales of traditional Japanese music, and both traditions shared a fondness for timbral finesse and, on a broader level, for extra-musical reference to picturesque, naturalistic subject matter. All this was hardly to be wondered at, considering that the Japanese were working with a European reflection of deep structures to be found within their own culture – a process of that type which Takemitsu, himself a devotee of Debussy's music, was many years later to describe as '"reciprocal action" – musical art which was reimported to Japan'.[21] Yet perhaps at this insecure stage of Japanese musical history, it was necessary that the 'Oriental' in art be exported and reimported in this way, in order that it might return home stamped with the endorsement that would ensure its acceptance in the post-*Meiji* intellectual climate – the seal of Western legitimation.

Soon, however, a school of composition was to emerge in Japan which would abolish such cultural customs officers entirely and work directly with the indigenous materials of its own heritage. In the years leading up to the Second World War a new voice began to make itself heard, one which eschewed the imitation of European models favoured by more 'academic' composers and substituted for it the expression of a distinctly 'national' identity. One cannot be sure to what extent individual composers associated with this movement harboured nationalistic sentiments in the broader, political sense of the term, but it is certainly true that the ascendancy of the pre-war 'nationalist' school in Japanese composition coincided with the period in modern Japanese history when attitudes towards the West had swung to the opposite extreme from the receptivity which characterised the early *Meiji* era. Furthermore, this isolationist stance was not without its impact on the composers of the 'nationalist' school in at least one respect, inasmuch as few of them underwent the course of 'foreign study' in Europe deemed so essential by many of their predecessors, and indeed one or two – notably Ifukube and Hayasaka – were largely self-taught. Japanese composers closely associated with this movement include Akira Ifukube (1914–), Kishio Hirao (1907–53), Shirō Fukai (1907–59), Fumio Hayasaka (1914–55) (on whose film scores

Takemitsu would later work as an assistant), Shūkichi Mitsukuri (1895–1971), Yoritsune Matsudaira (1907–), and the composer usually cited as Takemitsu's only formal 'teacher', Yasuji Kiyose (1899–1981) – the last three of whom formed the *Shinkō Sakkyokuka Renmei* ('Progressive Composers' League', later to become the Japanese branch of the ISCM) in 1930.

Strictly speaking, the descriptive term for this tendency here translated as 'nationalism' – *minzokushugi* – also carries with it connotations pertaining to the word for 'folk' or 'race' (*minzoku*), and this provides a clue as to the manner in which these composers tended to operate, working (as one Japanese commentator puts it) 'with folk-music and folklore in the same manner as the Hungarian composer Béla Bartók'.[22] Thus Ifukube, for example, produced 'complicated polymetres and instrumental combinations learned from years of listening to Ainu melodies in Hokkaidō';[23] while Mitsukuri – though educated under Georg Schumann in Berlin, and in many respects closer to the German Romantic tradition than the other composers named above – made a scientific study of the elements of traditional music, deriving from them a unique method of harmonisation based on the intervals of a fifth, which he described as his 'oriental harmonic system' (*tōyōwaonteikei*) and to which he gave theoretical expression in his publication *Ongaku no Toki* ('The Moment of Music') in 1948.

But while there are obvious similarities between such procedures and the methods of composers like Bartók in the West, there are also important differences. For example, in the case of Bartók the 'folkloristic' input tends to be counterbalanced by features drawn from the broader tradition of European art music, such as the rigour of the constructional method or the 'avant-gardism' of the chromatic harmony. This is not generally the case in the music of Japanese 'nationalists', in which folk-derived materials tend to be stated baldly, often in rather crude harmonisations, and developed as often as not by simple repetitive devices. Furthermore, whereas Bartók and Kodály did not limit their researches to their own country, but recognised instead a deeper structural unity between various folk musics transcending national boundaries, the Japanese composers preoccupied themselves exclusively with traditional Japanese music, conveniently ignoring whatever features it shared with other musics of the Far East. In addition, the Japanese regarded both popular songs and highly sophisticated genres like *gagaku* indiscriminately as expressions of the 'national'; they did not see the fundamental binary opposition as consisting of a social one between 'folk' and 'art' music, and neither was the 'regional' – for example the Ainu melodies with which Ifukube worked – viewed as differing from the 'national', despite the distinct racial and cultural identity possessed by

such minorities. Instead the fundamental duality perceived by this generation of composers was that between 'Japanese' and 'Western'; between the
'nationalistic' and the academic, pedagogical and derivative. In all of the
above respects, then, the music of these Japanese *minzokushugi* composers
bears less resemblance to the work of Bartók and Kodály than to that of
their nineteenth-century European forebears – to artists from the period
when for the first time 'folk art came to be regarded as a national, rather
than a regional or social, phenomenon'.[24] Indeed, as we have already seen,
such an identification is implicit in the very semantics of the term conventionally used to describe them.

Music by *minzokushugi* composers nevertheless appears to have enjoyed
a considerable vogue in pre-war Japan, and even today Japanese orchestras
visiting the West have a habit of surprising their audiences with bombastic
encore pieces in the *minzokushugi* vein, usually delivered with an appropriately passionate, *kamikaze*-like conviction. In general, however, outside
Japan music of this sort is today little heard of, and the judgement of
musical history has not been especially generous towards those composers
'who have been unable to see greater possibilities in their native idioms
than merely the harmonisation of Japanese tunes'.[25] Such judgements
reflect rather more than changing tastes in musical fashion: they point to
intrinsic weaknesses in the method of procedure, as becomes readily
apparent to anyone who has heard the works of certain of these composers. Although it is unfair to single out one particular work as emblematic
of a whole artistic tendency – and although the time is long past when
music written for the cinema was somehow considered intrinsically infe-
rior – it might nevertheless serve to conjure for the modern reader some
aural image of this type of music by referring to the creation of Akira
Ifukube that has undoubtedly received the widest public exposure: his
music for Inoshiro Honda's (in)famous 1954 'monster movie' *Gojira*
('Godzilla'). Most modern listeners would, I think, agree that the kinds of
excesses typified by such works do not constitute a very imaginative
attempt at East–West integration. The folk-like materials tend to be presented in crude harmonisations and orchestrated with thick instrumental
doublings, underpinned by a massive and hyperactive percussion section –
devices which seem to have the effect of battering out of them whatever
vitality they might originally have possessed. Ultimately, one comes to the
same regretful conclusion as Robin Heifetz, when he notes that 'generally,
the results of these "folklorists" were not successful';[26] but a discussion of
the precise reasons for this 'failure' must be postponed for the moment,
until the time comes to consider the very different approach adopted by
composers such as Takemitsu in the concluding chapter of this book.

As already suggested, the years which saw the ascendancy of this musical 'nationalism' were also those which witnessed the rise in Japan of its political namesake – which finally erupted to such spectacularly destructive effect in World War II. The immediate post-war years were harsh and deprived in the extreme, affording little opportunity for formal musical study, but eventually – and in particular, from the 1950s onwards – Japanese compositional activity began to rise out of the ashes. Furthermore, much of the work undertaken in those years can still be categorised in the same terms used to describe the old pre-war 'schools' of compositional thought. Thus once again there emerged composers of 'academic' bent who took their cue from developments in Europe and often travelled there to study, and once again these may be divided into composers of 'French' or 'German' inclination. To the former category, for instance, belong composers such as the Ikenouchi pupils Akio Yashiro and Akira Miyoshi, both of whom studied in Paris (under Nadia Boulanger and Raymond Gallois-Montbrun, respectively); while under the latter heading one might subsume the three pupils of Saburo Moroi already referred to: Yoshiro Irino, Makoto Moroi and Minao Shibata. However, there was by now of course a great difference in the European musical scene from those days when Yamada went to assimilate the methods of German late Romanticism, or Ikenouchi those of the French impressionists, and these developments find their echo in the more up-to-date preoccupations of post-war composers. Irino, for instance, was the first Japanese to compose a twelve-note work, his *Concerto da Camera* for seven instruments of 1951, while Shibata's activity in the 1950s ran the whole gamut of post-war techniques and styles, experimenting with twelve-note method, integral serialism, *musique concrète*, electronic music and electric instruments. In later years all of the composers listed above were additionally to experiment with works employing traditional Japanese instruments, often in combination with Western resources: for example, Irino's *Wandlungen* 'for grand orchestra with two *shakuhachis*' of 1973, and Shibata's intriguingly described *Leap Day's Vigil* for '*kokyu, san-gen* and electro-acoustic devices' of 1972.

While it is hardly surprising that composers with an 'academic' outlook should be turning their attention to the new developments in post-war Western music, what is less to be expected is that many composers who continued to follow in the 'nationalist' tradition – what Judith Ann Herd refers to as 'the neonationalist movement' – should also exploit the wealth of new sound resources now available to them, rather than simply the Japanese tunes and pentatonic harmonies that had satisfied their pre-war counterparts. Amongst the many groupings of Japanese composers that sprang up in the 1950s, two in particular came to be associated with this tendency. The first was the *Yagi no Kai* ('Goat Group'), initially formed in 1953 by Hikaru Hayashi (1931–), Yūzō Toyama (1931–) and Michio Mamiya (1929–), to be joined five years later by Toshiya Sukegawa (1930–). The second was the *Sannin no Kai* or 'Group of Three', founded (also in 1953) by Yasushi Akutagawa (1925–89), Ikuma Dan (1924–) and the most famous of Ikenouchi's pupils, Toshirō Mayuzumi. Admittedly these composers varied in the degree to which 'modernist' devices were assimilated into the essentially 'nationalist' aesthetic. Members of the *Yagi no Kai*, for instance, admired Bartók's example, and Mamiya used folksong material more or less directly in his own work, whereas Hayashi tended to experiment with more unusual forms of vocal technique, or used motifs from traditional music as the starting point for more chromaticised, quasi-serial procedures (a similar method is to be found in the post-war 'serial *gagaku*' compositions of the older 'nationalist' composer Yoritsune Matsudaira). And at the opposite extreme from Mamiya, perhaps the most technically radical of all these composers was Mayuzumi, who was for a spell during the 1960s quite well-known in the West as well as in Japan, partly as the result of his score for the John Huston film *The Bible* (1965). Mayuzumi studied under Tony Aubin at the Paris Conservatoire from 1951 to 1952, where he not only assimilated the techniques of Varèse, Messiaen and Boulez but also visited Pierre Schaeffer's studio, completing soon after his return to Japan both the first ever specimen of *musique concrète* to be composed in that country (*Œuvre pour Musique Concrète x, y, z*, 1953), and the first Japanese example of *elektronische Musik* (*Shūsaku I*, 1955). Within a few years of his return to Japan, too, he was placing the wealth of new-found techniques he had mastered at the service of his own 'pan-Asian' vision. In particular, his researches into timbre led him to study the overtone structures of Buddhist temple bells, thereby applying the most advanced techniques of his day to a sound-material powerfully symbolic of Asiatic identity. It was as a result of these researches that he produced probably the most remarkable achievement of his early career: inventing a kind of 'spectral music' decades before its emergence in the work of Europeans such as Murail or Grisey, he used the partials of a Buddhist bell as pitch-material for what is perhaps one of the unsung eccentric masterpieces of post-war music, his *Nehan Kōkyōkyoku* ('Nirvana Symphony') of 1958. Perhaps it is therefore a little dispiriting to learn that the composer of this impressive score was one for whom musical 'nationalism' did, for once, most certainly go hand in glove with its political equivalent. Even in these early works, Mayuzumi seems a little too concerned with his identity as a Japanese, and, as the years progressed, this concern was to express itself ever more in the form of active involvement with the political right – culminating in his work as Chairman of an organisation which styled itself the 'Council for the National Defence of Japan' (*Nippon o Mamoru Kokuminkaigi*) between 1981 and 1991. In this respect, Mayuzumi reveals a close spiritual kinship with another outspoken critic of Japanese society whom he had first met in Paris in 1952: the famous novelist Yukio Mishima (1925–70). It was upon one of the latter's best-known short stories that he was to base one of the most substantial works of his later years: the opera *Kinkakuji* ('The Temple of the Golden Pavilion'), commissioned by the Deutsche Oper of Berlin, and first performed there in 1976.

Yet alongside the 'academically' trained composers working in their own interpretation of a translocated 'European' tradition, and the 'neonationalists' asserting by contrast what they believed to be their own 'uniquely Japanese' identity, there was possibly a third force in operation in post-war Japanese music. Amongst the various groupings that sprang up in the 1950s alongside such affiliations as *Yagi no Kai* or *Sannin no Kai*, there was at least one whose constitution was radically different. Its membership comprised not only composers but artists working in other media; furthermore, the composers working within this group were autodidacts who had received almost no formal education in music, and were thus somewhat marginal to the 'official' Japanese composing community. The group in question was called *Jikken Kōbō*, the 'Experimental Workshop', and its presence on the map of post-war Japanese music marks one of the beginnings of the emergence of a true avant-garde, of an alternative to 'academic' tradition or 'nationalist' rhetoric. Composers associated with this tendency wished rather to distance themselves from the discredited pre-war traditions, as they 'diligently tried to rid themselves of the wartime stigma of existing nationalistic models'[27] – a task in which they were assisted in the early post-war years by the policy of the Occupation forces, who strictly limited outward displays of nationalism, while affording ample opportunities to gain access to the new styles currently enjoying vogue in Europe and the United States. Rather like their counterparts in a devastated Germany, composers of this persuasion wanted more or less to return to a *Nullstunde* and start from scratch, and thus found themselves in peculiar sympathy with the post-Webernian generation's desire for a new 'international' music, as well as – later on – with the aesthetics of Cage and the American experimentalists. One of the founder members of the particular association mentioned above – *Jikken Kōbō* – was a young man who had just celebrated his twenty-first birthday, Tōru Takemitsu.

Throughout this chapter, the reader will observe, the focus of attention has been gradually narrowing: from the broad perspective across Japanese history with which it began, via a concentration specifically on the development of Japanese music, to the history of Western-style composition outlined in the preceding pages. Now, in order to continue the story, it will be necessary to narrow the focus even further – to revert from the generalised to the particular, and examine how the ongoing dynamics of the relationship between Japan and Western music came to express themselves in the career and work of one individual. The detailed investigation of both the life and music of this individual, Takemitsu, will form the matter for discussion in the chapters which follow.

2 Music and 'pre-music': Takemitsu's early years

Encrypted at one point in the music of Takemitsu's late work *Family Tree – Musical Verses for Young People* (1992) is a kind of coded biographical allusion. When the girl narrator, introducing us in turn to each member of her family, comes to her father, the music launches suddenly into something like pastiche big-band jazz of the swing era. For the listener familiar with the biographical details of Takemitsu's earliest years, his private reasons for considering 'jazz' an apt metaphor for the paternal at this point are easily fathomed. Although born – on 8 October 1930 – in the Hongō district of Tōkyō, within a month of his birth Tōru Takemitsu had joined his father Takeo at his place of employment, the town of Dalian (Luda) in the region of China then known to the Japanese as Manchuria, and administered by them as a colony. There, enjoying a privileged lifestyle as a member of the expatriate community, Takeo Takemitsu had been able to indulge one of his favourite passions more frequently than might otherwise have been possible: the performance of jazz records from his vast personal collection. He had one or two other musical enthusiasms too, which it is just possible might have had some influence on the developing musical sensibilities of his son: the Takemitsu biographer Kuniharu Akiyama notes that he was for a while 'fanatical' about playing the *shakuhachi*,[1] and won first prize at a competition for making imitation bird sounds.[2] But it was his parent's constant rehearsal of his favourite 'Dixieland, New Orleans Style' discs that clearly left the most indelible impression on the fledgling composer, to the extent that nearly half a century later, in conversation with Seiji Ozawa, Takemitsu could still recall such names as 'Kid Ory and his Creole Band' from those days, adding that 'a little of this jazz music still remains inside me'.[3]

This assessment is indeed borne out by the composer's mature music in several ways – and not simply in those instances where jazz music is directly parodied, such as the passage in *Family Tree*, or the skilful jazz pastiches in the soundtracks for such films as *Karami-ai*,[4] *Tōkyō Sensō Sengo Hiwa*[5] and *Natsu no Imōto*.[6] In Takemitsu's mature 'concert' works as well, the traces of jazz influence are palpable in such features as the suave harmonic language (in part arrived at through the influence of George Russell's 'Lydian Chromatic' theories) and even, towards the end of the composer's career, a certain 'big band' style of orchestration. But in more general terms, the point to be noted at this stage is that the strongest musical impressions of Takemitsu's earliest years stemmed from a source that was 'Western' in origin, and that his reactions to this stimulus, as vindicated by later developments, were unambiguously positive in nature.

The situation was to prove otherwise with regard to traditional Japanese music. At the age of seven, Takemitsu was sent back to Tōkyō to commence his primary schooling, his father following him a year later on account of ill-health, and dying at Kagoshima in 1938 (his mother Raiko was to survive until 1983). Takemitsu stayed in the Akebonochō district with his uncle, whose wife taught the *koto*,[7] and it was perhaps the association of this constant musical presence with a period of such unhappiness in the composer's personal life which caused him to react as negatively as he did to this early encounter with traditional Japanese music. 'When I was a child I lived in Tōkyō with my aunt, a *koto* teacher', the composer was later to recall. 'I heard traditional Japanese music around me all the time. For some reason, it never really appealed to me, never moved me. Later, hearing traditional Japanese music always recalled the bitter memories of the war.'[8]

As this quotation suggests, the aversion to traditional Japanese music was intensified by the experiences of the war years, when – for reasons hinted at in the previous chapter – 'Japanese' music became associated with the dominant culture of militarism, while, as in Nazi Germany, other genres were vilified as so much *entartete Musik* (or, as the equivalent Japanese expression had it, *tekiseiongaku* – 'music of hostile character'). And it was precisely at this point that an experience occurred which was not only to reaffirm the positive connotations with which Western music had become imbued for Takemitsu, but which, in the musically deprived context of the war years, was to strike him with such force as to change the subsequent course of his life.

Appropriately enough, it was once again a form of American popular music – or, at least, an American popular musician – that was responsible for Takemitsu's epiphanic conversion. With mobilisation in 1944, Takemitsu's formal education was abruptly curtailed, and he was sent to work at a military provisions base in Saitama prefecture, lodged in an underground dugout deep in the mountains; 'the experience', the composer later confessed, 'was an extremely bitter one'.[9] On one occasion, however, a newly graduated officer cadet secretly took a number of the internees into a back room for a clandestine recital of proscribed music, using a wind-up gramophone with a carefully sharpened piece of bamboo as a needle. One of the first items he played, apparently, was Lucienne Boyer singing *Parlez-moi d'amour*; and for Takemitsu at least, accustomed by this time to a musical diet consisting solely of patriotic war songs, the experience of this music had a revelatory impact which he was to remember for the rest of his life. 'For me, hearing that music came as an enormous shock; I was stunned, and for the first time I suddenly realised the splendid quality of Western music.'[10]

As well as reawakening Takemitsu's dormant musical sensibilities, then, this revelatory moment also confirmed the Occidental bias of his musical preferences. And with the cessation of hostilities this bias was to extend to far more than matters of musical taste alone. Like many Japanese of the post-war years, Takemitsu eagerly embraced a decidedly 'Herodian' attitude of reaction against the discredited nationalism of the immediate past – 'a kind of gut-level response that whatever was Japanese should be rejected'[11] – coupled with an enthusiasm for all things Western. The ideological climate of the post-war American occupation was to afford the young Takemitsu ample opportunity to cultivate this predilection for Western culture, and in particular for modern Western music. The occupying US government established what the composer has described as a 'very big library' in Tōkyō to which he went 'every day to look at scores – all from America, none from Europe', with the inevitable result that he 'knew American music first, before I knew Schoenberg or Webern'.[12] They also set up a radio station called WVTR, and Takemitsu, at this period frequently bed-ridden on account of ill-health, was able to spend 'all my time listening to the US Armed Forces network',[13] who 'played various kinds of music (George Gershwin, Debussy and Mahler)'.[14] (And Messiaen too, at least according to Kuniharu Akiyama, who recalled hearing Stokowski conduct *L'Ascension* around 1948, and applied to the station for a copy of the recording to perform at a concert of works on disc.)[15] But – according to Takemitsu's later testimony, at least – it is to none of these modern masters that thanks are due for the young Takemitsu's decision to become a composer, but rather to the unlikely stimulus of César Franck. Hearing a radio broadcast of the latter's *Prelude, Chorale and Fugue* for piano, the composer was struck as profoundly by the quality of Western instrumental music as he had been by the vocal artistry of Boyer. 'I had discovered a second kind of music, namely the instrumental, the absolute kind. In Japan, word and sound cannot be separated. But here I was hearing an instrument being played alone and awakening astonishing feelings in me. It seemed to me like a song of peace, a prayer or an aspiration, after I had lived through so much suffering . . . At that moment, I decided to become a composer.'[16]

Takemitsu's later self-assessment as 'almost an autodidact, a self-taught composer'[17] is certainly lent credibility by the manner in which he set out initially to realise this ambition without professional guidance or encouragement of any sort; but at the same time one should not fall into the error of thinking that these earliest musical efforts were undertaken in utter isolation and solitude. For instance, Takemitsu became a member of an amateur chorus, and it was at the house of the choir's conductor, Tokuaki Hamada, that he met another young composer, Hiroyoshi Suzuki (1931–), who was to become something of a comrade-in-arms during these early years of struggle.[18] Together the pair pored over Rimsky-Korsakov's *Orchestration* and the scores that lined the shelves of Hamada's home – already with a significant preference for the works of French composers such as Roussel, Fauré and (once again) Franck. Shortly after this – just before Christmas 1946 – there occurred yet another signal event in Takemitsu's life linked in some way with American popular music. The young composer obtained a year's employment at a 'PX' ('post exchange', or recreational facility) attached to the US Army camp at Yokohama, where it was agreed that, in return for playing jazz records to the GIs by night, he might make use of the piano in the unoccupied hall during the day. The luxury this opportunity represented for the young Takemitsu in those years of desperate post-war privation cannot be overemphasised: until then, the lack of a piano on which to try out his compositional experiments had reduced him to such extreme ruses as knocking on the houses of complete strangers to obtain access to one, or even fabricating a 'paper keyboard' which could produce sounds only in his own aural imagination.

In spite of Takemitsu's professed aversion for anything 'Japanese' at this period, both he and Suzuki nevertheless appear to have been interested in their own traditional music as well, and even to have made efforts to assimilate elements from it into the language of modern Western composition. Such, at least, was the opinion of Akiyama, who claimed that the young composers were at this period experimenting with the possibilities afforded by the *ryō, ritsu* and *in* scales of traditional music – a preoccupation which apparently bore fruit in a series of pentatonic-derived pieces which the seventeen-year-old Takemitsu produced at this time, such as the rather oddly named *Kakehi* ('Conduit').[19] The story which Takemitsu himself was to tell regarding the genesis of this work, however, is rather different: he claimed that he was so shocked to discover that these pentatonic elements, with their negative 'nationalistic' connotations, had crept into his work subconsciously that he later destroyed the piece.[20]

Whichever version of events is correct, however, it is clear that both Takemitsu and Suzuki were at this period more sympathetically disposed towards the previous generation of Japanese composers, and in particular the 'nationalist' school, than might be expected from the militantly pro-Western stance Takemitsu claims to have espoused. In fact one of the pastimes of both composers at this time was combing the shelves of the Koga second-hand bookshop in Kanda for pre-war sheet music, and it was here that they came across the *Flute Sonatina* by the Japanese 'nationalist' composer Kishio Hirao, to whom they turned in their first attempt to put their musical studies on a more official footing. Unfortunately, they elected to accomplish this by means of the rather naïve stratagem of simply turning up unannounced at the composer's house, and – perhaps unsurprisingly – the unsolicited and, by all accounts, somewhat shabby visitors were turned away at the gate. Six years later, however, when both Hirao and Takemitsu were in hospital together, the elder composer repented of his former *brusquerie* and promised the young man a significant propitiatory gift: a copy of his forthcoming translation of Messiaen's *Technique de mon langage musical*.[21] Unfortunately, his death soon afterwards prevented him from honouring this pledge.

Rather better fortune was to attend Takemitsu's next effort to apprentice himself to an established senior composer. While buying a ticket for the 'Nichi-Bei Contemporary Music Festival' of 1948, he revealed his ambitions to the business manager of the Tōhō Music Association, who offered to provide him with an introduction to another composer of 'nationalist' bent, Yasuji Kiyose. When in due course Kiyose agreed to meet the younger composer, the latter rushed to his house immediately, only to find him absent; but Takemitsu refused to be deterred a second time after his experience with Hirao, and remained outside the composer's home like a Zen acolyte until he returned in the evening. According to Takemitsu's version of the story, Kiyose then played some of his music at the piano and paid him a compliment that seems particularly apt in the light of his subsequent reputation for timbral finesse: 'He told me that the sound was beautiful, that I was welcome to come again with more scores; and I was overjoyed to hear such things, spoken by a figure for whom I had such respect'.[22]

Kiyose accepted both Takemitsu and Suzuki as pupils, and, later that month when the 'Nichi-Bei' event took place, introduced them to two other senior figures in the Japanese 'nationalist' compositional world: Yoritsune Matsudaira and Fumio Hayasaka. This pair – plus Kiyose himself, Kunio Ōtsuki, Akihiro Tsukatani (*b.* 1919) and others – had formed a composers' association, the *Shinsakkyokuha* ('New Composition Group'), to present their works, to which the young newcomers were granted admission two years later. Thus it transpired that an organisation founded to further the interests of a group of conservative and 'nationalist' composers provided the platform for Takemitsu's first exposure to the listening public. The seventh *Shinsakkyokuha* recital, in December 1950, included the première of Takemitsu's solo piano work *Lento in Due Movimenti*; but the reception afforded the newcomer by the Japanese critical fraternity appears to have been a cool one, to say the least. In conversation with Seiji Ozawa many years later, Takemitsu was to recall – still with obvious bitterness – how he had bought a newspaper in Shinjuku after the performance, and had read the harsh review with its crushing final remark: 'It's "pre-music"'.[23] 'Everything went totally dark in front of my eyes . . . there was a cinema right in front of me, I bought a ticket, went inside, and in a corner of the pitch blackness . . . I just wanted to cry, and so I cried, thinking it would be best not to write music any more.'[24]

Yamane's remark about 'pre-music' in fact turned out to be remarkably apt, for Takemitsu was to withdraw both this work and its companion piece from the *Shinsakkyokuha* years, *Distance de Fée* (for violin and piano, premièred at the eighth recital of the group in 1951). Both pieces are omitted from the work list which appears in the composer's manuscript score of *Tableau Noir* (1958), which acknowledges instead the first *Uninterrupted Rest* of 1954 as his 'Op. 1', and, additionally, the score of the *Lento* was – as the composer later expressed it in his preface to the score of *Litany* – subsequently 'lost'. Nevertheless, as matters turned out, some musical documentation of this period was to survive in one form or another, and it is on the basis of this that the following speculations on the compositional preoccupations of Takemitsu's 'pre-musical' years are offered.

Début of 'the *Lento* composer'

Takemitsu may have destroyed the score of *Kakehi*, but he did not succeed in eradicating all evidence of his juvenile pentatonic-nationalist sympathies. In the possession of the Documentation Centre for Modern Japanese Music in Tōkyō is the manuscript score of a short piano composition dated '26 June 1949' and bearing the title *Romance*.[25] The score is prefaced by a 'respectful dedication to Kiyose *sensei*',[26] and most of the music in the three pages which follow would have been very much in accord with the aesthetic ideals of the nineteen-year-old composer's folkloristic-minded teacher. The most immediately striking of such preoccupations is the modal and, specifically, the 'Japanese'-sounding character of the musical material. Throughout the work, only eight pitch-classes are sounded – G, G♯, A, B♭, C, C♯, D and E♭ – but, of these, C♯ is not heard again after bar 19, and both this pitch and G♯ clearly function only as

Ex. 1 *Romance*, bars 21–7

adjuncts to the basic six-note 'minor' mode. Furthermore, such passages as the melody which eventually emerges in bar 21 (Ex. 1) suggest that this six-note scale is in reality the conflation of two pentatonic scales of 'Japanese' origin: the descending form of the *in* scale (here D–B♭–A–G–E♭), which is employed as far as the B♭ in bar 24, and the same scale's ascending version (D–E♭–G–A–C), which is used from the following C♮ onwards.

Another marker which locates the work firmly within the Japanese-nationalist tradition is the 'non-functional' harmony derived from verticalisations of pitches abstracted from the basic modal collection, with particular emphasis on interval classes other than the major and minor thirds of traditional Western practice. For example, in bars 46–7, the falling fourth incipit of Example 1 is accompanied by a bass collection which, together with the A♮ of the melody, projects all five pitches of the descending *in* scale simultaneously. Such collections tend to be highly dissonant, of course, and it is as intensifiers of this dissonance that the extraneous C♯ and G♯ make their appearance, always occurring in close proximity, respectively, to the C♮ and G♮ of the basic modal collection, like 'out-of-tune' versions of the 'correct' pitches. This perhaps reflects an anecdotal intention, and one which again relates the work to the aesthetics of the 'nationalist' school: the attempt by such means to simulate the microtonal inflections of traditional Japanese instruments.

On the other hand, although there is clearly much that is derivative of that tradition within this early work, there are also many prophetic pointers towards Takemitsu's later development. One such feature is that most prominently 'nationalistic' aspect of the work itself, its use of modality – a technical feature which was to provide the foundations for a harmonic and melodic style that lasted Takemitsu throughout his creative life. The composer once confessed that he was 'seriously interested in the idea of mode',[27] and as Akiyama was to note, 'this is something which has not changed from his very early period up to the present day'.[28] What did change, however, was the type of modal material in which Takemitsu was interested: the Japanese pentatonic scales, with their negative nationalistic associations, were soon to be jettisoned, yet the basic methods of manipulating them which Takemitsu had learned were to serve him well when applied to other scale collections. Thus Timothy Koozin is surely right when he asserts that 'the idea of a scale-based compositional idiom' as found in these early works 'sets an important precedent for Takemitsu's later use of octatonic and whole-tone collections in the piano works'[29] (although the types of materials employed, as we shall see, derived from a far wider-ranging thesaurus of scales than simply the two types Koozin mentions here). In particular, the verticalisation of modally derived pitch-materials as a source of harmony was to prove a life-long resource of the composer's technical vocabulary; as was the intensification of such collections by the addition of 'chromatic' pitches external to the mode in question: 'mode', the composer once explicitly acknowledged, 'interests me because it does not reject sounds from outside the scale'.[30] And if the above assumption concerning the function of such extraneous pitches in *Romance* is correct, it is perhaps ironic that this powerful harmonic resource might have had its origins in an early, anecdotal desire to imitate the sounds of traditional Japanese music.

Another prophetic hint of what was to become something of a Takemitsu trademark is the literal repetition of whole passages – and especially, as here, the repetition of the opening material as a sign of imminent closure. But perhaps the most characteristic traits of all are those implied by the performance indications at the head of the score: 'Adagio sostenuto – nobile funeral [*sic*]'. Takemitsu once remarked in a film interview that 'Japanese people have no sense of *Allegro*',[31] and while this is not necessarily true of *all* Japanese music (which includes, for example, some quite lively folksongs), it certainly reflects the composer's own general predilection for slower tempo categories. Examples abound in his scores of tempo values that lie at the lower end, or even outside the range, of those to be found on a conventional metronome: for example, the first movement of *Uninterrupted Rest* has the indication '♩ = 48' and the second is prefaced by the instruction to perform whole bars at the tempo 'MM20 = 3 sec.'; while in *Autumn* the sub-metronomic tempo of 'Extremely slow, ♩= 30' is required at one point. According to the conductor Hiroyuki Iwaki, this absence of *Allegria* reflects Takemitsu's own technical awkwardness as he composed at the keyboard in those early years – in the same way that the composer's fondness for soft dynamics originally stemmed from a desire not to be a nuisance to his benefactors when practising at the houses of strangers.[32] But it is at the same time surely a reflection of a personal temperamental propensity, one revealed by the second part of the *Romance* performing directions. The obvious influence of composers such as Debussy and Messiaen on Takemitsu's musical language has tended to result in an emphasis among commentators upon the '*im*-pressionistic' qualities of his music; but, at the same time, it should not be overlooked that his music from the very beginning permitted itself the *ex*-pression of at least one emotional state as well: that of a profound, dignified melancholy. 'This may indeed be a personal feeling', Takemitsu was to confess at one point, 'but the joy of music, ultimately, seems connected with sadness. The sadness is that of existence. The more you are filled with the pure happiness of music-making, the deeper the sadness is.'[33]

These typical qualities of mood and tempo are of course implicit in the very title of the Takemitsu composition which marked the official 'début' of the artist Funayama was later to describe as 'the *Lento* composer'.[34] As noted above, the score of this work – *Lento in Due Movimenti* – has been 'lost', and while urban myths of its survival in some form abound amongst the Tōkyō musical community, no documentation of this work has been available for the present author's researches. Two textual sources do nevertheless exist to provide the commentator with materials for a certain amount of – albeit very tentative – speculation. The first is a reconstruction of the composer's sketches for the pianist Fujiwara, which exists as a CD recording played by Kazuoki Fuji;[35] the second is *Litany – In Memory of Michael Vyner* (1990), a work Takemitsu described as a 'recomposition from memory' of the original, and whose title perhaps suggests some cryptic word-play – the Japanese for 'litany', *rentō*, being a near-homophone of the title of the original work. There are considerable differences between these two versions, and of course in the case of the recorded version no score exists to support definitively any close analytical readings; but with these qualifications in mind, it is still possible to make some

Ex. 2 *Litany* I, bars 1–3

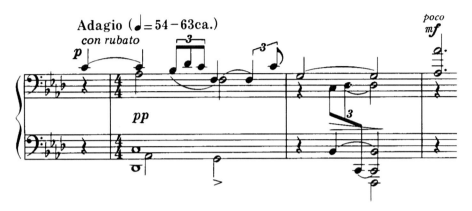

general observations about certain typical aspects of the work. For example, both versions begin with a characteristic Takemitsu gesture: a single, unaccompanied sustained pitch which here, as in many other instances, reveals itself as the first note of a melodic phrase. The actual notes of this melody are the same in both versions, but are accompanied differently; the 'harmonisation' as it appears in *Litany* is given in Example 2.

This emergence out of *niente* at the beginnings of works is complementary to the dissipation of works into silence which is the standard gesture of final closure in almost all of Takemitsu's music. It suggests a conception of music as contiguous with, rather than separate from, the silence surrounding it which is essentially 'Eastern' rather than Occidental in nature and which – as we shall examine more fully in the final chapter of this work – in later years, Takemitsu was to relate specifically to the Japanese aesthetic concept of *ma*. Examination of the uppermost, melodic voice in this example reveals something else about Takemitsu's musical language at this period: the continuing persistence of stylistic traits derivative of the Japanese 'nationalist' tradition. In this instance, what Akiyama refers to as the work's 'plaintively sombre pentatonic main theme'[36] begins by exposing all pitches of the same ascending *in* scale found at the beginning of *Romance*, in the transposed form C–Db–F–G–Bb. Curiously, when Takemitsu came to recompose this work as *Litany*, he added a passage not contained in the recording of the original *Lento* which lies entirely within the ambit of this mode (Ex. 3) – thus, paradoxically, including in a work written as late as 1990 a few bars which are probably the most superficially 'Japanese'-sounding in the composer's entire acknowledged output.

Such 'Japanese' elements apart, however, the composers whose influence

Ex. 3 *Litany* I, bars 17–18

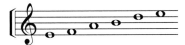

"In" scale ascending

(Transposed)

Litany, I, bb. 17 - 18

on the sound-world of *Lento/Litany* is most palpable tend to be French. Noriko Ohtake notes that by this time Takemitsu had acquired a rented Pleyel piano which possessed 'a sort of nasal sound as in the French language' and on which he played 'a lot of Debussy and Fauré, which suited the instrument'.[37] On the evidence of the second movement of *Lento*, he would appear also to have played a lot of a more recent French composer as well. Thanks to Toshi Ichiyanagi, he had by this time come into possession of a score of Olivier Messiaen's *8 Préludes*, and it would seem hard to disagree with Akiyama's assertion that the second movement of *Lento/Litany* is 'music in which the influence of Messiaen's *Préludes* can be seen'.[38] The most audible reflection of this new influence is the addition of a new resource to Takemitsu's modal vocabulary, and one not tainted with the pejorative connotations of the pentatonic forms employed hitherto: the octatonic scale ([0,1,3,4,6,7,9,10]), which, in the shape of the 'second mode of limited transposition', Messiaen had contrived to make so much his own. Although Takemitsu once claimed that he 'made use of the octatonic

Ex. 4 *Litany* II, reduction of uppermost voice, bars 1–3

collection before ever hearing it in the music of Messiaen, and that he arrived at it intuitively, using it as well as other modes of his own invention',[39] it has hard to overlook this synchronism between Takemitsu's first exposure to the French composer's music, and the incorporation into his musical style of what was, in fact, henceforth to remain one of the most consistent features of the composer's harmonic vocabulary for the remainder of his creative life.

The most obvious excursions into 'Mode II' occur in the middle section of the movement, 'Allegro con moto' (a rare instance, it will be observed, of this most 'un-Japanese' of tempo indications in Takemitsu's music), where substantial sections lie almost wholly within the ambit of one of the three available transpositions of the basic scale. Generally speaking, this aspect of Takemitsu's octatonic practice is a unique feature not shared by his handling of other modal materials: while the latter are generally used only as source collections for individual harmonies, or occasionally melodic lines, Takemitsu frequently uses the octatonic mode exclusively for extended passages, and it is this feature above all others which is probably most responsible for the 'Messiaenic' flavour exuded by so much of his music. But the outer sections of the second movement of *Lento/Litany* as well, though not exclusively octatonic, also contain several chords and short passages derived from 'Mode II', in promiscuous combination with other harmonies of decidedly 'impressionistic' character.

It is also possible to detect Messiaen's influence in the textural layout of much of these outer sections, for example at the very beginning of the piece. Whereas in the previous movement the texture had been clearly divided into melody and accompaniment, here the melody emerges as the uppermost voice of the harmony in a way that strongly recalls Messiaen's practice. Furthermore, the melodic line thus projected interestingly reveals a horizontal modal organisation which is distinct from the vertical modal derivations of individual harmonies. The uppermost pitches of bars 1-3, for instance, all lie within the ambit of a six-note collection comprising the notes of a 'D-major' scale (or one of its modal equivalents) minus B♮, as shown in Example 4.

While Miyamoto, with a certain justification, considers this opening

Ex. 5 *Litany* II, bar 30

section to be centred around a D tonality,[40] in my example it will be seen that I have highlighted the emphasis on F♯ and, to a lesser extent, C♯ that appears when the melody is abstracted from its harmonic context. The reasons for this emphasis are to be found in the overall tonal direction of this movement. The first movement of *Lento/Litany* is given an F-minor key signature, and ends in that key; the second movement, like the famous finale of Schoenberg's second string quartet, eschews key signatures but closes unexpectedly on a chord of F♯ major (spelt as G♭ major in Takemitsu's case). Unexpected as this tonal closure may be, Example 4 shows that it is not entirely unprepared: the emphasis on F♯ and its 'dominant' in this phrase, which is repeated twice during the course of the movement, subtly establish a precedent for its ultimate tonicisation at the work's close.

Moreover, the quasi-'diatonic' modalism revealed on the horizontal plane by Example 4 is found occasionally here in the vertical dimension as well. For example, the chord quoted above (Ex. 5) sounds all notes of a standard heptatonic collection simultaneously – in this case (perhaps significantly for Takemitsu's future development) of a 'D Lydian' mode. Since this chord appears in the original *Lento* as well (at least as far as the aural evidence of the recording can suggest), its presence here indicates another early instance of a practice that was to remain constant throughout Takemitsu's career.

Tonal closure – on an unambiguous E♭-major triad – is also featured in the second work from Takemitsu's *Shinsakkyokuha* years, the violin and piano duo *Distance de Fée* (1951).[41] Furthermore, the octatonic scale introduced into the second movement of *Lento* is here used with such frequency that it is easier to list the few passages *not* based on this mode than to identify all its occurrences; a factor which, not surprisingly, imparts to the work perhaps the most 'Messiaenic' sound of any surviving Takemitsu score.

Ex. 6 *Distance de Fée*, bar 5

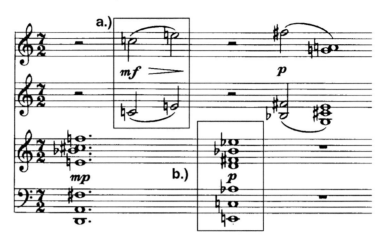

(Indeed in Japan, where it is possible to buy a recording of this work with the solo executed on the *ondes martenot*,[42] one writer on Takemitsu has confessed to mistaking it for Messiaen when playing his CD without reference to the liner notes![43]) Of the 'non-octatonic' passages referred to above, of particular interest is bar 47, where apparently for the first time Takemitsu makes horizontal use of another addition to his modal vocabulary, Messiaen's 'first mode of limited transposition', in other words the conventional whole-tone scale. But of even greater interest – and, for Takemitsu's future development, much more significant – is the harmony to be found in bar 5 (Ex. 6). The first chord here perhaps indicates Takemitsu's early familiarity with another of the modes in Messiaen's system, Mode III (of which more will be said with reference to later works), since its seven pitches lie within the gamut of nine available from that collection. The rising, quasi-'iambic' pattern marked 'a' is also of interest inasmuch as it prefigures what was to become a typical melodic gesture of the composer. But the greatest interest of all attaches to the chord marked 'b', generated by adding one extraneous pitch – E♭ – to the six pitches of a whole-tone scale. The pitch-collection resulting from this operation, [0,1,2,4,6,8,10], was to become such a distinctive signature of the composer's harmonic vocabulary that – since necessity henceforth demands that I shall make continued reference to it – I propose simply to refer to this 'pc set' by the shorthand it acquires in Allen Forte's theoretical system: '7-33'.[44]

The powerful harmonic resource which this technique of adding extraneous, semitonally dissonant pitches to modal forms represented for Takemitsu cannot be over emphasised. Koozin has suggested that the practice may have taken its cue from Messiaen's own hints on disguising modes in this way in his *Technique de mon langage musical*,[45] but, since this text did not appear in Japanese translation until 1954, it is uncertain whether Takemitsu could have acquired the technique by such means. A more likely explanation may be the suggestion already advanced: that it represents a refinement of the intensification of a mode by means of external, dissonant pitches seen in *Romance*, now devoid of the anecdotal, 'Japanese' associations which attached to the practice in that context.

As in *Romance* and (in its revised form) *Litany*, literal repetition plays an important structural role in *Distance de Fée*, and in particular the reappearance of the opening material is once again a clue that the work is drawing to its close. In other places, however, Takemitsu favours not so much a literal remembrance of things past as a sort of 'paramnesic' recollection of earlier material, in which various features are subjected to minute, apparently arbitrary, alteration in one way or other, and this too was to become a distinctive feature of the composer's style. Furthermore, the specific types of deviation from pre-established models that are revealed by this process suggest the manifold ways in which Takemitsu may have handled his *materia musica* in general: subjecting it to arbitrary change in a manner which contrasts sharply with the deterministic rigour of many of his Western colleagues. For both of these reasons, then, it will be profitable to examine more closely some of the ways in which the repetitions of material in *Distance de Fée* differ from their model.

Example 7 illustrates, on the uppermost system, the first five piano harmonies of *Distance de Fée* and, beneath them, three passages which derive in various ways from this original. Comparison of these versions with their model reveals various standard techniques of Takemitsu for altering and 'disguising' materials when they are repeated. Most obviously of all, for example, chord '4' of the original sequence is *omitted* completely from every subsequent version. Secondly, when chord '3' reappears in bar 20, the note density is not only increased by the *addition* of two extra pitches (E♮ and G♮), but the pitches are also reorganised horizontally to transform the single attack into a kind of falling major-second 'appoggiatura' figure which is retained as a consistent feature in bar 29 and reappears independently in bar 40. (This also relates to the falling major-second motif in the melodic line, highlighted in Ex. 8.) Thirdly, one observes that at its third appearance the material is globally *transposed* upwards by a whole-tone, and that the single event in bar 40 is a semitone lower than the corresponding chord of the original. Next, examination of the right-hand part of chord '5' reveals that two pitches (A♭ and E) are replaced by arbitrary *substitutions* at the equivalent point in bar 20 (respectively C♭ and F♮).

Ex. 7 *Distance de Fée*, transformations of opening materials

Interestingly, when this chord is transposed a tone higher in the third appearance of the progression, the C♭ duly rises to an enharmonically notated C♯, but the F♮ is raised by only a semitone to F♯ – in other words, it reverts to a 'correct' reading of bar 1 a whole-tone higher. Another kind of pitch substitution operates when chord '2' is rehearsed in bar 20: in this specific instance, Takemitsu selects a different pitch for octave doubling in the right hand, resulting in a *revoicing* of the harmony. Finally, with regard to chord '5', one notes that in the second version at bar 20, the right-hand part remains at the original pitch (with the substitutions referred to above), but the left-hand part is transposed down a minor third. This *global transposition of one segment of a pitch-collection by a different intervallic factor from the remainder* is also typical of Takemitsu. It will be noted that it implies a division of the harmony into certain autonomous 'strata' which are then treated as independent units for the purposes of further transformation – and that, in this particular instance, the division of these strata according to their allocation to the pianist's hands clearly points to the music's keyboard origins.

If all the above tends to give the impression – at least to a Western reader – of a certain imprecision on Takemitsu's part, it may be well to end by giving a description of a facet of *Distance de Fée* that displays a contrasting rigour: its thematic process. For the most part, the work is clearly divided into a number of phrases, in each of which the violin sings a long, expressive melodic line. A closer examination of these phrases shows that they are in fact quite artfully constructed out of a number of recurrent smaller motifs, and that the manner in which these are reconstituted to provide new material reveals the workings of a considerable compositional discipline. In Example 8, the pitches of the violinist's first phrase have been so displayed as to make this type of construction readily apparent. In this 'paradigmatic' representation, the unfolding of the melodic line 'syntagmatically' is to be read from left to right, and continuously from the end of one staff to the beginning of the next. The vertical partitions show how all this seamlessly unfolding *melos* can in fact be divided into three principal motivic categories – A, B and C – with the exception of two notes (X) which do not appear to fit into the scheme. The repeated pitches in this diagram, such as the E♭s in the second staff, do not correspond to actual pitch repetitions in the score, but rather illustrate an important device whereby Takemitsu overcomes and to a certain extent 'disguises' the potentially fragmentary nature of this type of constructional method: the use of certain notes as pivots, common to the end of one motivic unit and the beginning of the next. This kind of concatenation may, in its turn, generate higher-level motivic units which can reappear as melodic features: the overlapping of notes 2–4 of 'B' with notes 2–4 of 'A', found in the fifth and sixth staves of the example, gives rise to one such distinctive melodic turn.

Distance de Fée owes both title and inspiration to a poem by the colourful figure whose acquaintance Takemitsu had made the previous year, the Japanese surrealist poet Shūzo Takiguchi (1903–76). And although technically a product of the *Shinsakkyokuha* years, in reality this work, with its

Ex. 8 *Distance de Fée*, melodic construction of first phrase

Messiaenic harmonies, already belongs to the next period of Takemitsu's creative life – a period over which the personality of Takiguchi was to cast a long shadow. It is to a discussion of this next phase in Takemitsu's artistic career, then, and the artistic alliances that coalesced as a result partly of Takiguchi's influence, that attention must now be turned.

3 Experimental workshop: the years of *Jikken Kōbō*

Takemitsu's first exposure to public criticism may ultimately have ended in tears, but the *Shinsakkyokuha* evening which featured his compositional début was not without its positive side. In the green room after the performance, Takemitsu met two figures who were to become important allies: the composer Jōji Yuasa (1929–), and the poet and music critic Kuniharu Akiyama (1929–96). It was as a result of encounters with these and other kindred spirits over the course of the next year or so that a decision was made to found a new artistic alliance that would reflect their common aesthetic ideals. Thus it was that in September 1951 Takemitsu and eight idealistic young colleagues launched the new organisation which was to become such a colourful feature of the Japanese avant-garde landscape for the next six years; an organisation which, at the suggestion of the inspirational figure behind much of its activity, Shūzo Takiguchi, was given the name 'Experimental Workshop': *Jikken Kōbō*.

This switch of loyalties from the *Shinsakkyokuha* (from which both Takemitsu and Suzuki withdrew their membership in the following year) was a significant one for Takemitsu. The new grouping differed from the old in two important respects, both of which were to have far-reaching repercussions for Takemitsu's artistic development. First, it had a decidedly anti-academic bias – in fact, it seems that any kind of formal musical education was a barrier to membership, and this naturally helped consolidate Takemitsu's position as an outsider to the highly conservative world of the institutional Japanese academic establishment at this period. Secondly, whereas the elder composers' association had been a platform for exclusively 'musical' presentations of works in a conservative and 'nationalistic' vein, the youthful *Jikken Kōbō* membership embraced a variety of artists in different media, and aimed at an interdisciplinary meeting between them. This aspect of its activities was also to set an important precedent for Takemitsu, who for the rest of his life was to enjoy close friendships with a number of prominent writers, painters, sculptors and film directors in addition to his musical acquaintances, and whose musical philosophy was to be profoundly influenced by these 'synaesthetic' encounters with the other arts. One is reminded by Takemitsu's example, indeed, of what Morton Feldman once described as the 'painterly' quality of American music, and the whole *Jikken Kōbō* phenomenon seems, in retrospect, to

possess uncanny parallels with the manner in which the aesthetics of contemporaneous American 'experimental' composers were enriched by an
exchange of ideas with artists in other media. However, it would appear
that the Japanese group was unaware of these developments across the
Pacific, and that their role-models were instead such pre-war European
artistic coteries as the *Blaue Reiter* or *Bauhaus*. At precisely the period,
then, when in the West avant-garde art was beginning to be assimilated
into the establishment as the official language of academia, in Japan it was
still in the position of a subversive 'alternative' to the dominant tradition;
and much of the paraphernalia of the *Jikken Kōbō* movement, with its
strong echoes of the polemic tone typical of pre-war European artistic
movements, reflects this oppositional status. Takiguchi's exuberant
expression of the group's aims in 1955, for instance, reads somewhat like a
pre-war artistic 'manifesto': 'by using dance, film "autoslides" and television in a so-called "audio-visual" synthesis of the arts', he claims, 'the ultimate aim is that the experimental domain of new art will be infinitely
expanded'.[1]

These interdisciplinary aspirations of the *Jikken Kōbō* were reflected in a
membership which (besides Takemitsu and his fellow-composer Suzuki)
also comprised the writer already referred to, Kuniharu Akiyama; the
pianist Takahiro Sonoda; the stage producer Hideo Yamazaki; and the
artists Shōzō Kitajiro, Katsuhiro Yamaguchi, Hideko Fukushima and Naoji
Ima.[2] They were also reflected by the group's first public production: the
première of the ballet *Ikiru Yorokobi* ('Joie de vivre') on 16 November 1951
demanded the talents of all the above members, as well as Takemitsu who,
besides conducting the performance, wrote the score in collaboration with
Suzuki over the course of ten sleepless days and nights, and suffered physical breakdown as a result. The activities of *Jikken Kōbō* during the following six years of its existence assumed a number of forms. There was
continuing experimental exploration of new artistic media; for example,
the fourth *Jikken Kōbō* recital, on 30 September 1953, unveiled to the
public the new device mentioned by Takiguchi in the passage already
quoted, the *ōto suraido* or 'autoslide' created for the organisation by Tōkyō
Tsūshin Kōgyō, the forerunner of the Sony Corporation. In this contrap-
tion, pieces of metallic paper, attached to the reverse side of a conventional
magnetic tape, acted as switches to change the transparency being projected on to a screen, thus enabling a primitive 'multimedia' synchronisa-
tion between taped sounds and projected images. Three years later, on 4
February 1956, the group gave its first concert employing what has since
proved a more durable technology. It was at this recital of *musique concrète*

and 'electronic music' that – alongside works by Mayuzumi and Minao Shibata – Takemitsu's own inaugural venture into the medium, his *Relief Statique*, received its first exposure to the concert-going public.

Alongside these forays into more 'experimental' territory, however, the *Jikken Kōbō* was also responsible for conventionally staged musical performances, the programming of which clearly reflects two major imperatives. The first was the desire to introduce to the Japanese public the works of relatively 'advanced' Western composers still unknown to them. Thus Messiaen's *Quatuor pour la fin du temps* was given at the second *Jikken Kōbō* recital on 20 January 1952, and (according to Eiko Kasaba) his *8 Préludes* and *Visions de l'Amen* also featured amongst the works performed during the years of the group's existence.[3] Schoenberg's *Pierrot lunaire* was another piece which received its historic Japanese première under the group's auspices, an event which – amazingly – took place as late as 10 September 1954. But besides the work of such important Western figures as these, the *Jikken Kōbō* also provided a platform for the more advanced of the younger generation of Japanese composers – specifically, of course, for its own members. Besides *Relief Statique*, for example, two of Takemitsu's works from this period were given their first performances by the organisation: the original one-movement version of the solo piano *Uninterrupted Rest*, first heard on 9 August 1952; and a *Chamber Concerto* premièred on 12 July 1955 (and now lost).

But important as *Jikken Kōbō* was for Takemitsu's creative development, one should not fall into the error of assuming that his music in this period was circumscribed to the few performances which took place under its umbrella. The fact that so few scores have survived gives a distorted picture of Takemitsu's compositional activity at this time, which ranged far beyond the confines of conventional performances for the concert room. Mention has already been made, for example, of his tentative first experiments with *musique concrète*; another area into which Takemitsu first ventured during these years, and which in places overlaps with his electro-acoustic experimentation, is that of providing incidental music for various dramaturgical media. In the discussion of Takemitsu's music which follows, then, an examination of the one surviving printed musical text from these years – the first movement of *Uninterrupted Rest* – will be followed by brief discussions of Takemitsu's work in these other areas. Since textual support for a thorough investigation of the latter is mostly lacking, however – and since, in the case of the incidental music, the subject in question really lies beyond the professed scope of this book – it has been thought best to offer here only a general overview of each of these areas spanning the whole of the composer's career, and thereafter to refer to them only in those contexts where some relationship between them and Takemitsu's 'concert' music makes such reference absolutely necessary.

The music of the early *Jikken Kōbō* years: *Uninterrupted Rest I*

As noted above, the only work to have survived in the form of a fully notated and published text from the early *Jikken Kōbō* years is the movement which was eventually to form Part I of the triptych entitled *Uninterrupted Rest*, originally performed as an independent work under that title by its dedicatee, Takahiro Sonoda, in August 1952. The instruction (in English) with which this work is prefaced – 'Slowly, sadly and as if to converse with' – is very much in keeping with the general mood already established by 'the *Lento* composer' in previous works, and these verbal indications 'reverberate' in musical terms which translate their evocative sense with exact fidelity: a rather 'Messiaenic' tempo marking of $\downarrow$ = 48, plus the performance directions *Triste* and *quasi parlando*. The work's opening gesture, too, follows an established precedent: like *Lento/Litany*, it begins with a single unsupported pitch (here provided with an anacrusis a semitone higher) emerging out of the silence. Whereas in the earlier work, however, this pitch was sustained to become the first note of the melodic line, here it is tied to an inner voice of the supporting harmony, and the melodic line continues in the voice above (Ex. 9).

Like *Distance de Fée*, *Uninterrupted Rest* owes its title to a poem by Shūzo Takiguchi,[4] and like the earlier work too, this first movement clearly owes much to Messiaen's example – most obviously in its frequent use of the octatonic scale, and of a texture in which the melodic line is the uppermost voice of a homophonic harmonic movement. Yet at the same time *Uninterrupted Rest* represents a considerable advance in the handling of these derivative features. Gone are the triadic, tonal closures with which the phrases of *Distance de Fée* were periodically punctuated; gone too are the bars of regularly notated, if changing, metres in a basic minim pulse, to be replaced by a score layout in which solid and dotted barlines enclose irregular multiples of small durational values, in a manner very akin to that of Messiaen's keyboard music. The adherence to Messiaen's modal system is also far less literal than in the earlier work, with more frequent use of pitches extraneous to the locally prevalent octatonic collection, or passages which resist analysis in terms of that scale altogether. One such usage occurs at the climactic moment of the work's middle section (Ex. 10), where the uppermost melodic voice rises through four notes of a whole-tone scale to arrive on a chord which contains all six notes of the

Ex. 9 *Uninterrupted Rest* I, opening

scale at the same transposition, plus an extraneous B♭: the ubiquitous '7-33' collection again.

Musique concrète

Though it represented an advance on Takemitsu's previous work, the musical language of *Uninterrupted Rest* still, of course, lagged far behind the latest developments in the West. Yet within a few years Takemitsu was to venture into an area that represented one of the most advanced resources available to a composer of his time, and was to continue experimenting with it for several years alongside his more conservative instrumental offerings. As already narrated in chapter 1, it was Toshirō Mayuzumi's example that had made Japanese composers aware of this new resource, with his pioneering experiments in both *musique concrète* and *elektronische Musik*. But it is already significant of Takemitsu's aesthetic inclinations that – with the single major exception of some oscillator-generated sine waves in *Stanza II* for harp and tape (1972) – the composer's interests were to focus exclusively on the former means of production. The mathematical manipulation of sounds as 'quantitative' phenomena found in works such as Mayuzumi and Moroi's *Variations on a Numerical Principle of 7* was clearly already anathema to Takemitsu, who preferred instead to work in a much more intuitive fashion with the rich sounds of the 'concrete' world, considered in their 'qualitative' aspect. Takemitsu's *musique concrète* at the same time differs from Schaeffer's in that it does not necessarily avoid the anecdotal associations of his sound-material, but

Ex. 10 *Uninterrupted Rest* I, bar 6

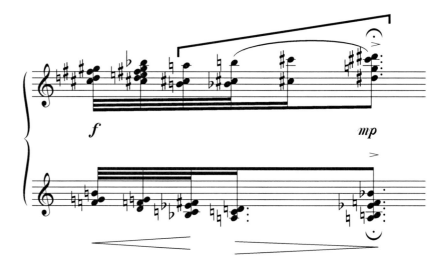

often actively encourages the listener's recognition of them. While Schaeffer laboured for hours over his steam-train and casserole sounds in an effort to 'abstract the sound from its dramatic context and elevate it to the dignity of musical material',[5] Takemitsu seems to have delighted in offering his listeners sounds drawn more or less recognisably from the natural world – lending to his work a 'radiophonic' quality that has made much of it especially suitable for use as accompaniment to dramatic presentations of various kinds.

In fact Takemitsu's first effort in the new medium began life – as did so many of his later tape compositions – in the form of incidental music. It was material originally realised in the studios of the commercial broadcasting station *Shin Nihon Hōsō* for Yasuji Inoue's 1955 radio drama *Honō* ('Flames') that, reworked, provided Takemitsu with his first acknowledged tape composition: *Relief Statique*, heard for the first time at a *Jikken Kōbō* concert in1956. The work was to be followed by no fewer than four compositions in the new medium within that same year: a triptych of pieces deriving from his incidental music for the Anouilh play *Eurydice*; *Tree, Sky and Birds*; *Clap Vocalism*; and – another *Shin Nihon Hōsō* commission – *Vocalism A.I.* This last exemplifies well the anecdotal quality of much of Takemitsu's tape music. A collaboration with the poet Shuntarō Tanikawa, it was originally planned as a tape montage on the single Japanese word *ai* (love) lasting seventy-two hours; mercifully the final version runs for only four minutes and five seconds, making it (in Takemitsu's words)

Tanikawa's 'shortest and longest love-poem'. The two phonemes of the Japanese word alone provide all the basic sound-material for the work, recited in various ways – sung, spoken, whispered, groaned, etc. – by a male and female speaker; and despite Akiyama's assertion that the work's title refers not only to 'the love that flows in the veins of lovers' but also to 'the love of which small birds sing . . . love such as that revealed in the inside of stones',[6] the overriding impression gained from this male–female dialogue is nevertheless often the very literal one of a certain playful eroticism. Certainly it is this quality that Yōji Kuri takes as the starting point for the scenario of his 1963 animated film *Love*, which uses Takemitsu's work as its soundtrack.

Similar anecdotal references, albeit partly of more metaphorical kind, pervade *Sky, Horse and Death* (1958), originally composed for a radio drama four years earlier. Here the three elements of the title are represented, respectively, by birdsongs, the neighing of a horse, and the cracking of a whip to simulate gunshots. A more concrete form of reference still is to be found in *Water Music* (1960), whose source materials consist entirely of various sounds produced with the aid of the medium which gives the work its title. In parenthesis, it is amusing to learn that some of the original recording sessions that eventually produced this evocative and poetic soundscape occurred in the most prosaic of locations. Takemitsu had wanted to record the sound of stones being dropped into a deep well, but at the same time he did not want to capture the sound of splashing water. The solution he eventually hit upon was to substitute for his 'deep well' a flushing lavatory in the bathrooms of the Sōgetsu Arts Centre in Tōkyō. As Heuwell Tircuit, who was privy (if that is the word) to Takemitsu's secret, noted: 'I seriously suspected that the audience might laugh, that someone or other might get wind of what was going on. Nobody laughed.'[7]

Of course, the source sounds from which these pieces are derived are not always presented in recognisable form: the usual repertory of studio treatments is employed to transform them in ways that run the whole gamut of recognisability. The droplet sounds of *Water Music*, for example, are often given highly percussive envelopes that make them sound like a traditional Japanese instrument such as the *tsuzuki*[8] of the *nō*[9] ensemble, and appropriately enough the work exists in a second version with three additional flute parts as accompaniment to a *nō* dance. This use of studio manipulation to confuse the listener's perception of sound-materials is taken to a high degree of sophistication in Takemitsu's music for Masaki Kobayashi's 1964 film *Kwaidan*, parts of which also exist in the form of an independent tape composition of the same name. Here Takemitsu goes so far as to blur the traditional distinctions between 'sound effects' and 'incidental music' (or indeed 'diagetic' (on-scene) music such as the *heikebiwa*[10] narrations required by the plot of the story *Hoichi the Earless*). For example, sounds usually categorised as 'effects', such as the splitting of wood and creaking of doors, are electronically treated and artfully arranged into a 'musical' composition. Conversely, sounds that the listener interprets in an illustrative fashion, such as the howling of a snowstorm or the roar of the ocean, turn out to be electronic metamorphoses of 'musical' sounds of a *shakuhachi* or slowed-down *nō* chanting: transformed so as to be longer recognisable as such, yet at the same time no longer 'realistic' and imparting to these ghost stories an eerie, dream-like quality.

After *Kwaidan*, however, there are only a few, widely spaced electronic works to be found in the Takemitsu catalogue: *Toward* (1970), *Wonder World* (1972), *A Minneapolis Garden* and *The Sea is Still* (both 1986). As with so many other composers of his generation, Takemitsu's brief flirtation with electronics did not blossom into a lifelong relationship. For all that, his excursion into this field was highly significant for his future development, enabling him to work directly with the raw timbres of natural sound without the mediation of instruments and their notation. In the early years of his career, the lessons gleaned from this experience were not, it is true, reflected in his instrumental output, which by contrast retained a relatively conservative idiom; but it was not long before Takemitsu's new-found awareness of timbre was to bear fruit in the domain of his instrumental music as well, as subsequent chapters of this study will show.

Music for dramatic media

While Takemitsu's period of most intense involvement with *musique concrète* may have been short-lived, the situation was to prove otherwise with an area of artistic activity already mentioned in passing: the provision of 'incidental music' for various dramaturgical media. As early as 1952, Takemitsu was already engaged in this type of work, writing a score for a film about the artist *Hokusai* to a scenario by Shūzo Takiguchi – although, in the event, owing to a change in production staff his music was never used. Over the course of the next few years, however, he was to begin writing music for both radio productions and live theatre in earnest, and it is interesting to note how many of the commissions for the latter came from the *Shiki* ('Four Seasons') theatre troupe, a former member of which had been the actress Asaka Wakayama, who – on 15 June 1954 – became Takemitsu's wife.[11] Reference to the worklist at the end of this volume will

give the reader some idea of just how much music Takemitsu was eventually to provide for both stage and radio (and later, television) – music
which is mostly unknown today, and indeed in many cases may have van-
ished altogether. But it is with the composition, in collaboration with
Masaru Satō, of his first full-length feature-film score – for Kō Nakahira's
Kuratta Kajutsu ('Crazed Fruit') in 1956 – that Takemitsu embarked on the
production of the particular form of 'incidental music' on which his reputation in this field today largely rests. This was to prove the first in a long
list of film scores to which Takemitsu continued to add right up to the year
preceding his death – amounting in the end to over ninety titles, and
including such artistic and commercial highpoints as his scores for Akira
Kurosawa's epic *Ran* (1986) and the Hollywood blockbuster *Rising Sun*
(Philip Kaufman, 1993), as well as countless other award-winning soundtracks.

Sadly, this important body of work lies outside the scope of the present
study, but a few general points should nevertheless be made. The first is
that the film music – or at least, those portions of it available on disc –
often reveals quite different aspects of Takemitsu's creative personality to
those found in most of his concert music. In fact, the picture that emerges
of Takemitsu the film composer is that of a highly skilled, professional pastiche artist who can turn his hand to a whole range of stylistic codes, each
of which is perfectly adapted for the scenario in question. For example, if a
film such as *Tanin no Kao*[12] contains a scene in a beer hall, Takemitsu provides a kind of Kurt Weill-soundalike 'German waltz'; if it deals with a
Puerto Rican boxer, as does Teshigahara's earlier *Jose Torres* (1959),
Takemitsu's music simulates an appropriately 'Latin' style. Furthermore,
many of the musical codes which Takemitsu employs to these ends are
obviously decidedly 'populist' and tonal in character, and as such constitute an area of musical activity radically divergent from the modernist preoccupations of his contemporaneous concert scores: an area which,
however, was increasingly to make its presence felt as an alternative to
'modernism' in Takemitsu's concert music as the language of the latter
developed over the years.

Takemitsu's decision to finance his career as a composer largely by
means of such activity (and also, in the early years, by means of detective
novels which he wrote under a pseudonym) had important repercussions
too, insomuch as it granted him a certain financial independence: in particular, it allowed him to eschew the form of remuneration which became
the staple resource of many of his Western colleagues – teaching in higher
education (a choice which had significant consequences for his aesthetic
priorities, as the final chapter of this book will reveal). It would be unjust

to assert, however, that Takemitsu's continuing involvement with incidental music was motivated solely by pecuniary imperatives. Among the many
other attractions it afforded, one was certainly that it offered him temporary release from the restrictive solitude of his composing studio into a
world peopled by other creative spirits – functioning as what he described
as a 'liberty passport'.[13] More pertinently for the topic to which this study
is devoted, however, Takemitsu's 'hands-on' experimentation with sound-
materials in his dramatic music often had direct consequences for later
concert-hall works: 'the film scores seem a sort of sketch-pad for concert
music, a place where he could experiment with new ideas and work out
musical problems before incorporating them into a work of abstract music
for the concert stage'.[14] On occasion, this relationship between film and
concert music might even take the form of direct quotation, or reworking,
of the same materials; more generally, however, the film music afforded
Takemitsu the opportunity to experiment freely with timbral, notational
and even – as has been suggested – stylistic devices which might later find
their way into his concert work.

But as suggested above, there are a number of instances in which the
relationship of Takemitsu's concert-hall work to his incidental music is a
direct one, consisting of actual quotation or reworking of the same materials. Towards the end of his life in particular, Takemitsu was to release a
whole succession of arrangements of his film and television work as
concert pieces, but his plundering of this vast resource had actually begun
much earlier. His music for the 1961 film *Furyō Shōnen*,[15] for instance, was
to provide the material for two concert pieces: *Bad Boy* for two guitars
(1993), and *Maru to Sankaku no Uta* ('A Song of ○'s [Circles] and △'s
[Triangles]'), the fifth number in the *a cappella* choral cycle *Uta* of
1979–92. In a more subtle manner, direct quotations from Takemitsu's
more 'commercially' orientated work had found their way into his 'serious'
music earlier still: such well-known concert pieces as *Requiem for Strings*
and *The Dorian Horizon* draw their materials in part from, respectively,
music for stage and screen. And, finally, this kind of derivative relationship
between concert music and film score could, on occasion, operate the
other way round: part of the composer's music for the film *Gishiki*[16] is a
reworking, for violin and string orchestra, of his *Hika* for violin and piano
of 1966.

Takemitsu's early embarkation on this long career as a film composer
had been considerably facilitated by the elder composer and fellow
Shinsakkyokuha member Fumio Hayasaka – nowadays best known in the
West (if at all) as creator of the music for such early Kurosawa films as
Rashōmon (1950) and *The Seven Samurai* (1954). Working as Hayasaka's

assistant, Takemitsu had gained invaluable experience of the practicalities of composition and performance, and the news of his mentor's sudden death – which occurred while Takemitsu was working on *Relief Statique* in 1955 – left him stunned. Yet out of this grief was to come the work which – as the next chapter will reveal – was to change the course of the composer's career irrevocably.

4 The *Requiem* and its reception

Two years after the death of Hayasaka, Takemitsu himself was obliged to take to his sickbed, and it was in this incapacitated state that he worked on a commission he had received from the Tōkyō Symphony Orchestra, sometimes managing to complete only a single bar, or even half a bar, during the course of a day. The work that eventually emerged from these painstaking efforts, *Requiem for Strings*, received its first performance in June 1957, and the composer's comments at the time certainly gave the impression that this intensely elegiac work was intended as a memorial to his departed mentor: while Takemitsu claimed he had not written the piece 'grieving over the death of any specific person', as he was writing it he 'gradually came to think about Fumio Hayasaka, and mourn his passing'.[1]

In subsequent years, however, Takemitsu was to give a slightly fuller account of the *Requiem*'s genesis, and hint at the presence of a second possible dedicatee. In one of his many conversations with Takashi Tachibana, for instance, he observed that 'at that time especially I was seriously ill, and since I finally realised that I didn't know when I myself was going to die, I ended up thinking that one way or another I'd like to create one piece before my death . . . I thought I ought to write my own requiem'.[2] This later version of events, in which the composer himself becomes the object of *déploration*, is corroborated by remarks made by Takemitsu in other contexts.[3] Nevertheless, as the composer went on to elaborate in the above interview with Tachibana, it was indeed as a result of Hayasaka's death that Takemitsu decided to turn the piece – previously entitled *Meditation* – into a *Requiem*; and it was the same stimulus that granted him what he had previously found lacking, the strength of resolve and clarity of image needed to embark on the project. The work thus ended up becoming both 'a requiem for Hayasaka and, at the same time, my own requiem'.[4]

Whatever the circumstances of its inspiration, the mood of *Requiem* is very much in harmony with that sombre tone which, as we have seen, had by this time already become a hallmark of Takemitsu's style. And once again, this gravity of mood is reflected in the choice of generally very slow tempi. Although Example 11, for example, may bear a metronome mark of 66, this refers to crotchet beats in a work whose basic pulse is for the most part the minim, making the actual tempo a sub-metronomic 33 beats per minute. At this speed it is certainly hard to perceive any higher-level metrical organisation, and it is perhaps to this quality that Takemitsu is referring by his enigmatic English phrase when he notes that 'the work is constructed on a "one by one" rhythm'.[5] Yōko Narazaki has noted that the frequent division of the beat into very slow triplets also undermines any sense of pulsation, inducing 'the feeling of suspension of sounds at the surface level',[6] and for a great deal of the time the overriding impression is indeed one of a profound desire to subvert any notion of regular pulse or metrical grouping. Takemitsu's choice of a string orchestra as medium for this threnody is also in accord with its sombre tone, creating a dark, monochromatic *film noir* sonority to which the composer was frequently to return in passages for strings alone in his mature orchestral music. This string orchestra medium was also to enter the lexicon of musical codes by means of which the composer identified his film music with the subject of the scenario in question: in this case, as vehicle for a certain kind of tragic lamentation. For instance, Takemitsu's scores for *Tōkyō Saiban*,[7] which deals with the post-war Tōkyō Trials, and *Kuroi Ame*,[8] whose subject is the Hiroshima bomb, both make exclusive use of the string orchestra to convey a very *Requiem*-like pathos.

As with the incipits of *Lento* and *Uninterrupted Rest I* quoted in the previous chapter, the opening gesture of *Requiem* is the emergence of a single pitch out of silence which – like its counterpart in *Uninterrupted Rest I* – then becomes the uppermost pitch of the harmony against which the melody unfolds (Ex. 11).

This melody apparently derives from a trumpet tune Takemitsu wrote as part of some incidental music for the *Shiki* theatre troupe in 1956: the production in question, *Semushi no Seijo*, was a reworking of Anouilh's *Ardèle, ou la Marguérite*.[9] It is an expansive, intensely expressive *cantilena* theme: Alain Poirier has commented on its relationship to 'neo-classical American lyricism',[10] and indeed one cannot help but wonder whether one of the items particularly favoured by the American radio station to which the invalid Takemitsu listened might have been that old warhorse of string orchestra repertory, Samuel Barber's *Adagio*. Like the melodic line of *Distance de Fée*, that of *Requiem* is clearly segmented into a number of phrases, articulated here by means of silences or *morendo* endings, and parallelisms of melodic contour – the second phrase, in bar 4, for instance, beginning as a transposed variant of the first a whole-tone higher. And while the working out of this melodic material over the course of the movement does not appear to proceed with quite the same degree of motivic rigour as that found in *Distance de Fée*, this opening melody obviously possesses a structural, 'thematic' significance – indeed Takemitsu himself describes the work in his programme note as based on a single

Ex. 11 *Requiem*, opening

REQUIEM
pour orchestre à cordes

theme.[11] One can perhaps gain some idea of what is meant by this assertion from Example 12, which compares the various forms assumed by this 'A' material during the course of the work. While clearly not identical, these nevertheless fall conspicuously into two types, each repeated more or less consistently in its appropriate context. Furthermore, each type is related to the other in various ways – most obviously in terms of the three-note head-motif, which differs only in the substitution of a minor for a major second between the first two pitches.

Ex. 12 Variants of main theme in *Requiem*

Takemitsu's programme note also observes that the work has no clearly differentiated beginning or end, and invokes a favourite metaphor of his: that of the 'stream of sound' running through humanity and the world, of which the composer has simply extracted a segment.[12] The origins of this concept, according to Takemitsu, date from a journey by underground train he undertook in 1948, in which he began to wonder whether it might be possible to incorporate sounds such as those he heard around him into instrumental music. 'To express it a little more precisely, I understood that "to compose" equalled "to attach meaning to" (*signifier*) the "stream of sound" flowing through the world around us.'[13] In the present context, this reference to the 'stream of sound' implies, yet again, that the work's initial emergence out of its ambience shall be balanced by a fading into nothingness at its close (Ex. 13) – both of these events, of course, at the same time being imbued with the quality of *ma* referred to previously.

The eight-note collection from which this final chord is constructed is

Ex. 13 *Requiem*, final bar

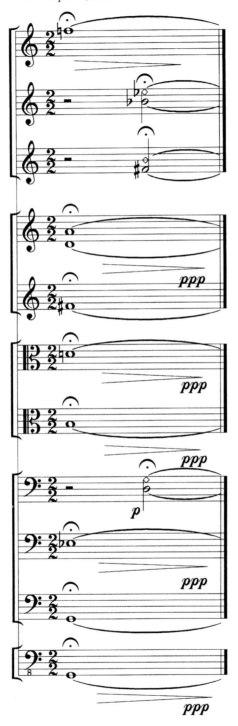

Ex. 14 *Requiem*, chords from bar 2 and bar 1

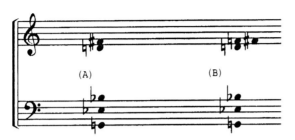

of considerable interest, inasmuch as it indicates the adoption of another
scale from Messiaen's system besides the octatonic: 'Mode III'
([0,1,2,4,5,6,8,9,10]), of which this harmony projects all but one note (C♯)
of the second transposition. In the specific context of *Requiem*, this particular chord is also significant since it expresses in its fullest form a recurrent
chordal type that gives the work much of its characteristic harmonic
flavour. This type is not always presented in a consistent form, like the 'referential' chord which we shall shortly examine in the second movement of
Uninterrupted Rest; rather, it appears in a number of guises, all of which
share one or more common features with each other and with Example 13.
Two such common features are: (i) reference to the 'Mode III' collection,
and (ii) a clear stratification of the harmony, often into triadic forms of
which the lowest tend to be in 'open' position and those superimposed
above it in 'close' position. For example, the 'Mode III' collection may be
segmented into three augmented triads a semitone apart, and the voicing
of Example 13 emphasises two of these in particular: an 'open'-position
augmented chord on 'G' in the bass, and one based on 'D' in harmonics.
Between these, the remaining pitches imply other, overlapping triads: B
minor, D major/minor. The second chord from bar 2 of the work, exclusive
of the melody note (Ex. 14a) is a subset of this concluding harmony, and
like it is clearly stratified into an 'open'-position (E♭ first inversion) triad
on the same root in the bass, and a 'close'-position augmented chord above
it. Addition of the F♮ found in Example 13 an octave lower adds to the 'E♭-
minor' implications of this composite sonority the further complication of
a B♭-major triad, yielding the very first accompanying chord of the piece
(Ex. 14b) – the work thus beginning with a close variant of the chord with
which it is to end.

Between this emergence from the 'stream of sound' and return thereto,
the music of *Requiem* unfolds a structure which, like those of the

Ex. 15 Form of *Requiem*

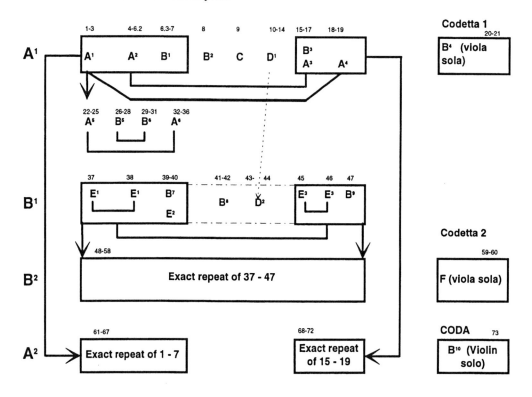

Takemitsu works already cited in previous chapters, relies heavily on repetition. Typically of the composer, this repetition often takes the form of the recycling of whole 'blocks' of material with note-for-note exactitude, and with an abruptness of transition that more frequently recalls the techniques of the studio splice than the well-prepared retransitions of Classical music. In other places, the material may be re-presented with minor alterations of some kind, transposed by a given intervallic factor, or both of these simultaneously. A complex pattern of repetitions of various kinds thus emerges, some of which are themselves nested within repetitions at a higher level, giving rise to an overall structure of which a schematised illustration is shown in Example 15.

Here, at the highest structural level, there are three exact duplications of material, identified as such in the diagram; while, occurring partly within these, there are also transposed repeats of bars 10, 37 and 45 as bars 11, 38 and 46 respectively. This particular form of repetition, in which a transposition immediately succeeds its model, is highly typical of Takemitsu, giving rise to patterns that have something of the character of a 'sequence' in tonal music (although without the implication of an ongoing tonal coherence which applies in the latter context). Transformed repetition is exemplified by the restatement of the opening material with a new, more rhythmically active accompaniment in bars 22–5, while both transposition and transformation operate together to generate the more radical reworking of the opening material offered in bars 18–19. And, as in *Distance de Fée*, this inexactitude in the recollection of previous material again operates here at the microcosmic level: pitches may be added or removed from individual chords or melodic lines, or different pitches substituted for them. Finally, one observes that the largest section of literal repetition is, in line with the composer's already established practice, once again a signifier of imminent closure.

It requires no more than a cursory glance at Example 15 to fathom that the overall structure of this work adds up to rather more than the sum of its parts, and that the pattern of repetitions operates to reinforce this formal articulation. The composer himself stated that 'roughly speaking, the work . . . is in a free three-section form . . . the tempo sequence of which is Lent – Modéré – Lent':[14] in other words, a no-nonsense 'Classical' ABA structure of a kind described by Seiji Ozawa as 'easy for Western people to understand'.[15] And it is easy (even for Westerners) to see how the arrangement of the repeated materials reinforces this ternary organisation. On the one hand, the final 'A2' section consists of a literal repeat of the opening and closing sections of 'A1'; at the same time, this outer pair of repeated sections encloses an internal repetition of the central section, 'B2' being an exact repeat of 'B1'; and, additionally, the outermost sections of 'B1' are closely related to one another in that they offer varied repeats of the same material, just as the outermost sections of 'A1' had done. Finally, the three *codette*, each affording a prominent role to a solo instrument, serve as landmarks to identify the end of each of the three principal segments, setting the seal on a structure which Ozawa describes as 'perfectly formed'.[16]

However, 'perfect' though this ternary organisation may be, its presence here is an indication that Takemitsu has not yet arrived at that individual attitude to formal organisation which is to distinguish his mature work. In general, the individual musical moments of Takemitsu's later music – which may or may not include repeated materials – do not add up to something like an overall pattern of organisation which may be apprehended as 'form' in the Western sense. Occasionally, it is true, they may suggest other types of formal organisation; but in most instances the arrangement of musical 'objects' simply *is* the form: the whole area of intermediary conceptualisation implied by that term, of a 'design' into which the material is poured as into a mould, is no longer present. The lingering presence of such a concept in Takemitsu's music in this period, then, is a sign that, on a formal level at least, his instrumental music has not yet had the temerity to transgress beyond the limits of what might be 'easily understood' by a Westerner.

Other orchestral music of the 1950s

The scale of *Requiem for Strings*, and the fact that it was commissioned by the Tōkyō Symphony Orchestra, are indications that by this stage Takemitsu was already embarking on more ambitious and prestigious projects than the modest chamber productions of *Jikken Kōbō*. In fact, over the course of the next two years, Takemitsu was to produce three more fairly substantial works for the Japanese national broadcasting service, the NHK – although he was subsequently to withdraw the third of these, *Scene* for cello and orchestra, and the composer's publisher was unwilling to make a copy available for the present author's researches. Of the other two works, the first appeared in July 1958, as part of the NHK's entry for the Italia Prize that year, which was a triptych entitled 'Three Forms for Words and Music'. Parts II and III of this project consisted of works by Hikaru Hayashi and Yoshiro Irino respectively; Takemitsu's contribution was Part I, *Tableau Noir*, a work for reciter and small orchestra to a poem by Kuniharu Akiyama. The instrumental forces employed for this seven-minute work are already unusual and idiosyncratic: in particular, the string section omits violins (with the exception of a violin solo), the woodwind parts consist of lower-register instruments only (bass flute, cor anglais and bass clarinet), and the keyboard instruments include organ and claviolin. As in *Requiem*, literal repetition has its role to play in the articulation of the work's overall structure, and as in much of the composer's music from *Lento/Litany* II onwards, the octatonic scale continually makes its presence felt: one of the work's thematic ideas, in fact, consists simply of an eight-note chord verticalising the whole collection, which is then transposed in parallel with an octatonic melodic line (bars 31–2). Whole-tone-derived materials also appear, and at one point there is a suggestion too that Takemitsu is referring to yet another of the 'modes of limited transposition' from Messiaen's system, Mode VI ([0,1,2,4,6,7,8,10]), perhaps best thought of as a whole-tone scale to which two extraneous semitones have been added, a tritone apart. Certainly the chord on the fourth beat of the bar at letter 'L' (Ex. 16) verticalises all eight notes of one of this scale's transpositions (whole-tone scale on C♯, plus G♯ and D).

Ex. 16 *Tableau Noir*, L/1

Only four months after the broadcast of the above work, in November 1958, NHK's listeners had the opportunity to hear yet another commission from Takemitsu: *Solitude Sonore*, for large orchestra including triple wind and two guitars. This new piece was dedicated to Toshirō Mayuzumi, who four years earlier, without ever having met the composer, had sent the newly married Takemitsu the unexpected gift of a small upright piano – a gift which he was to cherish for the remainder of his life. Once again the work's initial tempo indication ($\downarrow$ = 38-42) prescribes an extremely leisurely pace, and one which – as in *Requiem* – is subject to the constant fluctuations of a *rubato*; while any sensation of a regular pulse is again further undermined by extremely slow triplet formations. Furthermore, the overall mood is typically very grave: a rather intense, *Requiem*-like passage for strings alone from bar 22 onwards bears the indication 'Triste'. For those accustomed to the suave nuances of much of Takemitsu's mature music, however, the initial performance direction 'Quietment [a word not in my French dictionary!], avec sonore cruel' might come as something as a surprise – although it would be less surprising to pianists familiar with the second movement of *Uninterrupted Rest*, which bears the indication 'Quietly, and with a cruel reverberation', or to those members of the NHK orchestra who had participated in the première of Takemitsu's *Chamber Concerto* three years earlier, and had been instructed to play 'quietly and with a brutal sound'. Perhaps too Takemitsu's performance instruction may hit the mark in an unintended sense; for, compared with the finesse of Takemitsu's later instrumental style, the orchestration of the work is certainly rather basic.

Once again, the score contains passages of exact as well as inexact repetition: in fact, and unusually for Takemitsu, there is a rather old-fashioned instruction to repeat an entire section 'dal segno' before the Coda, resulting in an overall ABCB¹D form. Octatonicism and reference to other

Ex. 17 *Solitude Sonore*, bar 22

modal collections also reappear, and there is a particularly interesting usage of the latter in bar 22, where the final chord of the accompaniment verticalises all five notes of a 'black note' pentatonic scale over the extraneous pitches E, A and G in the bass: prophetic hint, perhaps, of the type of harmonic constructions that the composer was to use nearly twenty years later as the basis of *A Flock Descends into the Pentagonal Garden* (Ex. 17).

Early adventures in serialism

While such features of the harmonic language of *Tableau Noir* and *Solitude Sonore* as those quoted above indicate that Takemitsu was still to a large extent dependent on modal derivations, in other works of the same period he was already experimenting with a much freer exploration of the total-chromatic. The stimulus for such exploration almost certainly lay in his exposure to the music of the Second Viennese School, specifically Webern: mention has already been made of the *Jikken Kōbō*'s pioneer performances of the music of Schoenberg's circle, and whether Takemitsu first received his initiation into Webern's music by this medium or not, certainly by the end of the 1950s he was – like all good avant-garde composers of his day – 'enslaved'[17] by the music of the Austrian master.

There are unambiguous hints of this new 'enslavement' in *Le Son Calligraphié I*, first of a trio of works with this title for double string quartet. It received its première – appropriately enough – at what Poirier describes as 'the Japanese equivalent to Darmstadt',[18] the Karuizawa Festival of Contemporary Music, in August 1958, and its fragmented, 'pointillist' texture of angular, jagged, rhythmically irregular shapes clearly reflects the 'post-Webernian' aesthetics of the period in which it was written. Beneath this apparently typical 'avant-garde' surface, however, closer examination of the score reveals the continuing presence of many of the harmonic traits Takemitsu had developed over the course of the pre-

Ex. 18 *Le Son Calligraphié* I, bars 1–4

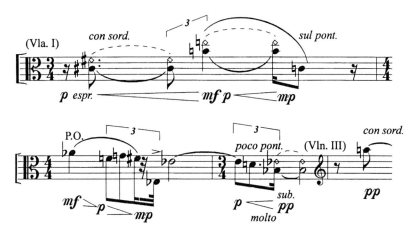

ceding few years. In particular, modally derived materials continue to occur: the second chord of bar 23, for instance, is a revoiced presentation of precisely the same pitches as those of Example 16, in other words, of the same 'Mode VI' collection; while the harmony on the first beat of bar 21 verticalises all pitches but one (G) of a diatonic scale (C major), and the work's final fading-out is preceded by a complete verticalisation of the whole-tone scale beginning on C♯.

But it is what happens in the work's very first bars that is perhaps most interesting. As Example 18 shows, the work begins with a typically angular viola solo containing ten pitches, to which the A of the third violin in bar 4 adds an eleventh. Of these eleven pitches, there is reason to believe that the first E♭ in bar 2 may be a misprint – certainly the octave leap up to the same pitch-class is hardly idiomatic within the norms of this style, and further-more, when the pitch-material of this bar reappears a perfect fifth higher in bar 21, a B♮ is 'correctly' substituted at this point, suggesting that the correct spelling here should be E♮. If this is so, then the twelve pitches exposed here comprise the total-chromatic, and the passage constitutes the historic first presentation in Takemitsu's music of a twelve-note 'series'.

This reading of the opening material is further corroborated by another passage near the end of the work, where the same dodecaphonic set is heard transposed up by an octave and a diminished fifth, with some varia-tions in the note-ordering from the eighth pitch-class onwards (b. 27ff). What is perhaps more interesting still, however, is that these two state-ments, plus the partial statement in bar 21, constitute the only passages in the work unambiguously derived from this 'serial' material. Takemitsu thus begins by offering what appears to be a clear signal that he is about to embark on some kind of exercise in 'twelve-tone' composition – and then proceeds, for the most part, not to write serial music at all. Chung-Haing Lee's observation that his techniques 'are similar to those used by Webern and Schoenberg, yet do not have the procedural precision of the set theory as in the music of the Second Viennese School'[19] is thus something of an understatement, to say the least.

Interestingly, the title of *Le Son Calligraphié* also constitutes an early reference to Takemitsu's own Japanese background, alluding as it does to the traditional Japanese art of calligraphy: a hint already that Takemitsu's self-professed negative stance towards his own culture was not absolute. Similar 'Eastern' connotations attach to *Masque*, the work for two flutes which Takemitsu wrote for the 1959 Karuizawa festival. Takemitsu's programme notes explicitly relate this work to the mask worn by *nō* actors to simulate a female character, and – on a less directly anecdotal level – to more abstract 'Eastern' conceptions of the temporal process: the work 'exists in that inner world of time that cannot be grasped by means of so-called "Western" ideas about metre'[20] and, like *Requiem*, is to be played in a 'one-by-one' rhythm. It is possible that in this work Takemitsu also makes an early attempt to simulate actual Japanese instrumental praxis: a handful of pitches conclude with brief quarter-tone glissandi, for which the composer devised his own unique notation – a long-held note tied to an acciaccatura value at the same pitch in an enharmonic spelling, with the indication 'port.' above it.

Alongside such traditional 'Eastern' elements, however, one detects once again the presence of a method that is decidedly twentieth century and Western in origin. The first of the work's two movements,[21] for example, contains passages of such obvious serial derivation as that quoted in Example 19 – the upper part of which, purely arbitrarily, will be taken as the 'prime form' of Takemitsu's basic series for purposes of further analysis.

Here the retrograde relationship between the two voices marks an advance on the application of the method in *Le Son Calligraphié I* where, it will be recalled, manipulation of the series was limited to the transposition operation only. The remaining two transformational tools of classic dodecaphonic practice – inversion and retrograde inversion – also appear unambiguously for the first time in this movement. This can be seen from Example 20, which gives a reduction of the second flute's pitch-material from bars 2 to 17. Here the technique of retrograde inversion appears in the guise of a global operation applied to both parts from bar 11 onwards;

Ex. 19 *Masque* I, bars 18–20

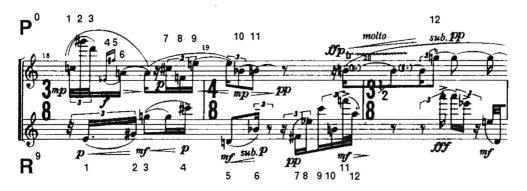

for this reason, the pitches of the *canzicrans* version (lower staff of the system) have been shown in reverse order, so that they line up with their equivalents in the 'prime' ordering.

The use of simple inversion of sets is also apparent here in the upper system, where a statement of the prime form in transposition (P^7) is followed by the first and second hexachords, respectively, of two transpositions of the inverted form (I^7 and I^0). At the same time, however, this presentation of two incomplete six-note sets already constitutes a solecism in terms of orthodox dodecaphonic practice, and further slight deviations from a literal adherence to the underlying pre-compositional method emerge as the passage progresses. Thus the second of the above two hexachords is reordered, while the material in the lower system contains one or two of the same kinds of arbitrary alteration that are also typical of Takemitsu's handling of repeated material: substitution of different pitch-classes in two instances, and the global transposition of a whole passage by a semitone upwards.

However, even this much compositional rigour is rather untypical of the movement, which displays an odd mixture of 'extravagance' of musical materials alongside the relative 'economy' with which these are occasionally handled. The second movement is even more freely composed, and makes no use of the first movement's serial materials. It is however linked thematically to the first movement by means of a somewhat older device, and one which had figured prominently in the pre-serial vocabulary of the Viennese atonalists. This is the device of motivic construction, using the four-note cell labelled 'x' in Example 20, which appears initially on the first flute in bar 2. When the opening bars of the first flute part are repeated a semitone lower at bar 22, this four-note idea is presented in retrograde,

Ex. 20 *Masque* I, bars 2–17, reduction of second flute part

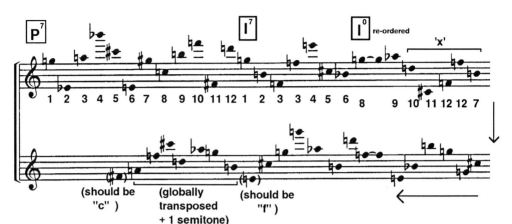

giving rise to a new form which is itself then repeated in bar 34. It is by means of this motif alone that Takemitsu forges some sort of link between *Masque*'s two disparate movements: in its original ordering, as in bar 1 of the second movement (Ex. 21), or in the retrograde version, as in bars 9 and 34 (Ex. 22).

These fleeting reminiscences apart, the two movements of *Masque* are quite different, not least in the matter of their contrasting textures: abrasive, fragmentary and '*pointilliste*' in the case of the first movement, more unified in the second, with the two instruments here sharing frequent simultaneous attacks, and even on occasion playing in rhythmic unison. A similar contrast of textural types emerged as a result of Takemitsu's decision, in 1959, to add two subsequent movements to his *Uninterrupted Rest* for piano of 1952. The extant movement projected a largely 'homophonic' texture, in which – as in the second movement of *Litany* – the melodic line appeared as the upper voice in a series of homorhythmic chords in a manner recalling much of Messiaen's music. In the new version, this was now supplemented by a third movement which opted for a contrasting hierarchical or 'melody and accompaniment' allocation of roles, with an upper melodic line in long notes supported by sporadic chordal attacks, and a second movement constructed from simultaneous chordal attacks like the first, but with these now separated from one another in time and register, so that few overall melodic shapes emerged. Yōko Narazaki makes great claims for this textural variety, observing that, although the work uses 'clusters of chords'[22] in the manner of Messiaen, 'in contrast to Messiaen, who uses his "clusters of chords" almost always according to the same pattern of textural types, Takemitsu, by making changes to the

Ex. 21 *Masque* II, bar 1

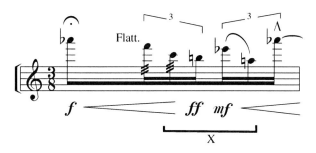

Ex. 22 *Masque* II, bars 8–9

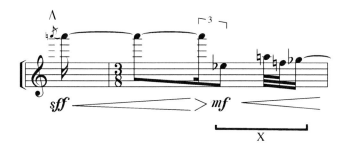

texture, transforms the latter into a structural element'.[23] While the invidious comparison with Messiaen may be a little exaggerated, Narazaki is
surely correct here in drawing attention to the highly individual contribution to the musical language which Takemitsu makes by this kind of formal
delineation according to textural type.

Once again there are fleeting, inconsequential allusions to serial method
in this newly composed material: specifically, in the second movement of
Uninterrupted Rest. Here, as shown in Example 23, Takemitsu also introduces a new, partly 'proportional' rhythmic notation, which allows the
performer a certain liberty in the placing of events within 'bars' of three
seconds' duration.

As the annotations here also illustrate, and as other commentators have
pointed out, these opening bars are guided by the application of dodecaphonic principles. A twelve-note collection in the first two bars (P^0) is followed by its transposition upwards by three semitones (P^3), with an
inverse registration which according to Koozin forms 'an arch shape of
antecedent and consequent'[24] (there is also perhaps an analogy here with

Ex. 23 *Uninterrupted Rest* II, bars 1–5

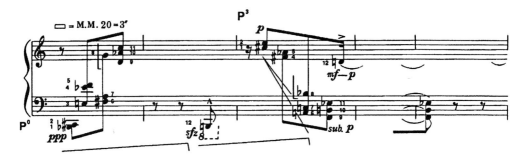

Takemitsu's favoured device of transposed, 'sequential' repetition).
Funayama, who also identifies this twelve-note series, adds the interesting
observation that the movement contains twelve gradations of dynamics
from *pppp* to *sfff* – although at the same time he wisely cautions that 'this is
not "integrated-serialist" music'.[25] In fact, of course – as one might predict
from Takemitsu's attitude to dodecaphonic materials in the above examples – it is not serial music of any sort. Already in the third bar of this
example, for instance, the 'integrity of the series' is destroyed by the omis-
sion of its third pitch (G♮), and while it is possible to continue the analysis
in terms of serial transformations for a few more bars (Ex. 24), to do so
involves the analyst in increasingly tortuous description, so complex are
the aberrations from serial rigour. Essentially this passage begins with
another statement of P^0 in which pitches 1 and 11 have been inter-
changed;[26] however the ninth pitch, D♮, is held in reserve, and the twelfth,
B♮, acts as a pivotal pitch to telescope the series with a statement of I^7 (here
numbered in italics to distinguish it from the preceding statement of P^0).
Pitch 2 of this new form, also D♮, is again 'held in reserve', eventually
appearing as part of the chordal attack in the third bar of the example;
while the tenth pitch of I^7, also omitted, perhaps appears in the form of the
sustained G in the bar following the passage quoted. One notes here, in
passing, that the cavalier attitude to pitch succession implied by all these
arbitrary reorderings and omissions is another general feature of
Takemitsu's manipulation of materials, whether the latter are serially
derived or not.

Beyond this point, however – with the exception of the unequivocal
statement of I^0 in bars 21–3, and a reminiscence of the opening bars at bar
31 – any attempt to analyse the work in serial terms would be foolhardy,
since it is quite clear that Takemitsu is no longer deriving his material in
this manner. Having set out what would appear to be the initial premises of

Ex. 24 *Uninterrupted Rest* II, bars 6–11

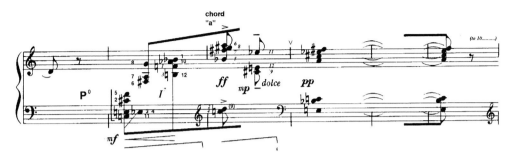

a serial argument, he leaves any expectation that such a discourse will ensue almost provocatively unfulfilled, and instead uses his basic material simply as a partial resource for a very free study in timbre and texture. However, this initial display of serial artifice is not without its repercussions for the rest of the movement. In Example 24, for instance, it will be observed that a specific vertical collection arising from this reordering of the basic materials has been labelled chord 'A'. This harmony is interesting for two reasons. First, the pitch-class set of which it is comprised, [0,2,3,4,6,8], is one of the four possible six-note subsets of the '7-33' collection introduced in the previous chapter, and a favourite vertical form of the composer. (As the '7-33' collection is in turn a subset of Messiaen's 'Mode VI', the present chord also lies within the ambit of that scale, which is how Koozin parses it.[27]) Secondly, within the context of this movement what Koozin describes as a 'referential meaning' attaches to this particular collection, in this particular voicing. In bar 25, for instance, it is heard in three different transpositions successively as part of a dramatic gesture utilising Takemitsu's favoured device of harmonic parallelism (Ex. 25), and reappears three more times when the same passage is repeated in a retrograde transposition in bars 32–3.

The second consequence of the serial process in this movement relates to the constructional rationale of serial method in general rather than the specific pitch-materials of the present instance. As shown in part by Example 20, in *Masque* the composer applied the basic transformational operation of inverted retrogression globally to a whole section (bars 4–10, repeated *al rovescio* as bars 11–17), reversing not only the pitch succession but also (with slight modifications) the durational values and even such timbral features as the first flute's 'quasi-fluttertonguing' in bar 8. Now, in the second movement of *Uninterrupted Rest*, Takemitsu took the important step of applying this technique of global reversal, which has its origins

Ex. 25 *Uninterrupted Rest II*, bar 25

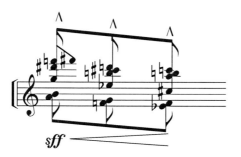

in serial practice, to materials which are not in themselves serially derived. All the pitches from bar 14 up to the high E♮ in bar 18, for instance, appear in reverse order in bars 38–41; in addition, the sequence of three chords in bar 24 is heard backwards, and in two different transpositions, in bars 34 and 48, and the three-chord pattern of bar 25 (Ex. 25) is heard in transposed retrograde in bars 32–3.

This kind of wholesale reversal of musical succession, which may have derived from Webern's or Berg's example (or possibly certain instances in the works of Messiaen), clearly exerted a great fascination over Takemitsu. As subsequent examples will illustrate, it was a technique in which he was to persist long after any deep interest in dodecaphonic materials had been abandoned. On one level, it is easy to guess at a simple practical reason for such fascination: retrogression and, to a lesser extent, inversion proved handy additions to the arsenal of devices by means of which wholesale repetitions could be varied and, indeed, 'disguised' in some way. At the same time, however, there can be little doubt that the arcane, 'esoteric' quality of these inaudible musical abstractions possessed for Takemitsu much of the same 'alchemical' appeal that it had clearly held for Webern and Berg. This is not only borne out by the many eye-catching 'palindromic' or mirror-image passages in his scores, that recall both of these Viennese masters: Takemitsu's affection for these kinds of patterning *per se* was clearly obsessive enough to spill over into the purely verbal medium of his theoretical writing as well. One of the subsections of an article of his – dealing, appropriately enough, with 'The Unpolished Mirror' – is given a Japanese title whose syllables themselves are arranged in a mirror-image sequence: *mi-ga-ka-nu-ka-ga-mi*.[28]

After the second movement's study in fragmentary textures and 'cruel reverberation', the final movement of *Uninterrupted Rest* – subtitled 'A Song of Love'– projects for the most part a contrasting stillness, with a

Ex. 26 *Uninterrupted Rest* III, opening

dynamic level that never rises above *mezzo-forte*; according to Luciana Galliano, it was intended as a homage to Alban Berg.[29] Like the first movement, it begins with the now-familiar gesture of an emergence out of the 'stream of sound' with which the music is contiguous (Ex. 26).

The opening E♮ proves to be the first term in the 'song' of the work's subtitle – what Koozin has described as 'the lyrical melody of this piece', which 'fundamentally consists of a chromatic descent from E^5 to C^5, extended over thirteen measures of music at very slow tempo'.[30] Ohtake goes even further, claiming that this whole melodic pattern outlines 'essentially three descending notes (E, D and C)',[31] and this apparently far-fetched reduction to an underlying 'Schenkerian' schema actually proves surprisingly convincing when one examines one or two features of the musical surface by which it is said to be projected. For instance, the 'D' in bar 7 which, according to Ohtake, forms the middle term in this progression is a whole semibreve long, and preceded by a characteristic falling triplet figure which also introduces the final 'C' in bar 11. However, while Ohtake's reduction identifies the middle term of the melodic descent with this particular 'D', there is also a strong case for granting this privilege to the 'D' in bar 9, which is given an even longer duration, and further emphasised by an accompaniment containing materials from bar 1 transposed down a whole-tone (Ex. 27). In passing, it is also interesting to note here that Takemitsu does not in any way consider the chord in brackets incongruous within the context of his highly chromatic and dissonant style.

The year following the première of the complete *Uninterrupted Rest* saw the addition of the third and final instalment to Takemitsu's string octet triptych. *Le Son Calligraphié III* (1960) returns, on a technical level at least, to many of the preoccupations of the second movement of *Uninterrupted Rest*. Once again retrograde motion is used to generate varied repetition of

Ex. 27 *Uninterrupted Rest* III, bar 9

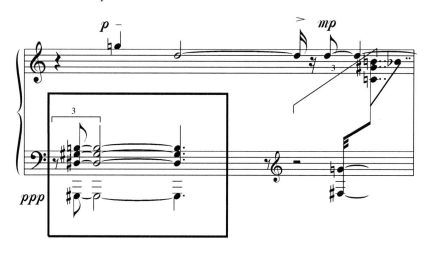

material, but here the technique is applied much more boldly: almost the whole third part of the work's A–B–A^1 form consists of a reworking of the pitch-materials from the first part in reverse order, turning the piece as a whole into a loose palindromic structure. And – as in the earlier piano movement – the work yet again begins with a strong suggestion of a serial ordering principle, which the composer then proceeds for the most part to ignore. Here the twelve-note series with which the work begins and (in its retrograde form) closes is of particular interest in that there is for the first time a suggestion of a certain care over the internal construction of the set, with a view towards the generation of specific harmonic forms. It is difficult to arrive at a definitive ordering of this series from the resultant musical structure as it appears in the score, particularly since pitches 4-6 always appear in vertical superimposition. Nevertheless, the basic set, heard at the work's very opening, can still be established with sufficient certainty to illustrate that it is built up from the concatenation of two sub-sets, each of which projects a collection occupying a privileged position in Takemitsu's musical vocabulary: the ubiquitous '7-33' collection furnishing the first seven pitches, and its chromatic complement – a fragment of the whole-tone scale – providing the remaining five (Ex. 28).

Reception of the *Requiem* and its aftermath

While the earlier works amongst those examined above were composed against a background of poverty and – from an international perspective,

Ex. 28 Series of *Le Son Calligraphié III*

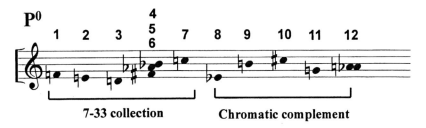

7-33 collection   Chromatic complement

at least – obscurity, by the end of the decade the signal event had occurred which was to transform Takemitsu's fortunes in both of these respects irrevocably. Furthermore, as the composer was often to recall in subsequent years, the lucky break came about only as the result of an almost miraculous fluke. In 1959 Igor Stravinsky was invited to Japan, and asked the NHK to play him some recordings of new Japanese music. There had been no plan to include anything by Takemitsu amongst the works selected for audition, but by accident someone appears to have begun playing a recording of the *Requiem* and – although the organisers were for stopping it – Stravinsky asked to hear the work through to the end. Later, at a press conference, asked if he thought any of the works he had heard were any good, Stravinsky mentioned only Takemitsu's name, commenting on the 'sincerity' and 'strictness' of his music, and apparently expressing his astonishment that 'music as passionate as this should be created by a man of such short stature'[32] – to which Seiji Ozawa[33] was several years later to provide the obvious rejoinder: 'Because he himself was short!'[34]

Stravinsky then invited Takemitsu to lunch – the latter was to retain a vivid recollection afterwards of shaking his hand, 'so big, and very soft, like marshmallow'[35] – and it was apparently through the senior Russian composer's kind offices that Takemitsu went on to obtain the Koussevitsky commission which eventually resulted in the composition of *The Dorian Horizon*.[36] To a certain extent, the whole Stravinsky incident reveals a gap between domestic and Western perceptions of Takemitsu's status that was to remain with the composer throughout his life, and indeed continues to persist after his death. Nevertheless, from around this point onwards, the critical reception of the composer's music, at home as well as abroad, begins to change dramatically. The prizes which the composer had received in the previous year, two from Japan and one from Italy, were to mark only the beginning of a long crescendo of prestigious awards, domestic and foreign premières, meetings with high-profile colleagues,

'residencies' at academic institutions and so forth – in short, of all the trap-
pings of a successful international composer in the latter half of the twentieth century. Surveying the composer's biographical details from around
this point onwards, one reads no longer of the touching, rather
'Bohemian' struggles of a dedicated young artist, but rather of the exhaust-
ing creative schedule of a member of the international composing élite.

From this time onwards, too, the style of Takemitsu's writing for the
concert hall begins to undergo change. So far, the stylistic imprints of the
models for his 'first period' works have been clear enough, and they are
predominantly European and American composers of an older generation
– Messiaen and Debussy, Webern and Berg, initially flavoured a little by the
'nationalist' school to which Takemitsu's teacher Kiyose belonged. But
now, around the turn of the 1960s, as Takemitsu becomes more aware of –
and, in many cases, often comes into direct contact with – his peers in the
international composing community, his career begins more and more to
run in parallel with, and reflect the preoccupations of, the avant-garde and
experimental musicians of his day. For roughly the next decade and a half,
his musical language is to be enriched by an eclectic exploration of novel
resources: the high modernist complexity of the Western avant-garde,
certain aesthetics of Cage and the American experimental school, as well
as – most famously of all – a renewed interest in his own traditional and
other 'Oriental' musics. Takemitsu's 'second period', the era of modernist
experimentation, begins here.

5   Projections on to a Western mirror

Takemitsu's theoretical writings about music abound in striking metaphors that have proved a fertile resource for commentators in search of an evocative title or handy descriptive phrase. The present writer is no exception to this general rule: the title of this chapter, for instance, is a reference to Takemitsu's famous essay of 1974, 'Mirror of Tree, Mirror of Grass',[1] in which he compares Western music, with its emphasis on the individual, to the tree, and contrasts this with non-Western musics which have 'grown like grass'.[2] The two mirrors thus symbolise the twin musical cultures into which Takemitsu was to 'project himself' as his musical language developed, and – as he makes explicit – for the first part of his life it was into the 'Western' mirror only that his gaze was directed: 'Once, I believed that to make music was to project myself on to an enormous mirror that was called the West.'[3]

Our examination of Takemitsu's career to date has corroborated the truth of this assertion. With one or two significant exceptions, most of his musical preoccupations have derived from the Western tradition, and one can generally agree with Poirier that the young Takemitsu devoted himself completely to this 'music from elsewhere' while 'abandoning completely the heritage of traditional music'.[4] Very soon things were to change dramatically, but this does not mean that Takemitsu abandoned his continued exploration of the 'Western' mirror. On the contrary: it is perhaps precisely at this period in his life, as his style is enriched by encounters with the burgeoning Western avant-garde of the 1960s, that his music approximates most closely to that of his international colleagues; in fact, many of his modes of adapting Eastern musical practices for a Western context would not have been possible without this exposure to the new technical resources being developed in the West. The present chapter, then, will examine some of these continued forays into Western musical territory, and the manner in which the fruits of these explorations were reflected in the mirror of Takemitsu's composition from this period.

Further adventures in serialism

For his first and only daughter, born in December 1961, Takemitsu chose – in somewhat Wagnerian fashion – a name intimately connected with his

Ex. 29 Series of *Music of Tree*

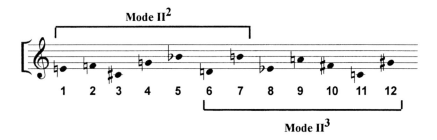

own recent creative work. The second syllable of Maki Takemitsu's given name is a reference to the 'tree' in the Japanese title of *Music of Tree* ('Ki no Kyoku') – an orchestral work which had received its première the previous May, and which, of all Takemitsu's scores from this period, perhaps most vividly reflects his professed 'enslavement' to Webern's music. Texturally, the work consists for the most part of a number of sparse, motivic aphorisms, as far removed as could be imagined from the opulent luxuriance of the composer's later work. Unusually for Takemitsu, too – and indeed somewhat in opposition to his own aesthetic principles – the work even emulates at one point some of the contrapuntal artifice associated with Webern's later scores. A passage beginning at bar 29 is constructed as a canon by retrograde; furthermore, the material utilised here is a twelve-note series, whose prime form (as suggested by the double-bass part) is given in Example 29. Once again, this is a series that shows evidence of a certain thoughtful internal construction: pitches 1–7 project a seven-note octatonic subset, overlapping with pitches 6–12, which project another.

A later work from the same year as *Music of Tree*, *Ring* for flute, terz-guitar[5] and lute also makes reference to serial technique, alongside more radical formal innovations which will be dealt with in chapter 7. The flute part at the beginning of the movement entitled 'N', for example, comprises a statement of the twelve-tone set shown in Example 30 (the apparent duplication of one pitch, 'E', in bar 7 on this occasion almost certainly being a misprint, since the note in question is tied over from a high 'G' three bars earlier).

As we might by now expect, however, this statement is not followed by any kind of consistent serial argument: the flute part continues with inexact references to I^0 and possibly the first three notes of RI^0, but for the remainder of *Ring*'s four movements unambiguous reference to this twelve-note row is conspicuously absent. However, exactly as in the second movement of *Uninterrupted Rest*, technical devices generally associated

Ex. 30 Series of *Ring*

with the serial method, and specifically with the later music of Webern, appear elsewhere in *Ring* independently of any serial context: the two movements entitled 'R' and 'I' are, respectively, retrograde and inverted forms of the movement entitled 'G', albeit very free ones.

The brittle, 'pointilliste' sound-world of *Ring*, with its combination of flute and plucked strings, was to be further explored and expanded in a work of 1962, *Sacrifice*, which adds a vibraphone player doubling on crotales to the combination of alto flute and lute, yielding a kind of scaled-down *Marteau sans maître* sonority. Here again, a twelve-note series makes an unambiguous appearance at one point in the score: to be precise, at the beginning of the second system of the first movement (*Chant I*), as shown in Example 31 (the alto flute part on the uppermost staff is notated in transposition).

Rather than being used as a recurrent ordering principle, however, this series is treated once again after the fashion of a resource from which materials, particularly of a harmonic nature, are freely derived. For this reason, it is perhaps more profitable to think of it as a series of four trichords, as suggested in Example 32, rather than any definitive ordering of the pitches of which the latter are composed.

Some idea of the extreme liberty with which this twelve-note collection is handled may be gathered from the opening of the second movement, *Chant 2* (Ex. 34). The materials for this derive from a transposition of the original row, P[2], which in Example 33 has been segmented into trichords as suggested above. It will be observed, however, that while the first hexachord of Example 34 at least respects this division into trichords (even if it does not respect the original note order), the presentation of the second part of the series violates the original ordering of events even at this level.

Nevertheless, despite the freedom with which it is handled, the series of *Sacrifice* once again reveals a certain thoughtful artifice in the manner of its internal construction. As can be seen from Example 32, the second trichord set ([0,1,3]) is the inversion of the first, as the fourth ([0,1,4]) is

Ex. 31 *Sacrifice* I, system 2

of the third; furthermore (and in somewhat similar fashion to the series of *Music of Tree*), pitches 1-7 constitute one octatonic subset (part of Mode II^2), and pitches 8-12 another (Mode II^3). This kind of care over the internal construction of a dodecaphonic set is yet again revealed by the series projected by the violin in the opening bars of Takemitsu's *Hika* for violin and piano (1966), of which a schematised version is shown in Example 35.

Like that of *Music of Tree*, this series is once again 'hexachordally combinatorial', in that the pitch content of the second half is simply a transposition of that of the first. That this should be the case in the present instance is hardly surprising, since both hexachords comprise the collection [0,1,4,5,8,9] or '6–20', a set possessing a number of interesting properties, one of which is that its chromatic complement is simply a transposition of itself. Among its other interesting features is the fact that, as suggested in Example 35, it may also be segmented into two augmented triads a semitone apart, making it a subset of Messiaen's third 'Mode of Limited Transposition', which may indeed be formed from three such semitonally

Ex. 32 Series of *Sacrifice*

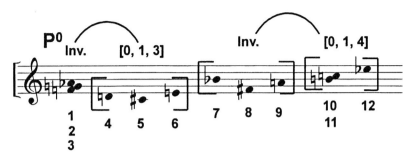

Ex. 33 Transposition of *Sacrifice* series

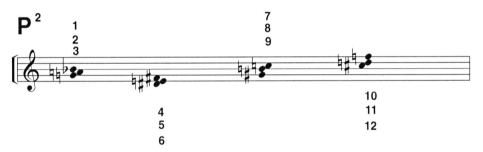

Ex. 34 *Sacrifice* II, opening

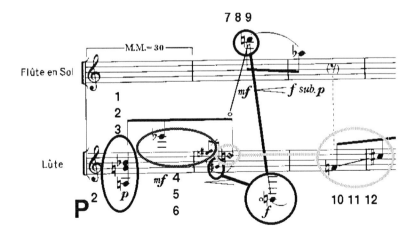

Ex. 35 Series of *Hika*

Ex. 36 Relationship of 'Mode III' to '6–20' collection

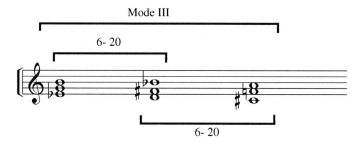

adjacent augmented chords, as shown in Example 36 (addition of a further augmented triad to this collection, of course, completes the total-chromatic).

Moreover, the '6–20' collection may be divided in three different ways into a major triad and a minor one, in such a way that the root of the former is always a major third above that of the latter. While fascination with such vertical, harmonic properties of this collection is revealed abundantly elsewhere in Takemitsu's music, however, it is ironically absent from the score of *Hika*. Once again the twelve-note series is referred to only intermittently, and for the most part the materials of the score are derived freely from other, independent sources. Some of them, in fact, derive from other works of Takemitsu altogether. For example, a brief 'upbeat' figure heard in the piano in bar 1 (Ex. 37), and subsequently repeated on a number of occasions, is quoted from the beginning of the third movement of the composer's *Uninterrupted Rest*, written seven years earlier and already quoted in the previous chapter (Ex. 26).

As in the second movement of *Uninterrupted Rest*, there are also a number of constant, 'referential' harmonic forms in this work, although in this instance there does not appear to be any obvious relationship between

Ex. 37 Opening of *Hika*

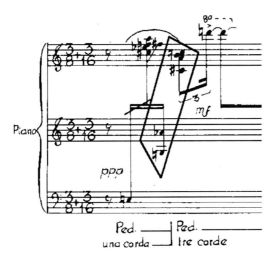

them and the work's opening serial statement. The materials for the work's
final bars, for example, consist almost entirely of reshufflings of three of
these basic harmonic types, labelled 'x', 'y' and 'z' in Example 38, and here
one also detects – perhaps not for the only time – the presence of something like a 'bass progression' in Takemitsu's music: as the music winds
down, the lowest pitches simply outline a chromatic descent from F♮ to B♭.

   Satisfying as this closure is from the purely musical point of view, it is of
course on a structural level in no way a fulfilment of the expectations
aroused by the opening dodecaphonic statement. In *Hika*, as in all other
works by Takemitsu making partial use of twelve-tone method, there is once
again absolutely no question of a consistent serial argument. Furthermore,
after *Hika* – with one or two exceptions – the composer was to abandon
almost entirely even this much interest in Schoenberg's method.
Takemitsu's involvement with serialism was therefore neither profound nor
long-lived; and a critic – particularly one with a strong academic bias –
might attribute both of these facts to a certain failure of compositional technique, a lack of the requisite theoretical rigour. However, as Miyamoto
points out, such passages as the canon by retrograde already referred to in
Music of Tree clearly demonstrate that actually 'the composer is in
command of a rigorous contrapuntal method'.[6] If for the most part it would
seem that he fails to make obvious use of this technical facility, therefore, the
causes must lie not in the limitations of Takemitsu's ability, but rather in the
exercise of his own free choice. In fact, far from suggesting a technical limitation, Takemitsu's lack of interest in such artificial procedures as serialism

Ex. 38 Ending of *Hika*

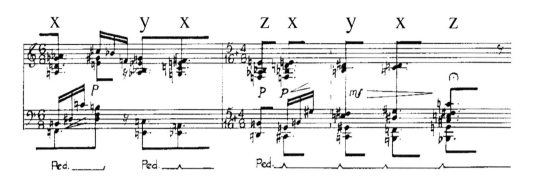

actually reflects profoundly held aesthetic principles – ideas relating to the primacy of 'sound' over 'syntax' in composition – which for the present it will be necessary to pass over, but to which we must return in the closing chapter of this book.

New adventures in timbre

While these aesthetic principles of Takemitsu's may have operated to extinguish most of his interest in serial method during these years, at the same time they had the effect of increasing the composer's interest in the tone-quality of individual sound-events. Takemitsu's keen ear for timbral subtleties had been evident from the very earliest phase of his career, but from around the beginning of the 1960s onwards his ability to conjure a wealth of differentiated sonorities entered on a new phase of refinement, one which was to continue unabated through the remainder of his life. One has only to compare the piano writing of *Uninterrupted Rest* with that of *Piano Distance* (1961), for instance, to see how much more radical and experimental Takemitsu's treatment of this instrumental medium had become in the space of a few years. While the three pieces comprising the earlier work are simply sensitive syntheses of established pianistic method, the new work demands of the performer a variety of carefully indicated tone colourings ('with feeling', 'hard', 'tenderly hard', 'like bell sound'), as well as the production of harmonics, tone clusters and meticulously pre-scribed pedal effects. Many of these refinements of instrumental technique – as was so often the case in Takemitsu's music – reflect the specific virtuos-ity of the performer to whom the work is dedicated: in this case the doyen of avant-garde Japanese pianists of the day, the composer and Xenakis pupil Yūji Takahashi (1938–).

Like the second movement of *Uninterrupted Rest, Piano Distance* also utilises a proportional notation in which attacks are placed freely inside nominal 'bars' of three seconds' duration. The texture is generally even sparser than in the earlier work, with much use of silence, and there is even less in the way of recognisable 'material' of a motivic or thematic kind. One or two events are however repeated: the bell-like chord of bar 20 which reappears at bar 76, for example, or the three-chord sequence which appears in various transpositions in bars 40, 42–3 and 66. It is perhaps to such repetitions as these that Koozin is referring when he describes the form of the work as one in which 'the repetition of more memorable events is spanned by passages of relative ambiguity and quietude'.[7] The apprehension of 'form' here, then, is dependent on the listener's recognition of certain fairly invariant gestures, which serve as points of orientation in the general flux: referential 'chords' or indeed referential 'motifs'. This use of such repeated events, which as Koozin observes may be 'sometimes invariant in regard to pitch and register',[8] as occasional landmarks within the formal scheme was to become another feature of Takemitsu's formal discourse; Miyamoto has also commented on the phenomenon, observing what he describes as a 'symmetry' of such 'analytical landmarks' or 'stations' in three more or less contemporaneous works: *Music of Tree, Ring* and *Piano Distance* itself.[9]

One vertical combination in *Piano Distance* is of particular interest, in that it shows that by this time Takemitsu had make another important addition to his armoury of available scalar types. The third chord in bar 41 (Ex. 39) verticalises all seven pitches of what is possibly, besides the straightforward 'diatonic', Takemitsu's favourite heptatonic collection: the so-called 'acoustic scale' with sharpened fourth and flattened seventh ($[0,1,3,4,6,8,10]$). Most probably Takemitsu had come across this scale in the work of Debussy, for example in the opening bars of *Nuages* from the *Nocturnes* – although at the same time there is by this stage a second possibility to be considered, namely that he had discovered it in the 'Lydian Chromatic Concept' of George Russell, where the seventh mode of this scale features under the guise of the 'Lydian Augmented Scale'.[10]

Takemitsu's explorations of new timbral resources during this period were not limited solely to instrumental music. One finds a similar exploitation of the possibilities afforded by the human voice in the settings of Kuniharu Akiyama's poetry which comprise *Wind Horse*, one of Takemitsu's very few contributions to the *a cappella* vocal repertory. In reality this cycle of five pieces is the conflation of two works: the first two movements, for women's voice alone, dating from 1962, the remaining three for full choir being added in 1966. But *Wind Horse* could also be

Ex. 39 *Piano Distance*, bar 41

considered the conflation of two works in another sense, and one which does not correspond to the above division of labour between the sexes: an interweaving and juxtaposition of works written in two apparently incompatible stylistic languages, one of them modernist and 'atonal', the other decidedly 'tonal' and populist.

It is within the former style that the 'experimental' vocal techniques referred to above occur: besides angular melodic lines and generally dissonant harmonies, Takemitsu here makes use of a whole repertory of extended effects such as speech, *Sprechgesang* and various kinds of breathing sounds, the last presumably in imitation of the 'wind' referred to in the work's title. In such a 'modernist' context – and especially for a listener unfamiliar with the whole breadth of Takemitsu's output – the sudden excursions into shameless major tonality come as something of an abrupt jolt, and one might wonder, with a certain amount of justification, whether the composer had no concept of stylistic congruity. Such a reaction, however, would be less likely from a listener familiar with Takemitsu's other major choral work, the collection of songs eventually published as *Uta* (1979–92) and dating from throughout his career. All of these songs are written in functional tonality, and scored with close, often unctuously chromatic, harmonies that recall the glee-club or even barbershop traditions: some of them are indeed so unambiguously light and tuneful that they have been successfully arranged and released in Japan as pop songs[11] (although this perhaps says as much about what passes for 'pop' in Japan as it does about Takemitsu's credibility as a pop musician!). Like his film music, too – from which some of the songs in *Uta* derive – these songs illustrate that from the very earliest years, outside the enclave of advanced experimentation represented by Takemitsu's 'serious' work, the 'sea of

Ex. 40 *Wind Horse* III, bar 12

tonality' that was to irrupt with such force into the mainstream of his compositional activity many years later was already flourishing unashamedly. And as an artist who professed to make no distinctions between 'high' and 'popular' culture, Takemitsu clearly saw no incongruity in incorporating passages written in this more populist style into the 'modernist' world of *Wind Horse* – thereby unconsciously giving his audience of the 1960s a foretaste of things to come.

Something of the 'barbershop' flavour referred to can be gleaned from Example 40, from the third movement of the work, scored for men's voices alone. Here Takemitsu makes use of a favoured harmonic device, the global transposition of a single harmony by a given intervallic factor: a practice which could, in a sense, be considered a minimal version of the kind of 'sequential' repetition of whole passages in transposition already encountered in works such as *Requiem*. However, when, as here, the direction of harmonic movement is downwards – and especially when the factor of transposition is a semitone, as between the last two chords – this kind of harmonic parallelism also strongly recalls the so-called 'side-slippings (steppings)' popular during the last phase of nineteenth-century tonality. And when such harmonic effects are in addition applied to chords of tonal origin, such as the six-note diatonic cluster used here, and conveyed by the suave timbre of unaccompanied men's voices, a comparison with the lubricious uses to which the more decadent of late Romantic musical genres put this device becomes irresistible.

The tonal 'centre' towards which those passages of *Wind Horse* written in this vein gravitate is clearly A♭ major, as exemplified by Example 41, which quotes the beginning of the fourth movement. Here one also observes that, with the exception of the anacrusis, the pitch-materials are derived exclusively from a further addition to Takemitsu's modal vocabulary, the implied heptatonic scale indicated on the uppermost staff. The

Ex. 41 *Wind Horse* IV, bars 1–4

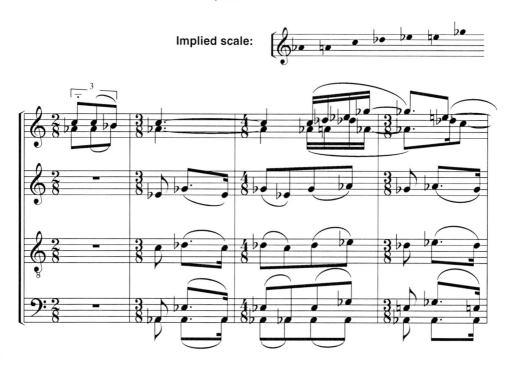

pitch content of the 'acoustic' scale encountered briefly in *Piano Distance* is identical with that of a 'melodic minor' scale in its ascending form; in similar fashion, the pitches of this present scale map on to the companion-piece of the above scale in the harmony textbooks, the rather theoretical 'harmonic minor' ([0,1,3,4,6,8,9]). However, although in the present instance the theoretical parsing of this generative scale would be 'D♭ harmonic minor', in practice Takemitsu uses this collection here only to give a certain 'Spanish-' or 'Moorish'-sounding modal piquancy to a passage whose tonal centre is unambiguously A♭.

Also of importance, besides the A♭ tonality, is the little three-note anacrustic figure with which this passage begins. This is actually a reference to the motif occurring for the first time in bar 3 of what Takemitsu describes as 'a lullaby of the Bantu tribe in Africa' (Ex. 42), a quotation of the South African song *Abiyoyo* popularised in the West by the American folk singer Pete Seeger (1919–). A simple tonal harmonisation of this appears three times in *Wind Horse*, on the last occasion serving as the gesture with which the work 'fades out', and this *volte-face* into a disarming simplicity is certainly the most flabbergasting stylistic shock in the whole piece. Such

Ex. 42 Bantu melody from *Wind Horse*

gestures as the insistence on an A♭ tonic, the incorporation of the lullaby
motif into Example 41, or the rocking thirds in A♭ in the previous movement (where the melody is first introduced) thus play a crucial role in
forging links between the quoted music and Takemitsu's own, and mitigat-
ing the effect of what would otherwise be an even more abrupt stylistic
rupture.[12]

In the sphere of Takemitsu's concert music, this represented the first
occasion on which the composer was to incorporate such a wholesale borrowing from an external musical source. However, in the less constrained
world of his film music he had already begun to experiment with musical
quotation at least a couple of years previously. His score for the 1964 film
Nijū-issai no Chichi,[13] for instance, makes use of a Schumann piano piece,
No.16 from *Album für die Jugend*, which he used again in his music for
Akogare[14] in 1966. Later he was to incorporate a Vivaldi violin concerto
and an Elvis Presley song into a *musique concrète* collage for the film
Moetsukita Chizu,[15] and, much later still, pieces by Josquin des Prés and
Eustache du Caurroy (1549–1609)[16] found their way, in period arrange-
ments, into the score for the film *Rikyu*.[17] As the years passed, his concert
music, too, was to include further examples of direct quotation, all of

which will receive due attention below. But – as in the case of a number of Takemitsu's other musical experiments – it was once again in the stylistically more liberal climate of his work for the cinema that the composer's first steps in this direction had been taken.

From 'Lydian Chromatic' to 'Dorian Horizon'

Further evidence of the degree to which Takemitsu was venturing into new areas of timbral exploration during these years is afforded by *The Dorian Horizon* (1966), whose writing for seventeen solo strings represents a considerable advance in this respect on that of the *Requiem* or even *Le Son Calligraphié*. Here, in addition to the formidable array of 'Western' extended techniques – harmonics, glissandi, 'Bartók' pizzicati, *col legno battuto*, playing behind the bridge, etc. – there are also perhaps one or two attempts to emulate the sounds of traditional Japanese instrumental praxis: Akiyama, at any rate, compares the sound of the sustained, senza vibrato string chords of the opening, and the pizzicati with which their attacks are emphasised, to those of the *shō*[18] and *kakko*[19] in the *gagaku* ensemble respectively. The work also incorporates a spatial dimension, and one in which sounds not only reach the listener from a variety of *directions*, but also occur at various *distances* both from the listener and from each other. Eight solo instruments, referred to as 'harmonic pitches', are placed in a horseshoe formation towards the front of the stage, while behind them a further nine soloists – 'nine echoes' – are arranged in two rows of violins and basses respectively; according to the preface in the score, these two groups 'are placed between as far as possible [sic]'. This physical separation has the effect not only of creating a kind of spatial perspective, but also of distinguishing the two groups in terms of dynamics: those of the 'echo' group are distorted by distance, so that, as one commentator has observed, 'the dynamic "forte" has different meanings for each group'.[20] Takemitsu exploits this acoustic phenomenon to great effect, for example, in the passage immediately preceding the central section, where the same chord is repeated by the 'echo' group at what is technically the same *ff* dynamic, but which in reality sounds quite different.

The Dorian Horizon is also the work which most explicitly manifests Takemitsu's debt to the harmonic theories of the American jazz composer George Russell (*b.* 1923), whose *Lydian Chromatic Concept of Tonal Organization for Improvisation* he had read five years previously. To quote the composer's own programme note, the work 'is based upon the idea of constructing the twelve notes of the octave out of the diatonic steps of the tonal Dorian mode, its augmentation ('Dorian Augment') and diminution ('Dorian Diminish'), as well as the whole-tone scale'.[21] It is the pair of somewhat mysterious terms in brackets here (which appear in English in the original) which betray the influence of Russell, even if the latter is never mentioned by name. Russell's system is designed to enable jazz musicians to improvise on chords and their sequences, and places at their disposal for this purpose a number of basic scales, amongst which are the 'Lydian' (i.e. the Lydian mode with sharpened fourth), the 'Lydian Augmented' (the same with the fifth also sharpened) and the 'Lydian Diminished' (a 'Lydian mode' with flattened third). Takemitsu, as his own terminology reveals, has clearly devised his own analogous scales to these using the Dorian mode as a starting point, adding to them the whole-tone scale (which also figures in Russell's system as the 'Auxiliary Augmented Scale'). And, just as the jazz improviser may choose to combine the scales of Russell's system freely, thereby using all twelve pitch-classes – the 'Lydian Chromatic Scale' – so too Takemitsu combines the pitches of his own modes to generate the total-chromatic, producing a 'pantonal' music which is offered as a 'humble protest against inorganic serialism'.[22] Furthermore, when one takes into account the fact that Russell admits of the possibility of both 'absolute' and 'chromatically enhanced' modal melodies, it becomes clear why Takemitsu felt such a strong affinity with his system, considering his own long-established precedent of enhancing modally derived collections with chromatic notes, as well as freely combining them to produce his own highly distinctive harmonic palette.

The bulk of Russell's theoretical text is concerned with the generation of horizontal melodies over standard, classifiable chord types, with a few thoughts on harmony appended as an afterthought, and Takemitsu's composition too, as its title indicates, is to a large extent preoccupied with the horizontal dimension. Although he uses his Dorian materials to generate vertical harmonies as well, in the outer portions of the work a melodic line clearly emerges from the uppermost voice of the chord changes or the long sustained pitches. The basis of this melodic line, despite excursions into other tonal areas, is clearly Dorian, with a tonal centre – the tonal centre of the work – on E♭ or D♯, as indicated, for example, by the emphasis that pitch receives in the passage quoted in Example 43. This type of writing, incidentally – in which melodic motion is suspended entirely in order to focus exclusively on timbral colourations of a single pitch – is another typical Takemitsu gesture. It has its precedents, obviously enough, in Webern's passages of monotone *Klangfarbenmelodie*, but at the same time it is clearly a practical demonstration of Takemitsu's aesthetic preference, already hinted at, for the sound-quality of individual events over the syntactical relationships between them.

Ex. 43 *The Dorian Horizon*, bars 22–7

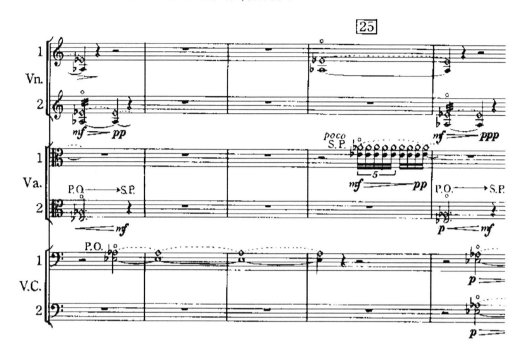

As suggested above, however, it is only in the outermost sections of the work that the 'Dorian Chromatic' technique is employed. Like *Wind Horse*, *The Dorian Horizon* is really two works interleaved into one, and the middle section of its ABA form in particular – as well as one or two inter-jections for the 'echo' group in the first part – are based to a large extent on material Takemitsu had written for the film *Woman in the Dunes*[23] two years previously. This material, at its first appearance, possesses a strik-ingly contrasting harmonic character to that of the 'Dorian' foreground, further intensifying the spatial separation between the two instrumental groups: the first entry of the 'echo' group, for instance, projects materials with a 'stratified' harmonic make-up in which the uppermost three voices clearly have a whole-tone basis (Ex. 44). One notes in passing, too, that this gesture is another version of the type of upwardly mobile 'anacrusis' found in Ex. 6 (p. 34).

Much of the music of the central section of this work still retains ele-ments pertaining to the specific dramatic purpose for which it was written. The eerie close-ups of sliding sands which appear in Teshigahara's film, for instance, have their musical analogue in the high clusters of glissandi over

Ex. 44 *The Dorian Horizon*, bars 21–3

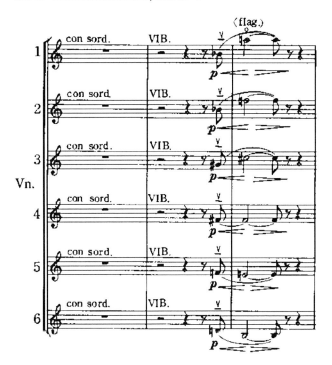

slow-moving, chromatic ostinati for the double basses, or the strange, 'Bartókian night music' of Example 45, with its weirdly chromatic slidings.

The contrapuntal device used here is a rather 'Bartókian' one as well, and a very straightforward one at that: simple canonic imitation at the unison. In a musical language of such sophistication as Takemitsu's it is perhaps, as Dana Richard Wilson pointed out, 'surprising when the obvious device of canon is incorporated,'[24] but such usages were nevertheless a consistent feature of his technical apparatus. A further instance, in fact, occurs immediately prior to the above example (Ex. 46). Here the 'theme' subjected to imitative treatment is in itself interesting insomuch as it consists of a single pitch articulated by the same series of durational values at each entry. This construction of a kind of 'mode de valeurs' by multiplication of a basic unit pulse (here the quaver) to build up a 'rhythmic canon' once again recalls Messiaen's example; at the same time, however, the insistent and dramatic emphasis on the same monotone in each entry also suggests that category of monorhythmic device that Alban Berg might well have designated *Hauptrhythmus*.

Ex. 45 *The Dorian Horizon*, bars 130–4

Ex. 46 *The Dorian Horizon, bars 128–31*

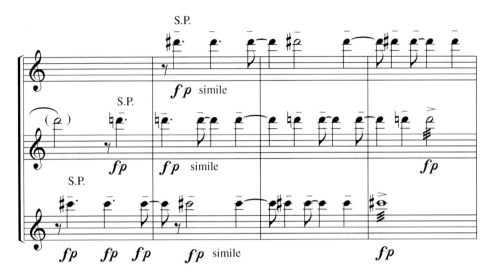

In the outer sections of *The Dorian Horizon,* a number of 'reference' chords are used with such frequency and consistency that it is almost possible to speak of composition using free selection from a 'gamut' of such devices. A similar type of construction had also featured in Takemitsu's *Landscape* for string quartet (1960),[25] which had additionally used similar vertical forms to *The Dorian Horizon,* in which foreign pitches in the bass form a dissonant relationship to modally derived collections above them. The manner in which chord changes take place generally in rhythmic unison in the earlier work, and at a very slow tempo, is also very much like its later counterpart. However, the typical string writing of the outermost sections of *The Dorian Horizon* may also have been influenced by a work by another composer whose acquaintance Takemitsu had made by this time: the *String Quartet in Four Parts* (1949–50) of John Cage. The following chapter, then, will take as its initial theme the crucial impact Takemitsu received from his encounter with this particular American master.

6 'Cage shock' and after

The unconscious parallels that existed between the ideals and performance practices of the *Jikken Kōbō* and those of the New York 'experimental school' have already been commented upon. It is, therefore, perhaps no surprise to learn that as early as 'shortly after the war', and via the 'intellectual antennae' of two figures intimately associated with the group's foundation – Shūzo Takiguchi and Kuniharu Akiyama – Takemitsu had already begun to hear about John Cage's innovations.[1] He was to gain more direct knowledge of the new possibilities the composer had uncovered after 1961, when Toshi Ichiyanagi returned from his nine years of study in the United States, which had included attendance at Cage's composition class. In particular, a performance which Ichiyanagi gave in August of that year, at the fourth Ōsaka Contemporary Music Festival, of Cage's *Concert for Piano and Orchestra*, made such a deep impression on Takemitsu that, thirty-one years later, writing an obituary notice for Cage, he could comment that 'I still feel the shock of hearing that piece'.[2] The works written under the influence of what Ohtake refers to as this 'Cage shock'[3] form the matter for discussion in the first part of this chapter.

Graphic scores and indeterminacy

Although there is evidence that Takemitsu had absorbed a number of the American composer's ideas as early as 1956, it is after Ichiyanagi's return from the United States in 1961 that his period of intensest involvement with the theories of Cage really begins. Indeed, Ichiyanagi himself was directly involved in Takemitsu's first experiment with one of Cage's most celebrated 'inventions', the prepared piano. Takemitsu introduced two such instruments, played by Ichiyanagi and Yūji Takahashi, into his score for the 1962 film *Otoshiana*,[4] as well as a third part for harpsichord played by himself. Subsequently he was to exploit this newly found instrumental resource, usually in conjunction with electronic treatment, in a number of other film scores of the 1960s: for example those of *Ansatsu*[5] (1964), *Kwaidan* (1964) and *Yotsuya Kwaidan*[6] (1965). And while it is true that the instrument was never incorporated into any of the composer's 'serious' scores, this may have had more to do with the practical problem of the enormous preparation time that such works require when performed in the concert room, than with any aesthetic preference.

More dramatic reflections of Cage's influence than this, however, are felt for the first time in *Ring* (1961). This work has already been referred to in passing as an exemplar of Takemitsu's use of serial method, but such a description gives a very distorted view of the degree to which the musical materials are determined. For the score of *Ring* also incorporates two radical innovations of Cage with which Takemitsu continued to be preoccupied in a number of works over the course of the next few years: indeterminacy and graphic notation. The notated movements of *Ring* – of whose four initials the work's title forms an acronym – are called 'R' (Retrograde), 'I' (Inversion), 'N' (Noise) and 'G' (General Theme). The notation of these movements is not fully determinate, however, in that they are devoid of tempo markings or dynamic and interpretative indications, and often use forms of imprecise rhythmic notation as well. Moreover, the four movements may be played in any order, giving rise to twenty-four possible permutational variants of the cyclic scheme. It will be seen at once that this indeterminacy of succession militates against any sense of an ongoing structural logic in which, for example, the 'General Theme' may be taken as a starting point from which its 'Retrograde' and 'Inverted' forms are then derived. Of course, there must have been an order of composition, and Miyamoto is probably right when he says that the other three movements were composed on the basis of the last.[7] But in the finished work as presented there are no real grounds for according 'primogeniture' to any of the three forms in which the basic material appears. This is a specific instance of a general observation that can be made about Takemitsu's music: the order in which materials appear in the score is rarely a reliable guideline to the sequence of their evolution from one another. If, for example, a chord when repeated contains one extra pitch – as in the example from *Distance de Fée* already quoted (Ex. 7) – it is equally possible to consider the earlier chord a 'filtered' version of the later, as it is to consider the second a 'thickened' version of the first. On such points as these, in almost every instance, the would-be analyst of Takemitsu's music is forced ultimately to concede defeat to an ineluctable ambiguity.

The indeterminate element in *Ring* is not confined merely to the free ordering of the movements, however. Between the four notated movements, the performers are requested to play three interludes, and it is for the execution of these that Takemitsu devises his first graphic performance materials. Each player is equipped with a circular ('ring'-like) design which may be read in either clockwise or counter-clockwise sense, and at a choice of two speeds. The outermost circle of the 'ring' prescribes dynamics, within which there are graph-like contours suggesting pitch – the circumference of the circle here indicating the lowest pitch, and the centre the highest. Further specialised notations indicate specific playing techniques for each of the three instruments, and with the aid of all of these indications, the three performers are enabled to realise the same material in ways that differ totally in each of the three interludes, or indeed, every time the work is performed.

There appears also for the first time in *Ring* a certain theatricalisation of the performative act, albeit a very discreet one. In yet another reference to the work's title – which according to the composer also alludes to Wagner's operatic tetralogy – Takemitsu requests that the 'flute player should have a ring which looks very gay'. This ring, however, does not serve merely decorative purposes. In 'N', the player is instructed to 'knock between the mouth piece and a joint by ring', the effect being only one of a whole catalogue of 'extended' techniques which appear in this 'noise' movement: for example, the terz-guitar is directed to produce an 'S.D. effect' and something called APAGA DOS, while the recurring 'referential' chord assigned to the lute is always accompanied by the performance direction 'Tam'. In *Ring,* then, the Cage-inspired 'indeterminate' elements coexist with a number of Takemitsu's other preoccupations from this period: serial organisation, wholesale retrogression/inversion, proportional notation, expansion of timbral possibilities, dramatisation of the performance gesture.

In the works employing graphic notation which followed this initial enterprise, however, Takemitsu was to engage more exclusively with this particular performance tool. A whole spate of such works was to appear within the relatively short time-span of the years 1962–3, thanks in part to Takemitsu's collaboration with the graphic designer Kōhei Sugiura (1932–). Evidently he must have found the circular motif of *Ring* very satisfying, too, since similar basic designs are to be found in all these subsequent experiments. Thus *Corona for pianist(s)* and *Corona II for string(s)* (both 1962) provide the performer with a number of coloured circular patterns, printed on cards which may be interlocked by means of incisions in the first instance, and on transparent sheets which are overlaid on a white sheet in the second. In *Crossing for pianist(s)* (1962), a number of interlocked circles are presented in the form of a folding booklet, while the score of *Arc for Strings* (1963) consists of a number of circles or arcs each containing a small dot like an orbiting satellite.

All these designs are of great visual appeal, and not only have they been much reproduced as illustrative material in books and articles on the composer, but – in the case of *Corona II*, at least – were exhibited in a Tōkyō gallery in March 1963 alongside other graphic scores by Ichiyanagi, Takahashi and Mayuzumi as works of art in their own right: exactly as Cage's own scores had been in New York (and, some might add, exactly in accord with the Japanese penchant for imitation). Moreover, Takemitsu was to exploit the potential of some of these scores to generate densely 'chaotic' materials by specifying their use as adjuncts to the performance of two of his grander orchestral statements of the 1960s. The graphics of *Corona II* thus enable the string players in the *Accumulation II* movement of *Coral Island* to furnish a backdrop of suitably 'anarchic' instrumental effects, while those of *Arc for Strings* perform the same function in the movement entitled *Your Love and the Crossing* from *Arc for piano and orchestra*, with the solo pianist here using the graphics of *Crossing for pianist(s)* in order to add a further layer of indeterminate sounds to the dense overall texture.

Shortly after these experiments, however, one has the sense that Takemitsu's interest in a direct, musical realisation of Cage's ideas is beginning to wane. To be sure, another set of striking visual images – those for the composer's 'event musical' *Blue Aurora for Toshi Ichiyanagi* – were to appear in 1964, and Takemitsu's catalogue also lists two other 'happenings' of this kind which took place in the mid-1960s: the 'theatre pieces' *Time Perspective* (1964) and *Seven Hills Event* (1966). There were also to be two more, comparatively late, ventures into graphic notation: *Munari by Munari* for percussion (1969–72), in which Takemitsu was assisted (as he had been in the production of *Crossing*) by the Italian designer Bruno Munari (1907–98); and *Seasons*, for two or four percussionists plus magnetic tape (1970). Beyond this point, however, there were to be no more such graphically notated, wholly indeterminate works modelled on Cage's example. Moreover, the notation of *Seasons*, with its 'plus' and 'minus' signs indicating, respectively, 'accumulation' and 'diminution', and its directions to 'imitate what is being played by the performer in front/on the right/on the left' etc., suggests the influence of such Stockhausen works as *Prozession* just as much as it does that of any Cage score. In Takemitsu's case, then – as in the case of many of his contemporaries, Stockhausen himself included – it seems that ultimately the 'Cage shock' was to wear off, and the fascination with coloured shapes and musical origami prove only a passing phase in the composer's development. But this abandonment of the practical musical consequences of Cage's philosophy does not mean that Takemitsu wholly abandoned his commitment to Cage's ideas in the abstract. On the contrary: many of these ideas were to remain essential tenets of faith for Takemitsu for the remainder of his creative life.

Of particular importance amongst such ideas were: the concept of a pluralistic, many layered, spatialised music; the idea of silence as *plenum*
rather than *vacuum*; and the preference for the individual timbre of the
single sound-event over and above the syntactical relationships between
such events which have traditionally formed the discourse of Western
music. There was of course an obvious congruence between some of these
ideas and those which Takemitsu already espoused, or indeed some of the
ideas of traditional Japanese musical aesthetics. Thus Cage's philosophy of
silence affords close parallels with both Takemitsu's own ideas about the
'stream of sound' and the traditional concept of *ma*, and his interest in the
individualised sound-phenomenon accords well with the concept of
sawari which – as we shall see in chapter 12 – Takemitsu was to make very
much his own. That there should be this affinity between Cage's own and
traditional 'Eastern' ideas is perhaps hardly surprising, for Cage – as is well
known, and as Takemitsu himself readily acknowledged – was himself
'influenced through Zen through his encounters with the Zen master
Daisetzu Suzuki'.[8] Superficially, therefore, the operation of Cage's
influence on the younger generation of Japanese composers at this time
appears to present another example of that kind of 'feedback loop'
whereby 'Eastern' ideas are reimported from the West to their point of
origin, as had happened half a century earlier with Debussy's music. Once
again, too, this export–import manoeuvre had the important consequence
of lending the seal of Western endorsement to ideas that were fundamentally 'Eastern' in origin, and thereby freeing Japanese composers to explore
aspects of their own tradition without fear that they might be lapsing into
some kind of pre-war nationalistic 'Zealotism'. This kind of legitimation
was to have particularly far-reaching consequences in the case of
Takemitsu's involvement with traditional Japanese music, as the events of
the subsequent chapter will show.

On the other hand, however, despite the many points of coincidence
between Cage's and Takemitsu's artistic philosophies, it should be pointed
out that there were certain crucial differences between them as well.
Probably the most important is that revealed by a very early commentary
of Takemitsu's on Cage which appeared in the journal *Bijitsu Hihyō* in
1956. Takemitsu's article certainly suggests that he possessed a remarkable
level of sympathy with Cage's ideas, despite his relatively isolated situation.
He notes that the use of sounds as vague 'functions' is now exhausted, and
that the future task of composers will consist of rehabilitating them to
their 'pre-artistic' condition. At the same time, however, he sees the composer's role as that of one who uses these tones, liberated from dry, forma-
listic ends, in the service of those same purposes which had been the goal

of composers at some golden age of the past: an age when 'composers explored the essence of human existence through the emotional world of sound'. For 'a true artist is a person who, descending to the bottom of his inner mineshaft, reveals his own self like a piece of unrefined ore', since – to express it more exuberantly still – 'music is song and song is love'.[9]

In other words, Takemitsu here compares composition explicitly to a natural, spontaneous emotional self-expression. Such a conclusion should indeed hardly occasion any surprise for us, coming as it does from a '*Lento* composer' whose tendency towards a rather melancholy 'expressionism' has already been remarked upon. But it is a conclusion that is diametrically opposed to Cage's philosophy of non-intentionality, to his belief that tones should simply be themselves, not vehicles for personal theories or human emotions. In this respect, Takemitsu's musical thinking differs profoundly from Cage's; and it may be for this reason that Takemitsu ultimately never became the 'experimental' composer that his explorations of the 1960s might have led one to expect, but rather ended his days producing music whose highly personal emotional tone was to be far removed from the 'Zen-like' absence of intention in these early graphic experiments.

Consolidation of avant-garde experimentation

As Takemitsu absorbed more and more of the innovations of his Western contemporaries, his technical vocabulary expanded rapidly, and works began to appear that have something of the character of 'compendia' or 'thesauruses' of the avant-garde devices available to a composer of that time. Often, too, these scores partake somewhat of the nature of the grandiose, epic gesture associated with the modernist ascendancy of that epoch, betraying the date of their composition simply by virtue of their sheer bulk and complexity. *Coral Island* for soprano and orchestra (1962) is the first example of this newly found confidence in the handling of large-scale forces and forms.

The work consists of two vocal movements, settings of poems by Makoto Ōoka (1931–) called *Poème I* and *Poème II*, interleaved between three purely orchestral pieces called *Accumulation I, II* and *III*, and – in a similar manner to that observed in *Uninterrupted Rest* and *Masque* – these various sections are distinguished from one another partly by means of differences in texture. Takemitsu divides his orchestral forces into six independent groups, and lays out the score of the *Accumulation* movements in accordance with this 'layering', but in the two *Poème* movements the instruments appear above one another in the score according to the conventional ordering. These notational differences correspond to differences in the type of texture the orchestra is being used to project. In the vocal movements, the various instrumental groups interact freely with one another, creating freely 'pointillistic' textures, *Klangfarbenmelodie* or even just conventional 'ensemble' accompaniment to the solo voice. In the *Accumulation* movements, however, each of the six groups is independent from one another, and has a clearly defined and consistent textural role. The strings provide a static harmonic backdrop; the tuned percussion washes of coruscating tintinnabulation; the brass disjointed, 'pointillistic' utterances; and the woodwind quasi-aleatoric, repeated 'mobile' passages. While the orchestral texture in the vocal movements is more unitary, therefore, in the instrumental sections it consists of a number of spatially and timbrally defined, independent strata. Takemitsu, whose own preferred term for this latter type of pluralistic, many-layered treatment of the orchestral apparatus was 'pan-focus',[10] appears to have arrived at such textures partly through a study of Debussy's orchestral music, which 'combines several things at the same time . . . two or three, or sometimes four together . . . and this music is also very spatial'.[11]

If Debussy is one of the more distant precursors of Takemitsu's stratified orchestral texture here, some aspects of the individual, compartmentalised textures contributing to this overall effect derive from more recent precedents. The use of constellations of freely repeated figures for the wind, for example – 'mobiles' – suggests Berio's influence, or even perhaps that of Witold Lutosławski, whose *Jeux vénétiens* had appeared in the previous year. The sustained string 'background', however, which mostly consists of slow-moving cluster formations, may reflect the influence of a number of other contemporary composers: Xenakis, Penderecki and, perhaps most obviously, György Ligeti. Comparisons with figures such as these have certainly occurred to other writers on the subject: Heifetz, for instance, with specific reference to *Coral Island*, speaks of 'wind and percussion sounds' which 'accumulate and envelop string sonorities that softly and gradually develop into dense vertical structures, not unlike the building-block structures that are typical of Penderecki's and Ligeti's music'.[12]

Alongside these references to more recent musical trends, however, some of the techniques employed by Takemitsu indicate his continuing 'enslavement' to the music of Webern. One passage from the score, indeed, contains perhaps the most directly imitative homage to the Austrian master to be found in the whole of the composer's music (Ex. 47).

Webernian influence is also, once again, tangible here in the shape of Takemitsu's continuing obsession with retrograde and loosely 'palindromic' constructions. These may take the form of local, literal reversals of

Ex. 47 Comparison between themes from *Coral Island* and Webern, op. 6

Webern, *Six Pieces* op. 6, VI, bars 2–5 (harp)

Takemitsu, *Coral Island*, p. 12, bar 4 (harp)

Ex. 48 Local retrograde relationship in *Coral Island*

(i) *Coral Island*, cl. 1, p. 5, bars 2–3

(ii) *Coral Island*, cl. 2, bars 1–2

material of the kind shown in Example 48, where the second clarinet part is simply the first clarinet part presented in retrograde at transposition T^1. At the same time, there are also global repetitions of whole passages in retrograde throughout the three *Accumulation* movements, the disposition of which – as shown in Example 49 – is in itself roughly symmetrical about a central axis, rendering the whole work in effect loosely 'palindromic', or at least 'arch-like'.

Ex. 49 Global retrograde relationships in *Coral Island*

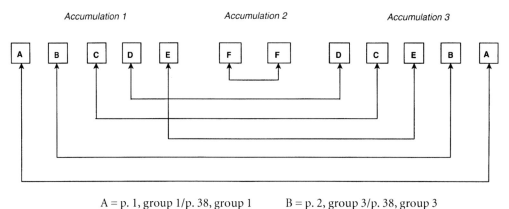

A = p. 1, group 1/p. 38, group 1   B = p. 2, group 3/p. 38, group 3
C = p. 4 (fig. 4)/p. 35 (fig. 2)   D = p. 5, group 1/p. 34, group 1
E = p. 5, group 3/p. 35, group 3   F = p. 16, group 3/p. 20, group 4

The two interpolated vocal settings are also linked by means of the familiar Takemitsu device of interlocking repetitions of material, and like the *Accumulation* movements reveal a coexistence of technical features which Takemitsu had acquired during the previous decade, alongside others of more recent origin. To the former category, for instance, belongs the soloist's first utterance, which exposes all eight pitches of the octatonic collection comprising Messiaen's Mode II[3] before appending to them an extraneous E♮ (Ex. 50). Takemitsu's practice here accords well with a phenomenon that Koozin has identified as a general preference of the composer in the handling of octatonic materials: for example, in bar 7 of the piano work *For Away*, the composer first exposes all the pitches of an octatonic collection and then, according to Koozin, 'veils his octatonic reference by introducing a pitch foreign to the locally predominant collection, B♭'.[13] As Koozin observes elsewhere, such a practice 'would not have displeased' the author of the *Technique*, who does indeed discuss there 'the disguising of a mode through the inclusion of foreign notes'.[14] At the same time, however, Example 50 is also a clear demonstration on the horizontal plane of Takemitsu's long-established practice of enhancing modally derived collections with 'chromatic' additions: a practice which, as we have seen, on the vertical plane at least, dates right back to the time of *Romance*.

The author of another harmony 'textbook' whose acquaintance Takemitsu had made more recently may also have had an influence on the materials of *Coral Island*. Amongst the family of scales that form the basis of Russell's *Lydian Chromatic Concept* is the 'Lydian Diminished'

Ex. 50 *Coral Island*, p. 8, soprano entry

Ex. 51 *Coral Island, Poème II*, bar 30 (marimba)

[0,1,3,4,7,8,10], in effect a kind of melodic-minor scale with sharpened fourth, or major scale with flattened sixth: an inversion of the traditional 'harmonic minor' scale, it is analogously known as the 'harmonic major' in jazz theory. Whether in conscious emulation of Russell or otherwise, Takemitsu certainly uses the pitches of precisely this scale as a repeated marimba upbeat to the melodic phrases of the final lines in *Poème II* (Ex. 51).

These final lines of text, describing the speaker's metamorphosis into a 'transparent coral island', also provide Takemitsu with a pretext for some hauntingly mysterious 'crystalline' orchestration making much use of celesta and tuned percussion, and referring harmonically for the most part to the various octatonic transpositions. Furthermore, the construction of this passage makes interesting use of another of Takemitsu's favoured devices, the repetition of a melodic pattern or sequence of harmonies as an ostinato. In the present instance, a one-bar ostinato for crotales, and another one-bar repeated pattern for strings, alto flute, celesta and marimba are superimposed over a two-bar ostinato for the bells, and – most interestingly of all – a two-bar 'basso ostinato'-like pattern in the lower register (Ex. 52), imparting to the whole something of a 'chaconne' character. This last pattern – anticipated earlier in the score at p. 28, bar 1 – is particularly unusual given how infrequently Takemitsu's music projects anything resembling a 'bass progression'; the composer once remarked, indeed, that because he was Japanese, his music was 'bottomless'.[15] It is

Ex. 52 *Coral Island, Poème II,* 'basso ostinato'

also interesting on account of its untypical projection of a regular pulse: Wilson, in fact, has suggested that precisely on this account the appearance of regularity here may create a sense of 'arrival' for the listener,[16] bringing the vocal part of *Coral Island* to a satisfying climactic conclusion. Beyond this point, the rough symmetrical organisation already referred to automatically generates a convincing movement towards closure: just as the texture of *Accumulation I* gradually increased in density, so now that of *Accumulation III* gradually attenuates, pointing up the loose 'palindromic' scheme by textural means, and finally dissolving the music into that 'stream of sound' whence it emerged.

Complex and 'modern' though *Coral Island* might be, Takemitsu was to surpass its grandeur in the following year, when he began work on the first of the scores which would eventually grow into the massive *Arc* cycle for piano and orchestra (1963–76). As the dates indicate, this work had an extended period of gestation. The first and third movements were premièred by the pianist to whom they were dedicated, Yūji Takahashi, as early as 1963, and the fourth, *Textures*, in the following year. But it was not until 1977, under the direction of Pierre Boulez in New York, and with Peter Serkin as soloist, that the full cycle of weighty, oversize tomes comprising the finished work received their first performance. In this final, revised form, the work now consisted of six movements: *Pile* (1963), *Solitude* (1966) and *Your Love and the Crossing* (1963) forming *Arc Part I*, and *Textures* (1964), *Reflection* (1966) and *Coda . . . Shall begin from the end* (1966) forming *Arc Part II*.

Once again, this ambitious avant-garde statement consists of a kind of inventory of almost all the influences Takemitsu had absorbed to date: tone-clusters, elements of serial technique and Messiaen's modal system, aleatoric writing, Cage-inspired graphic notations, and so on. In this sense, the aesthetic preoccupations of the work would appear, superficially at least, to be very much in sympathy with those of Takemitsu's Western contemporaries. But what distinguishes the piece from the work of Takemitsu's colleagues in the West, and identifies it as the work of a highly independent creative spirit, is the aesthetic vision in the service of which this vast technical apparatus is employed – one which is both highly personal, and specifically Japanese. For – as the composer made explicit in his commentaries on this work – various aspects of its formal patterning are modelled on the layout of a traditional Japanese garden. This was, indeed, a source of inspiration to which Takemitsu was to turn repeatedly in his search for specific formal organisations; but it was also one which he was to interpret in different senses as the years passed. In the present instance, for example, he envisages the solo pianist as an individual 'taking a stroll' through a garden represented by the orchestra, and even apparently incorporates into his writing some of the mannerisms of gait of the particular performer for whom the work was written. 'In *Arc* for piano and orchestra, written in 1963 for Yūji Takahashi as soloist, the stroller is Mr Takahashi. He has a unique way of walking that resembles limping, which is important in this piece.'[17]

It would appear that this rather nebulous-sounding metaphorical comparison to a garden is actually realised musically with a certain degree of precision. Unfortunately, Takemitsu's commentaries on the subject only go part of the way towards elucidating fully the manner in which his metaphor is translated into sound. His own drawings of an imaginary Japanese garden, with typical elements such as rocks, trees and grass all in their place, have been much reproduced by commentators;[18] yet despite such apparent candour, as one writer has noted with respect to his 'garden' works in general, 'to make out clearly what sort of role the spatial layout of Japanese gardens plays in this series of compositions is a perplexing task'.[19] In the case of *Arc*, however, it is at least clear that Takemitsu was using the elements of a Japanese garden as metaphors for various kinds of spatially and texturally differentiated musics which, in combination, could produce an overall 'pan-focal' texture similar to that found in *Coral Island*. Moreover, he associates each of these musical elements with its appropriate horticultural equivalent largely by drawing parallels between the 'time-cycles' of the two.

Some of the musical elements thus analogised are not unlike the textural types already encountered in *Coral Island*. Thus densely chromatic webs of sound for the strings, similar to the 'clusters' which had formed the background to the earlier work, here represent 'sand', the timeless, underlying medium in which the garden exists: Takemitsu, revealingly, applies to these the rather Xenakis-like description 'metagalaxy'. 'Grass' (and flowers), whose time-cycle is the shortest of all the elements in the garden, is represented by 'mobile' patterns for two out of the four groups of wind and percussion instruments in Takemitsu's unorthodox orchestral arrangement, similar once again to their counterparts in the earlier work. Interestingly, Takemitsu's preferred metaphor for the manner in which the dissimilar periodicities of the various melodic cycles constituting such a texture create ever-changing relationships with one another is taken from the rather unlikely field of molecular chemistry: 'these varying time-cycles contain what could be called heterocyclic relationship'.[20] Takemitsu conceives the time-cycle of 'trees' as similar to that of 'grass', but operating more slowly, and the role of impersonating it is allotted to the other two groups of wind and percussion instruments. Finally 'rocks', the most immobile element of all, are represented by sustained notes in the lower strings – although Takemitsu at the same time grants rocks a certain 'eloquence', portrayed at times by dissonant 'mobile' writing for the brass instruments.

It is in such an orchestral garden as this, then, that Mr Takahashi – and, vicariously, the listener – take their 'stroll': a 'multiply focussed musical garden',[21] a conception of the orchestra which differs radically from the classic Western view of this medium as a single, monolithic instrument. Takemitsu equates this latter outlook with the unitary perspective of Western art, in contrast with which, in his own music, several points of view coexist simultaneously. Once again, the metaphoric usage which Takemitsu appropriates to describe this is borrowed from a traditional Japanese form of artistic expression: 'by allowing the solo piano to stroll through the garden with changing viewpoints', the composer observes, 'the piece is freed from a set frame and becomes a mobile reminiscent of the Heian Period [794–1185] handscroll painting'.[22] In other words, just as there is no overall global perspective point from which the onlooker views the various scenes of an *emaki*, but rather a multitude of viewpoints which constantly shift as the scroll is unfurled, so too as the music of *Arc* unfolds, the listener experiences a constant shift of focus between the various elements contributing to Takemitsu's stratified textures.

The role of the 'stroller' in this metaphorical garden is not entirely a passive, contemplative one, however. At one or two points in the score, the decision as to which elements of the sound-garden he wishes to 'view' is left to his own spontaneous choice. Thus in *Pile*, the aleatoric interventions of the instrumental groups depicting 'grass' are cued by signals from the soloist, enabling him, as Ohtake expresses it, to 'choose to see any part of the grass he desires'.[23] A similar thing also happens at one point in *Your Love and the Crossing*, where the pianist gives cues for various solo instrumentalists to work through their allotted materials at their own pace. Akiyama singles out this passage as being of especial interest, inasmuch as the conductor's 'metronomic tempo' or 'clock time', the pianist's own tempo and the 'personal tempi' of the soloists constitute 'three kinds of musical time' which are superimposed upon one another.[24] But, as Poirier has observed, this kind of 'polyphony of time'[25] is prevalent throughout the score of *Arc* – is indeed an inevitable consequence of the manner in which Takemitsu interprets his 'garden' schema in terms of differentiated 'time-cycles'. At another point in the score, for example – Fig. 2 of *Textures* – two conductor's 'clock times' are superimposed upon one another simultaneously: a tempo of $\downarrow = 56$ is allocated to group 1 of the orchestra, and another of $\downarrow = 84$ to group 2. Since these two tempi are in a 2 : 3 ratio to one another, a $^2_4$ bar in the upper system will be equivalent to a $^3_4$ bar in the lower, and a $^4_4$ bar to two such $^3_4$ bars. This allocation of differing tempi, in a simple geometric ratio to one another, to spatially differentiated instrumental groups inevitably recalls the similar relationships between the three orchestral groups in Stockhausen's *Gruppen*; but, in Takemitsu's case, only one conductor appears to be on hand to deal with such complexities!

A further remark in Takemitsu's commentary on this 'stroll' observes that 'the work is in two sections and the direction walked in the first section is reversed in the second'.[26] The reader who has followed the development of Takemitsu's technical obsessions thus far should by now have no difficulty decoding what this infers in concrete musical terms, and two movements from the second part of *Arc* do indeed contain material from previous movements in retrograde orderings: *Textures* and the final *Coda* (which actually draws these materials, in turn, from the *Textures* movement). Furthermore the beginning of *Coda* consists of a reworking of materials from *Solitude*, further enhancing the sense of a 'return home'. And, in the context of *Arc*, this arrival back home can mean only one thing: the return of a recurrent, languorous melodic idea that appears intermittently throughout the work, aptly referred to by Funayama as 'the *Leitmotiv* of *Arc*, what should perhaps be called its principal theme, a Romantic melody'.[27] In the context of the 'high modernism' which *Arc* appears, superficially at least, to proclaim, such an incursion might strike the listener as an incongruity, something of an anachronistic throwback; but, as subsequent events were to demonstrate, it is actually at the same time a prophetic pointer towards a future beyond the 'avant-gardism' with which Takemitsu is presently preoccupied.

'Mr Takahashi' was to take a stroll through another of Takemitsu's gardens later in the 1960s, as soloist in the composer's *Asterism* for piano and orchestra (1967). This work takes its title from one of the obscurer entries in the English lexicon: the word 'asterism' may refer (among other things) either to a 'group of stars' or 'constellation', or to a printer's mark consisting of 'three asterisks ($\ast\,\ast\,\ast$ or $\ast\,\ast\,\ast$) placed before a passage to direct attention to it'. The former meaning identifies the work clearly as the first member of Takemitsu's 'star' series – to which he would later add several other titles, such as *Cassiopeia, Gémeaux, Star-Isle* and *Orion and Pleiades.* The second meaning, however, perhaps suggests a translation of the patterns of stellar phenomena into visual groupings on the page – a kind of *Augenmusik.* Certainly the percussion part of the later *Cassiopeia* is full of W- and M-shapes suggesting the layout of the stars in the eponymous constellation. While a similar correlation between visual configurations in the *Asterism* score and those of the star patterns Takemitsu describes is less easy to identify, it is perhaps possible that the contour of the triplet theme with which the work opens is intended to echo the ^-shape suggested by the second of the above typographical figures. At any rate, there are passages in *Asterism* which are incontrovertibly visually conceived, such as the symmetrical 'horseshoe'-shape created by the entry of the violin parts at letter 'D', and writing of this kind in general suggests that, although by this stage Takemitsu has almost abandoned his interest in graphic scores, the refined visual sense that is revealed by those scores is still operative in a more orthodox notational context. It also suggests the lingering influence of Cage. On the occasion of Cage's second actual visit to Japan, which took place in 1964, one of the works which Takemitsu heard when he travelled with him to the Sapporo Contemporary Music Festival was *Atlas Eclipticalis* (1961). This is the work which maps stellar configurations from an atlas of the heavens directly on to notations provided as performance materials, and it is scarcely conceivable that this audacious plan could not have had some impact on Takemitsu's own exploitation of astronomical phenomena as visual stimuli in such works as *Asterism* and *Cassiopeia.*

Though rather shorter than *Arc,* and scored for an almost conventionally seated orchestra, *Asterism* is no less of a grand modernist statement. Indeed it shares many of the same preoccupations as the earlier work: there are, for example, sections that are repeated in retrograde, densely chromatic passages in 'tone cluster' style, and passages of *senza misura* 'mobile' writing. There are even literal recyclings of materials from *Arc:* the mobiles for brass representing 'rocks' in the dense climax of *Your Love and the Crossing* reappear at Fig. F of *Asterism,* while the background harmony of the former passage – together with the opening chord of *Pile* – yields harmonic materials for the lower strings at Fig. E of the later work.

Perhaps the respect in which *Asterism* differs most markedly from *Arc,* however, is in its overall structure. Takemitsu here abandons his preferred cyclical forms for a kind of dramatic one-way propulsion towards total orchestral self-annihilation, followed by a brief coda: the work, as Ohtake puts it, is 'structured to have one long crescendo'.[28] What Roger Dettmer,

Ex. 53 *Asterism*, letter 'D' (vln)

in his sleeve notes for the original RCA recording,[29] describes as the 'anguishing, ultimately ecstatic climax' of this crescendo is a kind of shatteringly intense band of 'white noise' for full orchestra, built up like the textures of *Arc* from the superimposition of various strata: an accumulation of 'mobile' patterns, sustained tremolando harmonies for the strings and a massive percussion crescendo which finally engulfs the entire ensemble.

Harmonically this passage is of course chromatically saturated, or rather indeed 'super-saturated', with several pitches doubled at the octave. As such it is once again typical of the 'modernist' excursions of this period; Yōko Narazaki even goes so far as to speak of a ' "tone cluster" technique employed in such works as *Textures, November Steps*, etc.'[30] Closer examination of the various strata combining to produce this 'panchromatic' texture, however, reveals that they are not always themselves as 'atonally' conceived as the overall effect might suggest. For example, one of the first layers to be presented as Takemitsu builds up his climactic texture incrementally is the chord for violins at Fig. D, quoted in Example 53.

To be sure, this chord contains all twelve pitch-classes; yet a moment's consideration reveals that it does not consist of just an arbitrary jumble of notes. As the layout of the example emphasises, it is clearly the result of the superimposition of two hexachords – analogue, on this microcosmic level, to the macrocosmic superimposition of strata from which the texture is built up at this point. Furthermore, each of these hexachords is the chromatic complement of the other, and each the inversion of the other. Finally, the pitch-class sets of the two hexachords, [0,2,3,5,7,9] in prime and inverted form, are both segments of the diatonic major or 'acoustic'

Ex. 54 *Asterism*, bar 12 (harps)

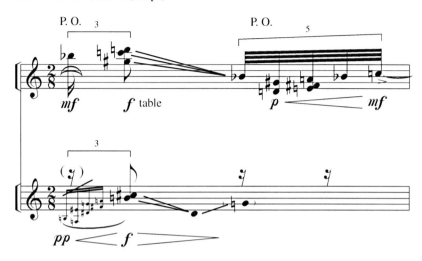

scales. In other words, although the collection may have the global effect of a 'panchromatic' cluster, its harmonic basis is obviously the superimposition of modal forms – another example of the kind of 'pantonal' writing that Takemitsu presented in the previous year as his 'humble protest against serialism' in *The Dorian Horizon*.

In fact, despite its often highly dissonant and 'atonal' surface, much of the harmonic material of *Asterism* is modally derived in this way. Layers in the richly chromatic texture prove, on closer inspection, to derive from the gamut of scalar types which Takemitsu had acquired by now, and in addition to 'absolute' modal types such as the two constituents of the above chord, Takemitsu also makes great play in this score with his favourite 'chromatically enhanced' modal collection, the 'whole-tone+1' form ('7-33'). By this stage, the discovery that the strings of the harp could be tuned to project this collection as a chord or even a glissando was evidently very much to the composer's liking, as Example 54 shows. Here two such collections, one for each harp, are superimposed upon one another: thus, once again, the total-chromatic is derived by means of the simultaneous projection of modally derived forms.

In the closing pages of *Asterism*, this underlying modalism emerges clearly into the foreground, and, in particular, the pitch-class G♯/A♭ is revealed as the work's ultimate tonal destination. Emphasis on this particular pitch-class can be found as early as bar 81, where it forms the uppermost pitch of a repeated two-chord gesture for wind, and the same pitch is

Ex. 55 *Asterism*, 'G'/7–8

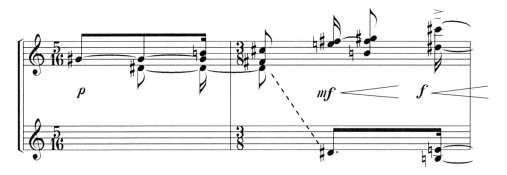

repeatedly re-emphasised over the course of succeeding pages. It is after the work's multi-layered, chromatic climax, however, that this pitch-class really begins to enjoy spotlit status in the musical drama. After the orchestral cataclysm, the music subsides to a sustained string harmony of which G♯ forms the uppermost pitch. Then, in a gesture which is highly typical of the composer, this same pitch is echoed by the solo piano, and thenceforth until the final G♯ attack for piano and harps is almost never absent from the musical texture. Furthermore, when one considers the effect of the piano passage quoted in Example 55, with its G♯-minor triad and pitch-materials confined to a six-note diatonic mode centred on that note, it is hard to dispute that this constant emphasis is designed to bestow upon this note the qualities of a convincing tonic. Akiyama suggests that the emphasis on this particular pitch might even represent an example of Takemitsu's direct transliteration of Roman letters into their equivalent musical note-names: 'G♯ = A♭ . . . is this sounding of the 'As' [i.e. German A♭] of *Asterism* the solution to the riddle?'[31]

While *Asterism* represents another summation of the technical devices Takemitsu had learned from the West, however, by the time it was written he had already composed the work that represents his most famous and direct confrontation with his own native Japanese tradition. It is to the steps leading to this confrontation that consideration must next be given.

7 Projections on to an Eastern mirror

Of all the effects the encounter with Cage had upon Takemitsu's musical thinking, perhaps the most significant was that of reconciling him at last to his own native musical tradition. As we have seen, Takemitsu claimed that at the outset he had 'struggled to avoid being "Japanese", to avoid "Japanese" qualities'; now, however, 'largely through my contact with John Cage' he was able 'to recognise the value of my own tradition'.[1] But despite these claims it is clear that Takemitsu had already become deeply interested in traditional Japanese music before Cage's appearance on the scene. In particular, a passage in *Mirror of Tree, Mirror of Grass* describes the moment in which he first recognised the intrinsic qualities of his own music in similarly epiphanic terms to those he used to describe his encounter with the music of Lucienne Boyer some years previously: 'It was ten years after I began studying music that I received a strong shock from a *bunraku*[2] performance. It was then that I became aware of Japan for the first time. In fact I saw Japan represented as distinct from myself, and acknowledged it as entirely different.'[3]

Takemitsu does not give an exact date for this revelation: Miyamoto supposes it to have occurred around 1958,[4] which was certainly 'ten years after' Takemitsu 'began studying music' in the official sense of taking lessons with Kiyose. At all events, Takemitsu's 'Japanese shock' clearly predated his 'Cage shock' by a number of years, and as we have already seen, specifically 'Japanese' musical ideas are referred to in Takemitsu's programme notes at least as early as his references to the 'one by one' rhythm of *Requiem* (1957) or to the *nō* theatre in *Masque* (1959). Moreover, it was not long before these borrowings on a 'philosophical' level were supplemented by actual use of Japanese traditional instruments, and once again it was incidental music that provided the laboratory for Takemitsu's first experiments. Indeed, given the care he exercised to match the style of his incidental music to the content of each individual commission, it was almost inevitable that Takemitsu should end up using traditional Japanese instruments such as the *chikuzenbiwa*[5] and *koto* for a documentary on Japanese *kimono*, *Nihon no Monyō* ('Japanese Crest Patterns'), which the NHK produced in 1961. This initial venture was to be followed by similar 'anecdotal' uses of traditional Japanese music in the films *Seppuku*[6] and *Kwaidan*, and in 1966 Takemitsu went a stage further, blending such traditional instruments as *shakuhachi, shinobue*[7] and *ryūteki*[8] with the Western symphony orchestra in his music for the period television drama series *Minamoto Yoshitsune*.

Such experiments as these were soon to find their echo in Takemitsu's work for the concert hall. *Eclipse* for *biwa* and *shakuhachi* appeared in 1966, and in the following year Takemitsu combined the same two instruments with symphony orchestra in what has since become one of his most celebrated works: *November Steps*, commissioned to commemorate the 125th anniversary of the New York Philharmonic Orchestra. This piece occupies perhaps an even more important position in the history of Takemitsu's Western reception than does *Requiem for Strings*: recorded the following year by Seiji Ozawa and the Toronto Symphony Orchestra, it was released as the fourth side of an LP recording of Messiaen's *Turangalîla Symphony*, thus guaranteeing Takemitsu's work such a worldwide distribution that, even today, it remains for many Western listeners the piece by which he is best known. Unfortunately, this has perhaps also had the deleterious effect of creating the impression that the composer's career was dominated by the attempt to create some sort of 'bridge' between traditional Japanese instrumental praxis and Western symphonic music. In reality, however, there are relatively few further works in the composer's catalogue that employ traditional instruments. It is true that another work for *biwa*, *shakuhachi* and orchestra, *Autumn*, and a work for three *biwa*, *Voyage*, both appeared in 1973; and that Takemitsu was to employ another traditional Japanese instrument, the *shō*,[9] with solo oboe in *Distance* (1972) and with orchestra in *Ceremonial – An Autumn Ode* (1992). He was also commissioned to write a work for full-scale *gagaku* orchestra, *In an Autumn Garden*, the final version of which appeared in 1979. But, these instances apart, this form of literal and concrete incorporation of traditional Japanese music was a kind of assimilation in which, after *November Steps*, Takemitsu was to show almost no further interest.[10]

Miyamoto takes this abandonment of traditional Japanese instruments to indicate that the composer had finally concluded that 'it made no sense to unite Japanese music with European',[11] but my own view differs slightly. While acknowledging that the composer showed very little further interest in the direct importation of Japanese music into a Western context, I believe that there is nevertheless another sense in which Japanese music continued to exert a profound influence on the composer's thinking throughout the remainder of his creative life. Just as Takemitsu soon abandoned his interest in musical graphics and prepared pianos, yet still remained indebted to Cage's thought on a theoretical and ideational level, so even after abandoning his interest in writing for the *shakuhachi*, he was still strongly influenced by the aesthetics of traditional Japanese music.

Indeed, as was noted in the last chapter, there were a number of points of contact between the two aesthetic ideologies, and it is perhaps in this sense that Cage, after all, can be seen as the person who 'reconciled' Takemitsu to his own native music – even if he arrived sometime after the latter had already begun to take an active interest in it. For not only did Cage's approbation lend what Wilson describes as the 'stamp of Western legitimacy'[12] to tendencies that were already taking place; by identifying the common preoccupations of traditional Japanese and his own, contemporary Western aesthetics, Cage handed Takemitsu a tool for investigating his own tradition on a profounder and, ultimately, more fruitful level than the mere appropriation of 'exotic' instruments. And, as we shall see in the final chapter of this book, it was upon this level that, ultimately, Takemitsu was eventually to achieve the most successful integration of 'Eastern' and 'Western' elements of any Japanese composer to date.

The road to *November Steps*

Problematic for Takemitsu, as a result of this decision to work with traditional instrumentalists, was the necessity of devising an adequate notation, and an insight into one of his earliest responses to this question can be gathered from a study of his first work for the concert room using traditional resources: *Eclipse* for *biwa* and *shakuhachi*. Written in 1966, a few years after the bulk of Takemitsu's graphic experiments, the score looks superficially like a throwback to his 'Cage shock' period, but in fact these symbols are an eminently practical response to the problem of notating the sounds produced by these instruments, and have fairly precise prescriptive significances. The notation for the *biwa* is reminiscent of the 'tablature' method of transcription associated particularly with music for the *biwa*'s distant Western cousin, the lute. In other words, the physical actions required for performance, rather than the sounding result, are the object of graphic representation, and the score is thus able to render pitches and articulative methods with considerable fidelity, although the rhythmic aspect of the music is much less rigidly prescribed. The performance materials provided for the *shakuhachi*, on the other hand, are rather less precise. Here an upper system with symbols indicating pitch contours on a purely relative, 'more than/less than' basis, is placed above various signs associated with idiomatic instrumental effects; again, there are no specific rhythmic indications. Practical as both these systems of notation are, however, obviously neither is rigidly determinate, and much of the success or otherwise of the performance depends on the performers' skill in breathing life into them. In this respect, the close association of this work with two particular exponents of *biwa* and *shakuhachi* – respectively Kinshi Tsuruta and Katsuya Yokoyama – has been of particular importance in ensuring the work's successful realisation.

The same performers have also been the regular executants of the solo parts in *November Steps*, and in many ways the notations employed in *Eclipse* can be seen as a preparatory exercise for those used in the later score: at any rate, the same notational conventions are used for the unaccompanied cadenza for the two instruments towards its close. Elsewhere in this score, however, Takemitsu must evidently have realised that this form of notation might be impenetrable to anyone but the soloists themselves, including the conductor. For those sections of the solo parts in which some form of minimum co-ordination between soloists and ensemble is expected, therefore, Takemitsu employs a notational system of more familiar aspect to Western readers: although there are no barlines, and rhythmic values are 'proportionately' notated, pitches are given in staff notation as equi-tempered approximations, with a few microtonal inflections, and some special signs for idiomatic instrumental practice.

Though most dramatically manifested in its choice of instrumental soloists, the 'Japanese' input into *November Steps* is not confined solely to this most conspicuous feature. It is also to be found, for example, at the level of overall formal organisation, and, in this respect, Takemitsu's English title is revealingly ambiguous. On the one hand, it is meant to be understood in the purely straightforward sense that any English speaker would attribute to it; as the composer put it, 'It was performed in November, and to me that project represented a new step: thus, I titled the work "November Steps".'[13] It was to this everyday, prosaic sense of the words that Takemitsu was referring when he used the Japanese translation *Jūichigatsu no Kaitei* as the title for a 1971 essay on the work.[14] On the other hand, an alternative rendering of 'November Steps' into Japanese might be *Jūichigatsu no Dan*, and in this case the word chosen as equivalent to 'step' (*dan*) is one that has precise technical meanings in Japanese traditional music. To borrow Eta Harich-Schneider's definition, 'The term *dan* is used . . . for the scenes of *nō* plays; it is also a musical term and means the sections in ballads'.[15]

Works comprising several such *dan* are referred to as *danmono* ('matters in steps'), and one of the most celebrated of these is a work from the *koto* repertory called *Rokudan* ('Six Steps'). Since 'November' in Japanese is 'the eleventh month' (*jūichigatsu*), Takemitsu's title can be understood as an echo of this famous precedent, but one in which the number of formal sections has been increased to correspond to the ordinal number of the month in which it was performed. It is to this sense of the title that

Takemitsu is referring when he notes: 'In Japanese music, *danmono* are the equivalent of Western variations, and the word *dan* means "step". My "November Steps" are a set of eleven variations.'[16]

Despite the apparent candour with which Takemitsu describes his formal pattern, however, to determine conclusively how these eleven sections map on to the actual score is – to borrow Funayama's phrase from the previous chapter – 'a perplexing task'. While Takemitsu himself suggestively provides eleven rehearsal numbers, the only commentator I have come across who has attempted a definitive eleven-fold segmentation of the structure – Kuniharu Akiyama – deviates slightly from the obvious interpretation implied by these markings. Although he acknowledges an identity between 'steps' 3 to 11 and the corresponding rehearsal numbers, Akiyama labels the twenty-four-bar introduction '*dan* 1', and consequently has to locate the beginning of the second *dan* after this introduction, at precisely the point where Takemitsu's rehearsal number 1 appears.[17] Similarly, the description of the soloists' unaccompanied cadenza as the work's 'tenth step' when it was issued independently on a CD recording[18] again suggests a slightly different segmentation from that implied by the rehearsal numbers, since the tenth of these actually appears in the orchestral passage four bars before the cadenza begins. Perhaps the most that one can assert with any certainty, then, is that the work – as Ohtake cautiously expresses it – consists of 'eleven ambiguously separated sections'.[19]

The orchestral apparatus Takemitsu employs to project this eleven-fold structure is unorthodox both in its selection and its spatial distribution: with the two soloists occupying the foreground, two similarly formed and symmetrical groups of strings and percussion are placed to left and right of the stage, with a small number of trumpets, trombones, oboes and clarinets occupying the rear. Takemitsu takes advantage of this spatial layout at one point to furnish a new means of transforming repeated materials: when the material of bars 2–5 reappears at bars 40–3, in addition to making certain other changes, Takemitsu swaps over the 'left' and 'right' sides of his 'stereo picture'. In passing, one also notes that the formal layout of the work honours another fairly consistent 'rule' of Takemitsu's formal construction, and one that has analogues in the Western 'Classical' tradition: as in *Distance de Fée*, the placing of the instrumental cadenza is a sign that the closing gesture is imminent. Edward Smaldone has also drawn attention to this point, noting that in both *November Steps* and *Autumn* 'there are elaborate cadenza passages for both *shakuhachi* and *biwa* which seem to serve as the dramatic goal of the entire composition, followed by a closing orchestral statement'.[20]

Ex. 56 *November Steps*, brass chords at: (i) bar 32 (ii) bar 61

To the many Western listeners who encountered Takemitsu's music for the first time in the shape of this particular work, its harmonic abrasiveness and fragmented textures must have seemed very much in accord with the aesthetics of the composer's European and American avant-garde contemporaries. Closer reading of the score, however, reveals that this apparently 'freely chromatic' surface is – once again – largely generated by the juxtaposition and superimposition of harmonic structures which in themselves have a modal basis: the work is by and large 'pan-tonal' rather than 'a-tonal'. Embedded in the overall chromatic texture at two points in the score, for example, is a harmonic form which was to become something of a trademark sonority in the works of the composer's later years – the complete verticalisation of all five pitches of the pentatonic scale represented by the black notes of the piano, [0,2,4,7,9] (Ex. 56). Inappropriate as these commonplace harmonic devices might seem in the context of the work's avant-garde abrasiveness, Takemitsu here absorbs them into the music's overall sound-world without the least feeling of incongruity.

But at the opposite extreme from such harmonic simplicities, there are other passages in the score employing densely chromatic aggregates, or even intervals smaller than the semitone. In bar 54, for instance, the violas present a cluster built up from ten conjunct quarter-tones filling the space between G♮^{3} and a B♭^{3} raised by a quarter-tone. This particular manner of employing microtones simply as denser infillings of chromatic space, which recalls the preoccupations of Xenakis or the Polish school, is of course contemporary and Western in origin, and it is entirely appropriate that its use in *November Steps* should be confined to the passages written for symphony orchestra. But by contrast, the microtonal 'bendings' of pitch in the two solo parts clearly relate rather to the idiomatic performance practices of traditional Japanese music, and thus suggest once again that Takemitsu is exploring a common ground between contemporary Western and ancient Japanese instrumental praxis; the order of events in the score, in which the microtones appear in the orchestral part only after their use by the soloists, as if the result of an 'influence' by the latter, is at least suggestive of as much.

For the most part, however, in *November Steps* the worlds of 'East' and 'West' resolutely proclaim their separateness. Far from attempting a fusion of the two cultures, Takemitsu has explicitly stated that in this work he 'resolved to blend some intrinsically mismatched instruments in one ensemble so as to reveal, to the extent I could, their underlying differences'.[21] The work in fact consists, as Poirier has observed, almost entirely of 'sections allocated alternately to the traditional instruments and to the orchestra',[22] with very few passages in which the two are heard simultaneously. The points of contact which Takemitsu does manage to forge between what would otherwise be two independent works performed simultaneously, therefore, assume crucial importance.

One such form of communication between the two cultures consists of the relationships Takemitsu establishes in the realm of timbre. Wilson, for instance, notes that the harp, plucked *près de la table*, might sound like a *biwa*, thus creating an 'aural bridge' between the two traditions here represented.[23] One might extend this idea further to encompass other sonorous approximations of this kind. For example, in the key to notational conventions at the beginning of the score, the harpist is instructed in one instance to 'make a quick and powerful glissando on the string with a coin in the direction shown by the arrow', while the *biwa* player is required by another, visually similar, symbol to 'rub the designated string lightly from top to bottom with the point of the plectrum', and both players are requested to strike the bodies of their instruments with parts of the hand in various ways. Other such instances of timbral resemblance are the brief pedal glissando for harp in bar 22, with its suggestion of the microtonal 'bendings' of pitch by the soloists which soon follow; the manner in which the first harp's inwardly folding arpeggio here anticipates the *biwa*'s sharply attacked chords; and the way in which the various effects obtained from gongs and tam-tams with wood and metal beaters (not to mention the 'Bartók' pizzicati for cellos) suggest the typical 'slap' gestures of the *biwa* idiom. Such concrete, individualised examples of East–West contact on the level of timbre neatly symbolise *in nuce* the broad philosophical overlap which Takemitsu discovered between the two traditions in this area, to which more attention will be given in the concluding chapter of this work.

A second point of contact between soloists and orchestra is effected by means of a favourite device of Takemitsu's: the linking of sections by means of a pitch (or pitches) common to the end of one passage and the beginning of the next. Emphasis on specific pitch-classes, either in the form of sustained pedal points, or as reiterated notes, is a common feature of *November Steps*; Wilson has noted that such 'emphasis and repetition of a single pitch provide a pitch focus amidst the array of complex string textures',[24] and draws particular attention to the sustained 'F' with which the work opens, which according to him recurs 'thematically' elsewhere in the piece. Edward Smaldone takes the same argument a stage further, linking all such highlighted pitches throughout the work to yield a kind of Schenkerian *Urlinie*, 'a precious few pitches which guide our ear along a large arch'.[25] While one cannot easily agree with this rather sweeping conclusion of Smaldone's, one observation of his with regard to a specific pair of such nuclear pitches does seem incontrovertibly accurate. In bar 21 of *November Steps*, two double basses enter with a long pedal D♮ in harmonics, joined later by two more basses sustaining the pitch E♮; and after the ensuing silence 'the *shakuhachi* enters on D and E, making a strong sonic connection with the orchestral passage'.[26] One might make the further observation that the adjacent, semitonally dissonant pitches – the C♯'s and D♯'s – with which the preceding double pedal is periodically 'smudged', are perhaps intended to prefigure the wavering intonation, the microtonally inflected vibrato (*tate-yuri*), of the ensuing *shakuhachi* entry. If this interpretation is correct, then the aural link forged by the use of common pitches also relates to the attempt to find an approximation for Japanese intonational practices by the use of semitone dissonances within the equitempered system: a preoccupation which, we have seen, goes right back to the time of the composer's early *Romance*.

November Steps has a 'companion piece' in the shape of the orchestral work *Green*, originally entitled *November Steps II* – Takemitsu's new name for the work reflecting 'the foliation of spring as he composed the two *November Steps* of buds into young leaves'.[27] In contrast to the austere, avant-garde complexities of *November Steps*, however, *Green* for the most part presents a simplified and more luxurious harmonic and textural surface that recalls instead the music of Messiaen or even Debussy. Indeed, Takemitsu revealed that he took the scores of both the *Prélude à 'L'Après-midi d'un faune'* and *Jeux* to the mountain villa where both works were composed, 'from a wish to enter into the secrets of Debussy's music, which never ceases to assert a strong influence on my music',[28] and this Debussyan influence is certainly palpable as far as the score of *Green* is concerned. In particular, such details as the prominent use of antique cymbals, the inverted pedal point in octaves for strings just before Figure 2, the pedal B♮ at Figure 11 (at the same pitch as its celebrated counterpart at the opening of *Jeux*), and the 'layered' scoring of Figure 2, bar 2, with its bowed tremolando harmonies and inner parts of cascading woodwind figures – all point to Takemitsu's exhaustive study of the 'secrets' of the French composer's orchestral palette.

In *Green*, too, the modalism which, as we have seen, lies behind so much of *November Steps*' harmonic construction emerges more clearly into the foreground. This 'emergence' is in fact not merely metaphorical, but in one instance at least literal as well. As the original title of *Green* suggests, the work is related 'thematically' to *November Steps*, as can most clearly be seen by comparing bar 12 of the latter work with Figure 7, bar 1 of the former (Ex. 57).

It is immediately apparent from this juxtaposition that the passage quoted from *Green* is essentially a reworking of the *November Steps* passage a whole-tone lower. The relationship between the two works does not end here, though. Specifically, the material given to the violas in the *November Steps* example, and to the second violins and violas in that from *Green*, abstracted from this many-layered context, acquires an important and independent thematic significance throughout the score of the latter. It is, however, transformed during the course of the work, and by means of another of Takemitsu's standard devices for departing from literal repetition: the 'reharmonisation' of what is essentially the same uppermost melodic voice. These transformations can perhaps best be understood by examining them in reverse order to that in which they actually appear in the score of *Green*. Shortly before the above appearance, for example, at Figure 6, bar 2, the material appears in the form shown in Example 58: augmented rhythmically, and 'harmonised' in a manner closer to the form in which it appeared in *November Steps* (each chord now consisting of a transposition of its equivalent in the latter work, plus one added pitch).

A little while before this, there is another appearance of the same basic idea, albeit with slight modifications to the harmony. This time, however, the fourth and fifth chords are transposed down one octave (rather than two), imparting a highly distinctive melodic profile to the uppermost voice (Ex. 59).

And it is this reshaped melodic contour, supported now by a completely different set of accompanying harmonies, that provides the opening thematic statement of the entire work (Ex. 60 – the melodic line is in the third

Ex. 57 Comparison of *November Steps*, bar 12 with *Green*, 7/1

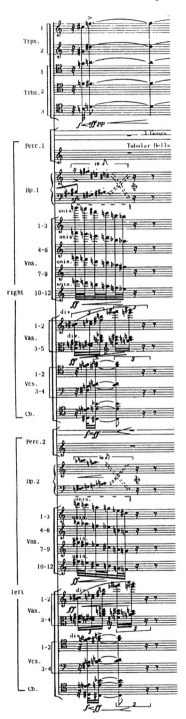
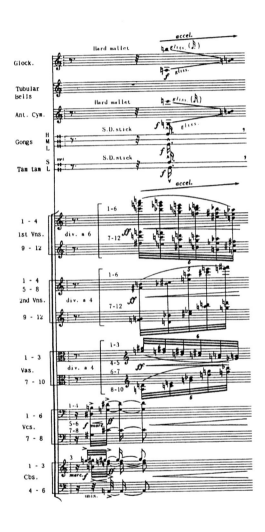

Ex. 58 *Green*, 6/2

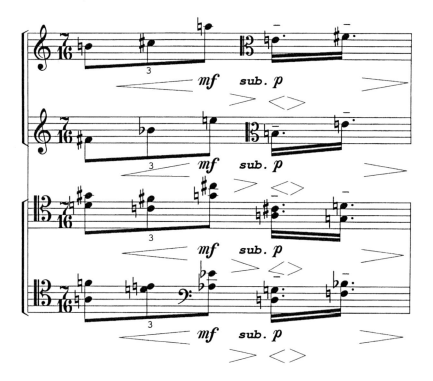

Ex. 59 *Green*, 5/1

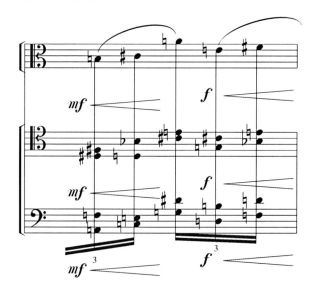

Ex. 60 *Green*, bar 1

Vln.1
nos.1-6
(div.)

Vln.2
nos.1-6
(div.)

Vlas.
1-6,
cello
solo

Cellos
2-4

staff down). Thus the lyrical, suavely harmonised opening idea of *Green* derives ultimately from one layer in the densely 'pantonal' web of Example 57: the modalism secreted in the complex texture of the *November Steps* passage is literally brought to the surface, manifesting itself clearly to the listener on both horizontal and vertical levels.

I have described this process of transformation as if it were clear that the composer's starting point was the material derived from *November Steps* which, in the context of *Green*, gave rise to these new variant forms. In reality, of course, no such unambiguous interpretation is possible, and it is equally feasible to consider that the *Green* material came first, and that one of its variant forms came to be incorporated into *November Steps* as the result of the wholesale lifting of one bar. As both works were composed in the same period, the composer's dating gives no hint of which interpretation of the sequence of events is correct. In the case of another borrowing in *Green*, however, there are more certain grounds for preferring one version of the material as the 'original' and the other as the 'quotation'. The passage in question is that quoted in Example 61, which is essentially a rescoring of Figure G, bars 7–8 of *Réflexion*, part of Takemitsu's gigantic *Arc* for piano and orchestra. As the latter work was composed in 1966, one can with more certainty grant 'primogeniture' to the *Arc* version.

Ex. 61 *Green*, 11/2

But while this interpretation resolves the ambiguity regarding the quotation's origins, it creates another type of ambiguity within the context of *Green* itself. Earlier in this work, the same material appears in a rhythmically varied form an octave higher, and minus the bracketed chord 'X' (Ex. 62). On the basis of the temporal order in which events unfold in the score, then, one would be inclined to describe Example 61 as a version of Example 62 with one chord *interpolated*. The prior origin of the latter, however, suggests that in reality it is Example 62 which is an elliptical commentary on Example 61 with one chord *omitted*. Depending on whether one's interpretation is based on the sequence of events within the score of *Green*, then, or on the order of composition of that score and *Arc*, the relationship of these two passages to one another is – once again – capable of ambiguous interpretation.

The modal basis of much of *Green*'s harmony can clearly be seen from the above examples – whether it takes the form of simple verticalisations of scalar forms (as in the case of the second, whole-tone-derived chord of Ex. 60), or scale verticalisations to which extraneous pitches have been added (as in the case of the third chord from Ex. 60, [0,2,3,4,6,8], the same subset

Ex. 62 *Green*, 5/1

of the '7-33' or 'whole-tone+1' collection used as a 'reference' chord in the second movement of *Uninterrupted Rest* (Ex. 25)). Vertical forms superimposing all seven notes of the '7-33' collection are of fairly regular occurrence in the score of *Green* too, providing in this work especially a good example of the potential Takemitsu had discovered in this harmonic form for a number of revoicings, each possessing a different harmonic character. Wilson, remarking on the ubiquity of this same harmonic type in the score of *Asterism*, noted that the addition of a 'non-scale note infuses a certain density and denies the obvious aural nature of the whole-tone scale',[29] and this increase in density also opens up a much greater range of harmonic possibilities. The nature of the whole-tone scale itself permits only the construction of vertical forms containing even-numbered interval classes: in Fortean terminology, the 'interval vector' of the whole-tone ('6-35') collection is a rather limiting 060603. By contrast, the addition of only one extraneous pitch greatly increases the range of available intervals: the 'interval vector' of the set now becomes a much richer 262623. Takemitsu exploits this increased potential to the full in the score of *Green*, where (as shown in Ex. 63) the collection is revoiced in various ways so that its lower parts project major triads in first (iii) and second inversion (v), or

Ex. 63 *Green*, versions of '7–33' chord

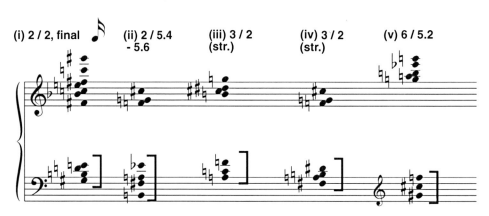

dominant sevenths in root position (ii), first inversion (i) and second inversion (iv).

Despite this preoccupation with modally derived forms, however, *Green* does not eschew the occasional use of more richly chromatic materials, or of even finer divisions of the octave, as in Example 64, where Takemitsu builds up clusters of quarter-tones rather after the fashion of the passage already referred to in *November Steps*. Furthermore, the passage illustrates another instance of Takemitsu's practice of building up such densely woven textures by means of canonic imitation. Here a twelve-part 'endless canon' is introduced *in medias res*; lacking as it does, however, any clear-cut presentation of the traditional *dux* and *comes*, and consisting in any case of featureless, microtonal 'slitherings', the canon is hardly likely to be perceived as such by the listener. Rather it operates here more as a notational device, to ensure constant movement on the one hand, coupled with complete verticalisation of the saturated microtonal harmony at any given point on the other.

Nevertheless, in spite of passages of such complexity as the above, the predominant impression the listener retains of *Green* is of its benign, modal elements, and at the time the work must surely have seemed something of an anomaly in the context of Takemitsu's contemporaneous works. With hindsight, of course, such qualities seem to afford a surprisingly prophetic glimpse of the direction his music was to take from the latter half of the 1970s onwards, and, viewed in this light, the coda of the work acquires an unintentionally ironic symbolism. The work ends with an early example of the 'panpentatonic' valedictions that were to become such a trademark of the composer from *A Flock Descends into the*

Ex. 64 *Green*, 8/2

Pentagonal Garden onwards, but at this stage the cadential effect is unbalanced by the voicing. Although the sustained harmony is indeed a verticalisation of the pentatonic collection A–B–C♯–E–F♯, the placing of the 'B' in the bass, and the D♯ of the horn's melodic turn, contrive to impart to it a 'B dominant seventh' feel which, instead of bringing the work to a close, suddenly and unexpectedly reveals a magical, evanescent glimpse of a possible E-major future. It is as if the music were offering a fleeting vision of that 'sea of tonality' into which the music of Takemitsu was to flow abundantly in the following decade, but which for the present existed only in the shape of some such dimly glimpsed potential.

Beyond *November Steps*

Takemitsu was to revisit the combination of *biwa*, *shakuhachi* and orchestra six years later in his much less well-known *Autumn* of 1973, but here, in contrast to the earlier work's 'confrontation' between the two cultures, Takemitsu 'wanted to do something which I hadn't done in *November Steps*, not to blend the instruments, but to integrate them'.[30] Thus passages in which orchestra and soloists play simultaneously are much more frequent, and as Poirier notes there is an increase in the number of 'points of common anchorage' between the two, an 'insistence on encounters at the unison or at the octave'.[31]

One passage of *Autumn* should be singled out for especial mention: the densely textured web of sound beginning at letter 'A' of the score which, as Smaldone points out, is 'organised by a complex procedure of transposition, ordering and transformation, which governs the nineteen individual string parts'.[32] The uppermost six voices constituting this texture are involved in the working out of the typical 'microcanonic' processes which Takemitsu frequently adopted for the generation of such sound-masses at this period: here there is a four-part canon at the unison for the violins, and another (two-part) canon for the violas. Beneath these two 'layers' are four more independent strata, comprising either unison melodic lines, or block harmonies moving in rhythmic unison within the layer. In all four instances, the material of these strata consists of a sequence of pitches or chords which is repeated cyclically, independently of the durational values by which it is expressed, somewhat in the manner of the *color* in an isorhythmic construction. However, in the case of the three uppermost strands, these durational values in themselves demonstrate no corresponding constructional organisation of their own: in other words, do not constitute a *talea*. In the lowest strand of the texture, however, a repeated cycle of eight chords is presented in rhythmic values determined by a cycle

Ex. 65 *Autumn*, A/1

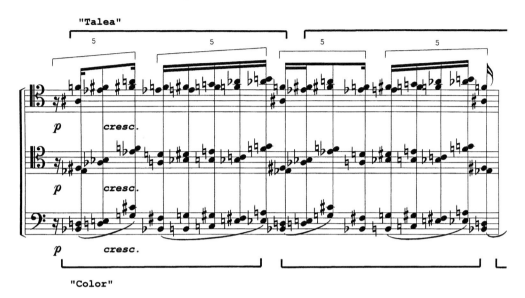

of nine durational values, the dissimilar lengths of the two cycles guaranteeing different combinations of harmony and rhythm at each repetition (Ex. 65). In other words, this is one of the rare instances in Takemitsu's output where *color* and *talea* of differing lengths mesh with one another to generate the classic isorhythmic structure.

Of course, despite the medieval connotations of the terms used above, there can be little doubt that this device was transmitted to Takemitsu not via a study of early music, but rather by means of the *Technique de mon langage musical* of Messiaen. But perhaps the most interesting feature of this passage is not Takemitsu's use of this technique *per se*, but rather the lack of interest he shows in pursuing the consequences of the mechanism he has thus constructed. The pattern quoted above clearly follows the same constructional procedures as the famous piano part of the *Liturgie de cristal*, but – in contrast to Messiaen's almost alchemical fascination with this type of arithmetical process – Takemitsu shows no interest in pursuing its workings for more than a few bars. Moreover, the fact that in the other 'isomelodic' strands in the texture at this point the *color* is changed after a couple of repetitions, and allied to a set of completely arbitrary durational values, indicates that Takemitsu is employing the device here for much the same reason as he employs canonic imitation in the upper voices: simply as a convenient means for generating a dense instrumental micropolyphony. He is as little interested in the opportunity for a display of compositional artifice afforded by the one as he is by the other, and the very rarity of this kind of writing in Takemitsu's music in itself points to his temperamental disinclination for the strict application of any 'constructivist' rigour of this sort.

Reflections in other Eastern mirrors

While, as we shall see in chapter 12, Takemitsu tended to think he was working towards a sort of cultural cosmopolitanism through his composition, there is repeated evidence in his writings that – despite such 'advanced' ideas – he still unconsciously thought in terms of the old binary opposition of 'Japan' and 'other' to which his nationalist colleagues had adhered. Rather than recognising any common ground between Japanese and other Asiatic musics, he found the latter as alien to his own sensibility as Western music, and as a result, the music of other Asian traditions was to exercise almost no influence on his ideas at either a musical or philosophical level.

There are however one or two exceptions to this general rule. In his music for the film *Shinju Ten no Amishima*,[33] Takemitsu included taped recordings of various 'ethnic' musics: a Balinese gamelan and, most tellingly, a Turkish *nay* solo to accompany the cathartic final frames. This was in 1969, and three years later Takemitsu was able to hear gamelan music in its native habitat, as a result of a two-week expedition to Bali in the company of, amongst others, Iannis Xenakis and Betsy Jolas. The experience clearly affected Takemitsu deeply, not only on a philosophical level but musically too, providing the inspiration for the only reference to an 'Eastern' musical tradition other than Japanese to be found in Takemitsu's writing for the concert hall. This occurs in *For Away*, written for the Australian pianist Roger Woodward in 1973 (Ex. 66).

The distribution of the music between the performer's hands here is clearly intended as a personal reflection of the interlocking 'hocket' patterns between metallophones on which Balinese gamelan music is based, just as the limitation of pitches to the four-note collection C–D♭–F–F♯ is intended to evoke the sound of the typical Balinese pentatonic scale, of which these notes form a subset. But perhaps this overt reference does not constitute the only evidence of a 'gamelan' influence on the score. For in one or two places elsewhere, one comes across passages such as Example 67, in which each pitch-class is allocated to a specific octave from the A♭ after the dotted barline onwards. As a result of this 'registral locking', the whole passage from this point onwards could be considered a projection of the 'harmonic field' shown in Example 68: Takemitsu's bracketing of the

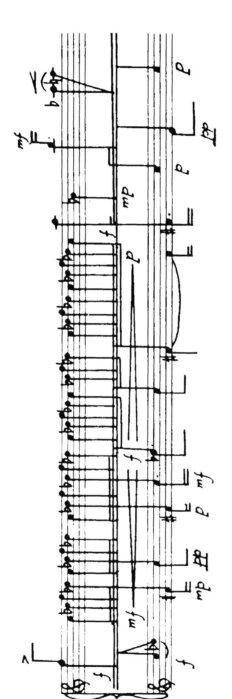

Ex. 66 *For Away*, bar 36

Ex. 67 *For Away*, bars 7–8

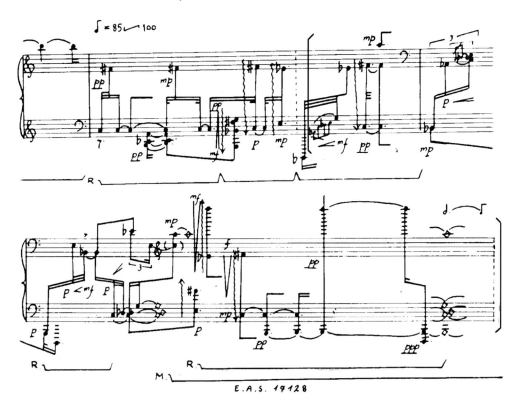

E.A.S. 19128

pitch-collection, and his use of the sustaining pedal to prolong the constituent pitches harmonically, supporting this view.

It will be observed that this latent pitch-field contains all twelve chromatic pitch-classes; moreover, that the core of this harmonic collection, from the B♭¹ to A♮⁴, comprises all eight pitches of the octatonic 'Mode II¹', with the remaining four pitches of the total-chromatic consigned to the margins of the keyboard on either side – fulfilling Timothy Koozin's observation that 'such foreign elements are most often found in registral extremities'.[34] This kind of harmonic construction, in which pitches are assigned to a specific octave in which they remain 'locked' for the duration of a given passage, may be traced at least as far back as later Webern: the opening of the latter's *Symphony*, Op. 21 could be said to project a single, twelve-note 'harmonic field' for this reason (although of course the contrapuntal nature of the writing here produces a quite different effect). Furthermore, in more recent times, composers such as Boulez, Berio and Lutosławski have all made use of the device as a means of constructing

Ex. 68 Harmonic field of Ex. 67

stable, static harmonic organisations. But it is perhaps also possible to speculate on another putative source for Takemitsu's adoption of this particular technique in *For Away*: is it wholly impossible that the manner in which the melodies of gamelan music move between the 'fixed pitches' of the metallophone bars, tuned to what to the Western ear sound like 'gapped' scalar formations, might have suggested to Takemitsu his own free meanderings between the widely spaced fixed points of the 'harmonic fields' in this and other parts of the score?

8 Modernist apogee: the early 1970s

By 1970, the perception of Takemitsu as member of the international avant-garde had become sufficiently well established to receive the most elegant of symbolic confirmations. In that year a lavish world fair, Expo '70, took place in Ōsaka, and Takemitsu became closely associated with this paean to progress and modernism in several capacities. While his music for the film *The Sun's Hunter*[1] played in the 'Electrical Industry Pavilion', an ambitious work for four soloists, female voices and two orchestras, *Crossing*, was being relayed over the sound-system of the 'Space Theatre' at the 'Iron and Steel Pavilion', alongside works by avant-garde stalwarts Xenakis and his Japanese pupil Yūji Takahashi. The sound-system in this hall comprised a total of 1,000 loudspeakers, many of which could be moved either by hand or by electrical power, and Takemitsu's notes at the time certainly share some of the futuristic optimism implicit in this project – although at the same time, they also accord very much with his own personal aesthetics of musical space as revealed through his instrumental writing in general. 'The conventionally arranged space of most halls initiates no movement, brings about no human experience (spatial or temporal) as a qualitative experience', he noted. 'Departing from the standard placement of former instruments, a free sound-source has become established, and the information supply has become pluralistic. Spatiality and spatial timbre . . . have been added as important parameters in the construction of music.'[2]

Expo '70 also provided Takemitsu with the opportunity to meet more of his colleagues in the international composing community. Karlheinz Stockhausen was in attendance, and in the sleeve-notes for his *Telemusik* numbers Takemitsu amongst his friends; while in April 1970, Takemitsu produced a four-day festival of contemporary music in the 'Iron and Steel Pavilion', whose participants included Lukas Foss, Peter Sculthorpe and Vinko Globokar. This last-named was also well known as a virtuoso trombonist, and Takemitsu was to employ him as one of the soloists in his *Gémeaux*, the first movement of which appeared two years later. Moreover over the next few years Takemitsu was to meet several more representatives of the new generation of avant-garde virtuosi who were then coming to prominence, and compose works with these soloists specifically in mind. Thus later in 1970, as a result of a commission from Paul Sacher and the

Zurich 'Collegium Musicum', he included solo parts for the flautist Aurèle Nicolet, oboist Heinz Holliger and harpist Ursula Holliger in his *Eucalypts I*, and subsequently went on to write solo pieces for each of these performers. Similarly *Cassiopeia* of 1971, a large-scale work for percussion and orchestra, was composed to showcase the talents of another rising star, the young Japanese performer Stomu Yamashita. The experience of writing for this kind of virtuoso modern performer left its mark on Takemitsu's music, enormously expanding the technical vocabulary of his instrumental writing – most obviously by means of the incorporation of the kind of 'extended' resources with which players such as Holliger and Globokar were especially associated. An examination of the complex instrumental works written as a response to the challenge of this new generation of soloists is, therefore, a particularly appropriate place to begin an exploration of those Takemitsu works from that period when his engagement with the Western avant-garde tradition had attained its zenith – even if it was a zenith from which, within only a few years, Takemitsu was to descend with spectacular swiftness.

Further adventures in timbre

Takemitsu's writing for string instruments in *Eucalypts I* is similar to that found in works from the second half of the previous decade such as *November Steps*: layers of solo instrumental lines are superimposed upon one another to create a densely polyphonic, richly dissonant texture. As with *November Steps*, however, the superficially 'atonal' impression created by this global texture is belied by a closer inspection of the harmonic details from which it is built up, many of which turn out to be of modal derivation. Once again, familiar favourites such as the octatonic and whole-tone scales, or the '7-33' collection, form the basis of a substantial number of Takemitsu's harmonic choices here. There are also one or two examples of types of harmonic construction more rarely encountered in Takemitsu's music, such as the chords marked 'A' in Example 69. Here each chord is built up from the same 'superset' form of the '7-33' collection, [0,1,2,3,4,6,8,10], in other words a whole-tone scale to which two semitones have been added, themselves a whole-tone apart. Chord 'B' here is formed from a familiar subset of the same collection, the whole-tone scale itself.

Eucalypts exists in two versions: the original *Eucalypts I*, for the three soloists and string orchestra, and *Eucalypts II* (1971), which consists of the three solo parts alone. The latter preserves the music of the former intact, and the relationship of the two might initially suggest the influence of

Ex. 69 *Eucalypts I*, D/6

Luciano Berio's practice of expanding his solo *Sequenze* into works for larger ensemble such as the *Chemins* series and *Corale*. But while there is indeed a possibility that this kind of recycling may have been influenced in very general terms by Berio's example, there are also important differences between the two composers' ways of proceeding. Apart from the obvious fact that, in contrast to Berio, Takemitsu worked subtractively, composing the chamber *Eucalypts II* after the version with string orchestra, Berio's reworkings also differ from his in that the original version and its expansion are intimately linked harmonically: by amplifying the harmonic implications inherent in the original, Berio creates pitch-fields which unite soloists and ensemble in a harmonically homogeneous texture. In Takemitsu's case, by contrast, the music for the three soloists constitutes such a wholly adventitious addition to that for the string orchestra that he is able to remove the latter and produce a completely satisfying, self-sufficient work without the least feeling on the listener's part that anything is missing.

This remarkable self-sufficiency of the solo parts in *Eucalypts I*, and the lack of thematic connection between them and the ensemble materials, rather recalls the similar independence of the soloists in *November Steps* – even if here the two groups play mostly simultaneously, rather than alternating as in the earlier work. So similar is the situation here, indeed, that Takemitsu even has recourse to one of the same devices to effect some sort of aural connection between the two otherwise disparate instrumental worlds: the common emphasis, at various points in the score, on specific pitch-classes. Examples are afforded by the C♮ of the harp at letter 'B', picked up by the cellos and basses and sustained in harmonics; the flute's sustained F♮ in bar 4 of 'C', picked up by the first violin; and the oboist's low B♮ in the next bar, which is taken up by the bass. It is rather as if the device which, in *November Steps*, had assumed the function of forging East–West contacts, were here forging similar contacts in a purely West–West situation.

The most adventurous aspect of *Eucalypts I* is, of course, the writing for its three prestigious soloists, where the 'new virtuosity' of the performers is exploited to the full in a multitude of 'extended' instrumental techniques. This can readily be seen from the opening gesture for Heinz Holliger's oboe, with its alternation of various fingerings of the same note, B♮ (Ex. 70). The notation which Takemitsu uses here to describe the alternation of normally fingered notes and harmonics at the same pitch, and which gives rise to such accidentally amusing phonetic combinations as ONO or NONO, was to become almost a cliché of his writing for this instrument.

However, *Eucalypts I* was written before Takemitsu came into contact with its three soloists, and the question therefore arises: how exactly did he manage to incorporate such a plethora of expanded instrumental possibilities in the score without their assistance? The answer to this is something of an open secret: as Funayama notes,[3] Bruno Bartolozzi's *New Sounds for Woodwind* had appeared in 1967, and in *Eucalypts* Takemitsu, like so many other composers of his day, made extensive use of the 'Bartolozzi sounds' it prescribes. In fact, anecdotal evidence supplied to the present author by various acquaintances of the composer suggests that he relied exclusively

Ex. 70 *Eucalypts I*, opening

Ex. 71 *Eucalypts I*, G/1 (final beat), harp chord (A) as written, (B) as sounding

on the Bartolozzi textbook for the multiphonic techniques used in such works as this – a view that gains support from the fact that Bartolozzi is actually mentioned by name in the performance directions for the solo flute work *Voice* of 1971.

The writing for the harp is similarly adventurous, and one cannot help but wonder whether Takemitsu might already have had another 'manual' to hand while writing it, that of Carlos Salzedo – certainly, as we shall see later, Takemitsu's use of a playing technique described as 'Æolian rustling' in some of his later scores suggests an acquaintance with Salzedo's theories.[4] Here in *Eucalypts*, one also encounters another favourite device of Takemitsu's when writing for this instrument: the prior tuning of selected individual strings to pitches other than those normally employed (scordatura). At one point in the score of *Eucalypts* Takemitsu hits upon an ingenious application of this device to enable the harp, whose seven strings per octave normally limit it to the same number of discrete pitch-classes at any given moment, to attack all eight notes of an octatonic scale simultaneously. Chord 'A' of Example 71 shows the pitches of this harmony as they are notated in the score; but, owing to the fact that the harpist is instructed to tune the D^3 and G^2 strings of the instrument a semitone lower than usual, the actual sounding result is chord 'B' – a full statement of all pitches of Mode II[1] in vertical superimposition.

As noted previously, Takemitsu was to provide solo works for each of the three instrumentalists of *Eucalypts* over the course of the succeeding two years; the first to appear was *Voice*, written for the flautist Aurèle Nicolet in 1971. A single example (Ex. 72) will suffice to indicate the general instrumental idiom of the work, heavily dependent on multiphonics, microtones,

Ex. 72 *Voice* for solo flautist

harmonics and other 'Bartolozziana' – an idiom which it is instructive to compare with the flute writing in the examples quoted from *Masque* in chapter 4, to illustrate how much more about flute technique Takemitsu has learned in the intervening twelve years, and how much bolder he has become in the application of that knowledge.

Takemitsu's description of *Voice* as 'for solo flautist', however, emphasises another important aspect of the work: that it involves the whole performer, and not merely the flute, in a kind of instrumental theatre. In particular, as well as utilising various kinds of breathing and attack that demand a certain muscular physicality, as the performance progresses the player appears to be struggling, between phrases, to bring verbal utterances to birth. These sounds eventually coalesce to form verses by the surrealist poet Shūzo Takiguchi, heard first in French and then in English:

> Qui va là? Qui que tu sois, parle transparence!
> Who goes there? Speak, transparence, whoever you are!

Elsewhere in the score, the performer is directed to 'shout' and 'growl', and to hum and sing into the instrument. Such extensions of instrumental performance by means of vocalisation are of course idiomatic to various traditional Japanese instrumental genres, for example the music of the *nō* and *kabuki* dramas, and an influence from traditional sources is also hinted at in some of the playing techniques, such as the instruction to produce a 'strong accent without tonguing as Japanese *nō* flute'. At the same time, however, this theatrical dimension was also very much in accord with the preoccupations of certain of Takemitsu's Western colleagues: hearing the flautist's whispered exclamations of 'Qui va la?' for example, one cannot help but be irresistibly reminded of the trombonist's interjection of 'Why?' in Berio's *Sequenza V.*

The second of the *Eucalypts* soloists to be honoured with a solo composition was Ursula Holliger, for whom Takemitsu wrote *Stanza II* for harp and tape, first performed in Paris in October 1971. The electro-acoustic dimension to this work is interesting, and not simply because it represents the brief revival of a genre which Takemitsu had by this time mostly abandoned. For the tape part of this particular piece – rarely for Takemitsu – incorporates certain devices associated with *elektronische Musik*, in addition to sounds prepared by the methods of the *musique concrète* tradition Takemitsu more frequently favoured. One wonders, indeed, whether the composer's encounter the previous year with the author of *Telemusik* did not leave its mark here in the shape of Takemitsu's decision to treat his taped harp sounds with a ring modulator (he also suggests live performance with this device as an alternative to performance with tape), or the use of four oscillators emitting sine waves of very close frequencies centred around F♯ to generate the drone-like pedal in the second part of the piece. Even the two 'concrete' intrusions here, in fact, have echoes of the type of thing found in *Hymnen*: brief snatches of birdsong and some sort of untreated, 'vox pop' sampling of a French conversation towards the close of the work, which strongly recalls Stockhausen's fondness at this period for the abrupt opening of a window on to the banal and everyday.

For the third of *Eucalypts*' trio of soloists, Heinz Holliger, Takemitsu composed *Distance* for oboe and *shō* in 1972. This is another work to lay especial emphasis on the spatial aspect of performance, and, as the title suggests, Takemitsu is here particularly concerned with the relative distances from which sounds reach the listener – a phenomenon which he had also explored, as we have seen, in *The Dorian Horizon*. To gain a similar kind of 'spatial perspective' to that found in the earlier work, the oboist is directed to stand in front of the *shō* player with a 'long distance' between them, creating a situation in which 'the oboe plays a phrase, stops, and the sound continues in the distant *shō*. The movement of sound gives a fresh experience of space.'[5] But the title of the work is also polysemous: as Ohtake notes, it refers not only to the physical distance between the players but also to 'the extreme distances of the intervals, dynamics and articulation'.[6] It also, of course, refers metaphorically to the 'distance' between the two instruments on a cultural and historical level, as Takemitsu once again places 'East' and 'West' in confrontation with one another as he had done in *November Steps*. At the same time however, as Poirier has observed,[7] there is a certain approximation between the two cultures as well, each instrument impersonating the qualities normally associated with the other: the oboe, by the use of multiphonics, becoming a polyphonic instrument like the *shō*, while the latter abandons its traditional harmonic function for much of the time to produce single monophonic drones.

These multiphonics and other 'extended' devices once again hint at an acquaintance with Bartolozzi's innovations, but there is also in *Distance* the strong suggestion of an influence from another of Bartolozzi's compatriots. Reference back to Example 70 will show that the invariant pitch selected for colouration by means of alternative fingerings in the oboe solo at the beginning of *Eucalypts* is B♮. This particular pitch also assumes a prominent role in *Distance*, as can clearly be seen from Example 73, in which the oboist modifies the timbre of a sustained B♮ by means of a typical Takemitsu 'NONO' pattern, while the *shō* (sounding an octave higher than written) maintains the same pitch as a long pedal-point.

This same focal pitch, however, had also been chosen by Berio for special emphasis in his *Sequenza VII* for solo oboe of 1969 – chosen 'because it can be produced by a greater variety of fingerings, each with its own timbre, than any other note on the instrument'.[8] It might be argued that both Takemitsu and Berio arrived at their common insistence on this pitch simply by virtue of the inherent acoustic properties of the instrument for which they were writing. But when one takes into account the fact that Berio asks for the note B♮ to be sustained throughout his *Sequenza* by an unspecified sound-source, and then turns to such passages in the score of *Distance* as that quoted below, in which the *shō* fulfils precisely this function, then the evidence for Berio's influence seems incontrovertible.

In 1976, encounters with further outstanding instrumentalists resulted in the composition of two more works in which the exploration of instrumental sonority is very much in the foreground. Takemitsu's close personal association with one of these performers is reflected in the very title of the work in which he was to take part: *Bryce*, for flute, two harps, marimba and percussion, was named after Bryce Engelman, the ten-year-old son of Robin Engelman, member of the Canadian percussion ensemble 'Nexus'. In fact, by means of the time-honoured device of transliterating words in Roman script into the equivalent German note names, Takemitsu was able to derive from the boy's name a musical figure, B [♭]–C–E, which – according to the composer – together with its adjacent quarter-tones provides the source of much of the musical material. Later in the same year, Takemitsu wrote another work with a North American virtuoso in mind: the clarinettist Richard Stolzman, who along with his Japanese colleague Toshiaki Morita became joint dedicatee of *Waves* for clarinet, two trombones, horn and bass-drum. Like *Distance*, this is

Ex. 73 *Distance*, p. 10 system 1

another Takemitsu score to incorporate a spatial dimension, placing the two trombonists at either side of the stage, with the other instrumentalists disposed at various points in between.

These two scores look remarkably similar, a fact not wholly unrelated to the type of performers for whom they were written, who differed somewhat from the three soloists of *Eucalypts*. Those three Europeans had been highly polished executants of fully determinate music, and had functioned in that work as an ensemble largely by means of a meticulously prescribed rhythmic notation. By contrast, while the instrumental writing in *Bryce* and *Waves* also demands considerable fluency in a wide range of 'extended' techniques, it additionally expects of its American executants certain abilities of a nature not found in the earlier work, skills which imply some experience of works not fully notated. Thus both scores employ a kind of 'spatial' notation, dispensing with barlines and rhythmic values – the later score even dispensing with timings as well, relying on cues between the players for the succession of events: a type of notation which obviously requires of each player a constant sensitivity to the performance of the others, of the kind demanded by improvised music. Similarly, a certain improvisational ability is also assumed by the inclusion at many points in these scores of general verbal suggestions for performance rather than strictly notated music. Such directions – which have been described by one commentator as 'providing acoustic effects with verbal imagery'[9] – are often of a highly poetic and evocative nature, as in the case of the instruction to the bass-drum player in *Waves* to 'rub the skin of the drum with finger to get various overtone as sound of the ocean [*sic*]'. In this particular instance too, of course, the metaphorical evocation of natural sound is very much in accord with the aesthetics of Takemitsu's own native tradition – for example those of *shakuhachi* performance, where the tone ultimately aimed at is supposedly that of wind sweeping through a bamboo grove.

As might be expected, from a superficial viewpoint neither *Bryce* nor *Waves* demonstrates a readily apprehensible formal outline, but further consideration reveals that in both pieces Takemitsu has actually exercised considerable care to avoid the impression of a totally free essay in timbral atmospherics. One means he employs to achieve this end is a clear segmentation of the overall structure. In both works there are a number of readily perceived sectional subdivisions: in *Bryce*, these are occasionally punctuated by pauses or fermatas; and in *Waves* – more interestingly still – largely by means of gestures, especially of a crescendo–diminuendo nature, for the bass drum, which thus acquires here something of the 'colotomic' function ascribed by ethnomusicologists to the gongs in gamelan music and – more relevantly perhaps – to the punctuating cycles of the *taiko*[10] in *gagaku*.

However, possibly the most effective means adopted by Takemitsu to guide the listener's ear through these loosely structured works are two devices already discussed with reference to *November Steps*. As in *Eucalypts*, the emphasis on common pitch-classes which had been used to associate the disparate worlds of 'East' and 'West' in *November Steps* is here appropriated to form connections in a more purely 'Western' context. But Takemitsu also makes use of the other connection established between the two cultures in the earlier work, the approximation of instrumental sounds in terms of timbre, as a further means of establishing clear aural relationships between consecutive events. Both forms of connection can clearly be seen from Example 74, the opening of *Waves*, where Takemitsu proceeds by a kind of 'timbral imitation'. Here the bass drum's opening roll, imperceptibly appearing out of the 'stream of sound', is imitated by the second trombone's similar emergence from *niente* on a deep pedal note; the microtonally sharpened E♭ with which the clarinet enters is echoed by the same pitch on the first trombone; the latter's progression from, and return to, muted *tenuto* tone via flutter-tonguing, variant fingerings of the same note and glissando is paralleled by the clarinet's movement away from, and return to, senza vibrato tone via vibrato and multiphonics; and the rapid alternation between different slide-positions to produce the same pitch in the middle of the trombone phrase is echoed by the clarinet's typical 'NONO' patterns shortly afterwards. The clear aural perceptibility of these kinds of relationship provides a valuable point of anchorage for the listener, lending a measure of coherence and comprehensibility to what might otherwise be a very informally structured and meandering score.

Large-scale works of the early 1970s – towards a new orchestral competence

To provide music for the 'Space Theatre' at Ōsaka of which he was director, Takemitsu turned to a work he had recently written for an ensemble of guitar, harp, piano/celesta, vibraphone and female voice. *Stanza I* (1969), composed in part to a text from Wittgenstein's *Tractatus Logico-Philosophicus* – with a final allusion to the title of Jasper Johns's painting *According to What?* – is a quintessential distillation of the avant-garde music of the decade that was about to come to a close. As Funayama has commented, with its 'combination of harmony instruments and voice' and its 'delicate phrases divided into small parts by the punctuations of

Ex. 74 *Waves*, opening

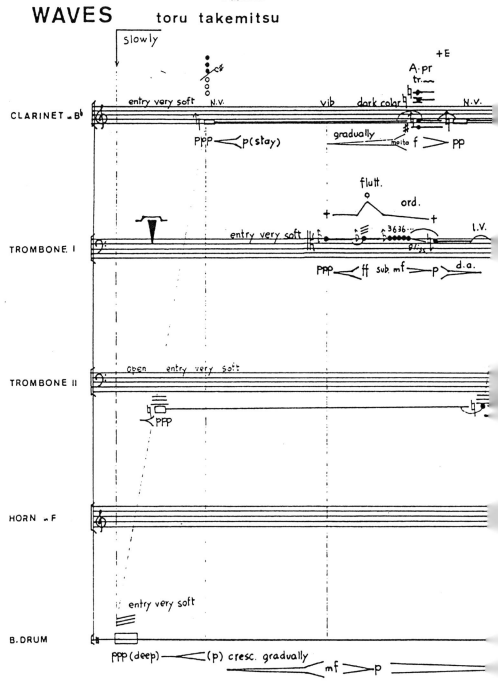

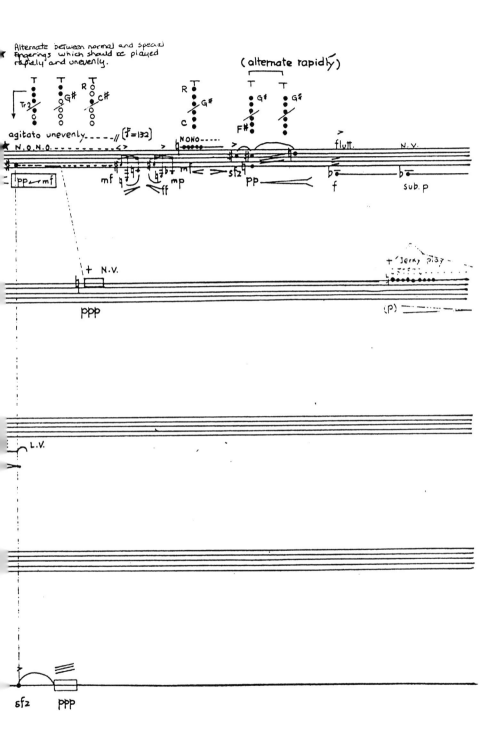

Ex. 75 Series of *Stanza I*

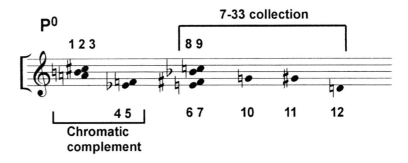

fermatas',[11] the work strongly recalls the example of Boulez's *Le Marteau sans maître*, and it is perhaps no surprise, therefore, to find that at the root of these angular, dissonant textures there is once again evidence of serial thinking. Moreover, the basic twelve-note series that Takemitsu appears intermittently to have used again shows evidence of a thoughtful internal construction using harmonic materials particularly favoured by the composer: as shown by the form in which it appears on the piano on page 2 (Ex. 75), it consists – exactly like the series of *Le Son Calligraphié III* – of a '7-33' collection (pitches 8–12) plus its chromatic complement (pitches 1–5).

Takemitsu took this modest chamber work as the basis of the piece which would be projected over the elaborate sound-system of the 'Space Theatre', enlarging the forces to produce a score of suitable grandeur for such a prestigious project. The result was *Crossing* (1969), a work in which the chamber original is more or less incorporated intact into a vast expansion of its materials for four instrumental soloists, female voices and two orchestras. The forces involved are indeed so large that Takemitsu had to paste together his own manuscript paper to fit them all in, and while the preface to the score optimistically suggests two possible seating arrangements for live performance, the piece had to wait over thirty years before it could be heard in any form other than the taped version relayed over the sound-system of the Ōsaka venue. A glance at the score, in fact, suggests that as he composed the work, Takemitsu probably had an eye, or ear, on performance over this elaborate network of loudspeakers already: most obviously at the end of the work, where the same harmony played by various instrumental groups fades in and out of the overall 'stereo picture', somewhat after the fashion of the famous brass chord in Stockhausen's *Gruppen*.

It is also possible that Takemitsu may have turned again to *Stanza I* for inspiration when he came to fulfil his next large-scale orchestral commis-

Ex. 76 *Cassiopeia*, letter 'B'

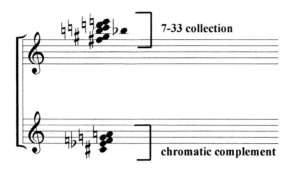

sion. At all events, the vertical arrangement of pitches in the twelve-note chord quoted in Example 76 is clearly patterned after the twelve-note series quoted in Example 75: the pitch-classes of the upper system in the former are identical to pitch-classes 6 to 12 of the latter, forming a '7-33' collection which is completed chromatically by notes 1 to 5 of the series in the lower staff.

Cassiopeia (1971), the work from which this chord is quoted, is another complex 'avant-garde' orchestral statement, as well as another exploration of the possibilities opened up by an innovative instrumental soloist, the Japanese percussionist Stomu Yamashita. It is also, like *Asterism*, a work inspired in part by stellar phenomena: in this instance the eponymous constellation, which among other things forms the template for a spatial redistribution of the orchestral apparatus of the kind which was becoming almost *de rigueur* in Takemitsu's work at this period. In this seating arrangement, 'the five stars forming a W (or M when seen above the pole in December) is the position in which Takemitsu places the solo percussionist and the four groups of instrumental soloists. The many clusters of nebulæ surrounding them are represented by one brass and two string sections.'[12]

Furthermore, the suggestion made that *Asterism*'s motif of three stars might be reflected in some *Augenmusik*-like patternings in the score may be asserted with rather more confidence in the case of the five stars of *Cassiopeia*. Example 77, for instance, a typical passage from the solo percussion part of the work, obviously makes great play with W- or M-shaped visual patterns, indicating that the spirit of 'graphic' notation was still to a certain extent alive in Takemitsu's music as late as 1971. The type of notation employed here also, once again, suggests a familiarity with Stockhausen's work: in this case *Zyklus* for solo percussion (1959).

Ex. 77 *Cassiopeia*, p. 21

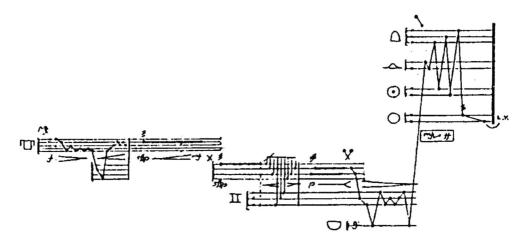

The percussion soloist of *Cassiopeia*, like the flautist in *Voice*, is also required to be something of an actor: at his first appearance after the orchestral prelude, for instance, he is 'suggested to walk (or running) to the regular place yo [*sic*] perform, and play castanets intermittently as Spanish dancer (or *Kabuki* actor) while his [*sic*] walks'. Nor is the work's theatrical dimension limited to these gestures by the solo performer; according to Wilson, at least, elements of traditional Japanese theatre – specifically the *kabuki* genre referred to in Takemitsu's performance notes – inform both the spatial layout of the forces, and the overall formal outline of the work,[13] whose sections bear the suggestive titles *Entrance–Scene–Solo–Scene*. Moreover, in addition to his theatrical flair, the soloist in *Cassiopeia* must also possess some of the quasi-improvisatory ability necessary to respond creatively both to Takemitsu's partly graphic notation, and to his sometimes rather enigmatic verbal suggestions. The direction given to the percussionist at one point to play 'softly as Cassiopeia', for example, could almost have strayed here out of the pages of Stockhausen's *Aus den sieben Tagen*; but it appears to have meant something at least to Stomu Yamashita, who in his recording of the work devises the same steel-pan figure in response to these words at both their appearances in the score.

It was during the 1970s that Takemitsu eventually achieved that consummate mastery of orchestral sonority for which he subsequently became so renowned, and in works such as *Crossing* and *Cassiopeia* one can see the beginnings of this expansion of orchestral vocabulary. At this

Ex. 78 *Winter*, F/4

stage of his career, however, when Takemitsu was still very much in sympathy with the aesthetics of the avant-garde, the expansion is most noticeable in the transference to large forces of the same type of instrumental experimentation already encountered in works for smaller media. Thus in *Crossing* the brass players are required to speak the text 'Things are different' into their instruments, and in *Cassiopeia* they are instructed to blow into the tubing of their instruments without mouthpieces. The latter device also figures in the score of *Winter* (1971), a work originally commissioned to commemorate the hosting of the Winter Olympics by the Japanese city of Sapporo. Here, however, as a reflection of the work's title, the device acquires a metaphorical significance: the players are advised that the passage in question 'should be played as wind', and various blobs of ink in the manuscript, reminiscent of marks on a film soundtrack, give them suggestions as to how this effect should be achieved. One is reminded of the manner in which, in the film *Kwaidan*, the breathy sounds of slowed-down *shakuhachi* notes evoke the howling of the wind across the frozen landscapes in the story *Woman of the Snows*.

Winter is also of interest in that it may possibly contain one of the earliest statements of a three-note motif that was to loom large in Takemitsu's later music: the three pitches E♭, E♮ and A which spell 'SEA' in German nomenclature. The version heard here is certainly at the correct transposition (Ex. 78).

This proves to be not the only forward-looking element in the score: in the final pages there is another prophetic hint of the 'sea of tonality' into which Takemitsu's music was later to flow. Here, in a similar fashion to that encountered at the end of *Asterism*, the music gravitates unambiguously towards a tonal centre of G♯, ultimately fading out on a G♯–A♯ dyad. Moreover – and again as in *Asterism* – this tonal final is prepared by a passage of modal writing unmistakably centred around the same pitch. The writing for strings at letter 'L' of *Winter* even *looks* rather similar to the piano passage from the earlier work quoted in Example 55, although the sounding result conjures up another work from the previous decade:

based as it is almost exclusively on the pitches contained in the Dorian and Phrygian modes on G♯, it is little wonder that this divided string passage often irresistibly recalls the sound-world of *The Dorian Horizon*, or that at one point it quotes one of the harmonies from that work at the same pitch.

Like *Arc for piano and orchestra*, the complete version of Takemitsu's next work for large forces – *Gémeaux* (1971) – was to have a rather protracted genesis. While the first part of the score was heard in 1972, it was not until 1986 that all four movements (*Strophe, Genesis, Traces, Antistrophe*) could receive their first performance. Like *Arc*, too, the work represents the large-scale modernist gesture at its most extravagant, and thus embodies stylistic preoccupations which the composer had already long abandoned by the time it received its première. The scale of the forces required is actually even grander than in the earlier work: to reflect the dualism of the work's title, there are two soloists (oboe and trombone), two orchestras and two conductors. As might be expected, these two solo parts – written originally for Heinz Holliger and Vinko Globokar – make great play with a full range of 'extended' techniques, and the writing for the two orchestras is similarly adventurous. The instrumental line-up includes amplified guitar, keyboard glockenspiel and the inevitable prayer-bells-on-timpani combination which was becoming almost a standard feature of Takemitsu's instrumentarium at this period, and among the many sonorous novelties in which this apparatus is involved is another passage in which the brass players are requested to speak through the tubing of their instruments. As in *Voice*, the verses they recite derive from Shūzo Takiguchi, and constitute another reference to the 'twin' metaphor which pervades the work:

> Tes yeux, tes mains, tes seins . . .
> Tes une, et tu es deux, toi même.[14]

However, by the time Takemitsu came to write *Gitimalya* (1974) for solo marimba and orchestra – whose title comes from the same Tagore poem from which the soloists are asked to recite lines in the earlier *Eclipse* for *biwa* and *shakuhachi* – there were one or two hints that a stylistic change was in the offing. To be sure, there is still a wealth of innovative instrumental writing: the tam-tam player, for instance, is required to use a cardboard tube to coax harmonics from the instrument, and the timpanist is equipped with the usual array of Japanese temple bells. But the forces employed – an orchestra mostly of double winds, and without violins – are much more modest and conventional than in any of the works so far described. In places too, the style of orchestration contains strong hints of the direction this aspect of Takemitsu's writing was to take in the future: for example at the first entry of the marimba soloist, where for the first three or four bars almost every note of the solo 'theme' is doubled (albeit sometimes heterophonically) by some orchestral sonority or other.

Prophetic, too, are the pentatonic forms which appear here from time to time – particularly the verticalised pentatonic harmony on B with F♯ in the bass before the final fade-out, another symbolic 'dominant preparation' like that at the end of *Green*. Like the numerous and clearly audible references to the 'S–E–A' motif, this gesture again hints at Takemitsu's exploration, in the following decade, of the 'sea of tonality'; but, as in *Green*, it is an exploration which the composer clearly does not feel it appropriate to undertake yet in the present aesthetic circumstances.

The purely orchestral work *Marginalia* of 1976 also has something of a transitional character. The title, taken from a 1970 work by Takiguchi, is perhaps a reference to the manner in which, as the composer puts it, 'in this piece, two different notations were used. Proportional indeterminate and conventional determined'.[15] As the two forms of notation alternate in the score, conventionally barred music constantly fades into a kind of timeless suspension which might function as a kind of 'marginal commentary' to the more rigorously scripted 'text' that precedes it. Undoubtedly the most impressive of these unmeasured passages occurs on page 2 of the score: over a very deep, very long sustained D♮ pedal, a handful of instrumentalists work through individual *ad libitum* materials rich in captivating sonorities. The harpist is instructed to play with the tuning key; the timpanist is again equipped with the ubiquitous Japanese prayer bells; and – most magically of all – one of the percussion players is instructed to float various objects in a tub of water and improvise quietly to produce glissandi and portamenti that must be 'transparent and dreamy'. The wonderfully evocative performance direction Takemitsu writes above this section sums up the effect obtained perfectly: 'Spacious calm – water mirror'.

Perhaps in order to create as effective a foil as possible to this kind of timeless floating, Takemitsu in one or two parts of the measured sections opts for a form of material whose metrical precision lies at the opposite extreme: what the composer describes as a 'German waltz', complete with *Wienerisch* double thirds that give an effect something akin to *La Valse* or *Jeux*. This German waltz, in fact, also has 'German' orchestration, of a kind which the composer has described elsewhere as 'very condensed, with emphasis; it is very strongly one thing, like a tight, concrete building'.[16] In other words, the instrumental writing at this point – unusually for the composer – consists of a thickly doubled, homogeneous and 'aspatial' musical texture that could easily be reduced to a 'piano score' format, and

Ex. 79 *Marginalia*, A/7

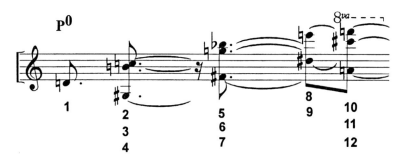

as such – by default – throws into relief his habitual preference for a many-layered, spatially compartmentalised texture all the more conspicuously. The 'German waltz' may also possibly make oblique reference to Teutonic technical rigour: the two [0,1,4] collections with which it begins are perhaps derived from pitches 2–4 and 5–7 of Example 79, another of the relatively rare occurrences of a twelve-note statement in Takemitsu's later music.

However, while these occasional references to serial technique, together with the unconventional rhythmic notations and innovative instrumental sonorities, indicate Takemitsu's continuing preoccupation with the 'modernist' tradition, there are other aspects of the score of *Marginalia* which point rather in the direction of his future adoption of a more 'Romantic' idiom. It is perhaps in the closing pages of the work, once again, that this tendency becomes most manifest. As Roger Reynolds has pointed out, 'Takemitsu's works often close with a strikingly lyrical coda',[17] a concluding passage on a heightened poetical level which often includes a particularly evocative instrumental, melodic or harmonic effect that seems to have been held in reserve to lend a 'magical' quality to the peroration. The 'epilogue' of *Marginalia* must surely rank as one of the most impressive of Takemitsu's achievements of this kind. Over a sustained triple pedal-point on E, B and D, which produces a 'dominant-seventh' effect similar to that found at the end of *Green*, an ensemble of wind, harps, vibraphone, glockenspiel and marimba ascends in parallel ninths through an 'acoustic' scale on D, producing an indescribable sonority – something like a polyphonic flexatone; then, over ostinato patterns repeated in canon by flute and clarinets, the piano and tuned percussion descend in parallel major sixteenths through a whole-tone scale with chromatically altered notes. The effect of the passage, like that of its counterpart in *Green*, is not simply unexpected and aurally ravishing. Strongly modal as the harmonic basis of these elements is, the gesture also affords the listener yet another glimpse of the 'sea of tonality', although again in the form of a 'dominant preparation' to a tonal future not here attained. In contrast to the ending of *Green*, however, that of *Marginalia* hints at a tonal resolution not so far distant: *A Flock Descends into the Pentagonal Garden*, with its unambiguously tonal valediction, was only one year off.

Homages to Bach and Messiaen

As *Wind Horse* had demonstrated, even more radically tonal elements than those just described could enter Takemitsu's 'middle period' music as a result of quotation, a further example of which was to occur in 1974, when Takemitsu included a citation from Bach's *St Matthew Passion* in the third and final movement of his *Folios* for solo guitar. Takemitsu is known to have revered this work, and as a form of purificatory ritual, would prepare himself for the act of composition 'by playing through the *St Matthew Passion* on the piano';[18] yet, for all that, the precise reasons why he chose to quote what he calls 'Matthew Passion Choral No. 72 by J. S. Bach' at this particular juncture – in other words the famous 'Passion Chorale' attributed to Hans Leo Hassler, *O Haupt voll Blut und Wunden*, in Bach's harmonisation – remain somewhat inscrutable.

Yet, though difficult to account for on a philosophical level, in purely musical terms this sudden departure does not sound quite as adventitious as might be expected. Takemitsu has actually prepared the ground for its appearance carefully, and two details in particular enable the listener to assimilate this unexpected excursion with the minimum discontinuity. First, the descending quaver 'passing notes' in the lowest voice at the opening of the Bach chorale strongly recall a similar anacrustic gesture found elsewhere in Takemitsu's three movements, an example of which is quoted in a later chapter.[19] Secondly, the chorale is in A minor, and this may loosely be described as the 'home key' towards which the music of *Folios* is directed. It is a key hinted at, for example, by means of such devices as the 'pedal note' on A in the final movement (achieved, on this non-sustaining instrument, by means of reiteration), the use of the bottom string of the guitar as a kind of 'dominant', and by the penultimate chord of the first movement, which is actually a verticalisation of the complete descending form of the *in* scale encountered already in Takemitsu's very earliest work (Ex. 80).

Elsewhere in *Folios* there is the suggestion of a kind of 'homage' to a second Western master, and one whose influence on Takemitsu's music is generally much more palpable than Bach's. The gesture in question takes

Ex. 80 *Folios I*, penultimate chord

Ex. 81 Takemitsu: melodic ideas with similar 'zig-zag' contours

(i) *Folios*, **p. 3, system 5**   **(ii)** *To the Edge of Dream*, **K/1 (guitar)**

(iii) *Vers, l'arc-en-ciel, Palma*, **G/7 (ob. d'amore)**

the form of a stock melodic formula found in several Takemitsu works: a kind of 'zig-zag' pattern formed by the alternation of ascending and descending intervals. Although the actual intervals in each case differ, Example 81 shows some typical uses of this same basic melodic contour in three works, all of which coincidentally contain a part for guitar. It is possible that this type of melodic pattern – particularly that from *Vers, l'arc-en-ciel, Palma*, with its characteristic falling tritone final – may have been suggested to Takemitsu by Example 76 from Messiaen's *Technique*, which the French composer claims to have derived from *Boris Godunov* (Ex. 82).

A rather more convincing case for this kind of melodic influence can be argued with reference to *Quatrain*, a work for violin, cello, clarinet, piano and orchestra which Takemitsu wrote for the ensemble *Tashi* in 1975. The instrumentation of the solo quartet here is of course identical to that of Messiaen's *Quatuor pour la fin du temps*, and Takemitsu explicitly intended this work as an *hommage* to the French master, who had given him a two-hour 'lesson' analysing the *Quatuor* during their meeting in New York in 1975. The similarities to Messiaen's example in various aspects of the score,

Ex. 82 Messiaen: examples of melodic type derived from Mussorgsky

(i) Messiaen, *Technique*, Ex. 75 (after Mussorgsky)

(ii) *Technique*, Ex. 76

(iii) *Quatuor pour la fin du temps, III, Abîme des oiseaux* (opening)

then, are in this case much more likely to be a matter of conscious imitation
– including the resemblance of actual thematic patterns. The principal
'theme' of *Quatrain* – shown in Example 83 – is in fact very closely related to
the melodic pattern shown as Example 94 in Messiaen's *Technique*, the only
difference being that the second interval has been reduced from a major to a
minor second. This means that it also bears a close kinship to some of the
melodic ideas in Messiaen's *Quatuor*, two of which are also quoted in
Example 83. And, as also shown in this example, the same basic pitch-
collection projected by the Messiaen formula – [0,1,2,6,7] – is also found in
inversion in a passage from *Valeria*, a chamber work of Takemitsu's from
1965. This last connection might seem, on paper at least, rather less convincing; but when heard in context, the lugubrious cello solo from which
this extract is taken irresistibly calls to mind the *Louange à l'immortalité de
Jésus* from the *Quatuor* – not least on account of its accompaniment of sustained harmonies for electric organ, which call to mind Messiaen's own
organ music if not also the multiple *ondes Martenot* of the *Louange*'s original transcription in *Fêtes des belles eaux* (although one cannot be certain
whether or not Takemitsu would have been familiar with the latter).

  Another melodic type associated with Messiaen, the *Thème de joie*
found in the *Vingt regards* and *Visions de l'Amen*, also has a close relative
amongst the thematic materials employed in *Quatrain*. Its triumphantly
rising pentatonic phrase is recalled by a similar emotional upsurge in the
extended melody first heard on the clarinet after letter 'C' of Takemitsu's
work, whose initial four pitches (Ex. 84) map on to the *Thème de joie*
exactly, and are elsewhere heard as an independent melodic incipit.

Ex. 83 Comparison of themes by Takemitsu and Messiaen with Ex. 94 of latter's *Technique*

(i) Messiaen: *Louange à l'immortalité de Jésus*

(ii) Messiaen: Ex. 94 from *Technique*

(iii) Messiaen: *Fouillis de l'arc-en-ciel, pour l'ange qui annonce la fin du temps*

(iv) Takemitsu: *Quatrain*

(v) Takemitsu: *Valeria*

Ex. 84 Comparison between Takemitsu, *Quatrain* and Messiaen, *Vingt regards*

(i) *Quatrain* (1975), G/1 (cl.)

(ii) Messiaen, *Thème de joie* (*Vingt regards sur l'enfant Jésus*)

Ex. 85 Comparison between Takemitsu, *Quatrain* and Messiaen, *Abîme des oiseaux*

(i) *Quatrain* **(1975), Fig. H (cl.)**

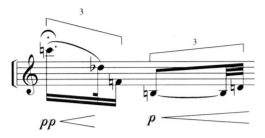

(ii) Messiaen, *Quatuor pour la fin du temps,*
"Abîme des oiseaux" (cl.)

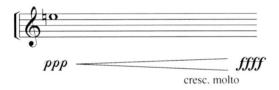

cresc. molto

The Messiaenic influence on *Quatrain* is not, however, confined to the matter of thematic resemblances. When the main idea of the work is first presented by the solo quartet at letter 'A', for example, the two string instruments, in contrary motion, provide a background of slow glissandi in harmonics between two pitches, each glissando repeated a number of times like an ostinato. The effect is so similar to the cello glissandi in the *Liturgie de cristal* of Messiaen's *Quatuor* that the resemblance has also been remarked upon by other commentators – for example Koozin, who, quoting the relevant passages one after the other, notes that Takemitsu's 'glissandos on harmonics and whole-tone implications in the strings' were 'very likely influenced by Messiaen's cello writing in the previous example'.[20] Takemitsu's writing for clarinet is another aspect of *Quatrain* strikingly evocative of Messiaen's *Quatuor*, and of the celebrated *Abîme des oiseaux* for solo clarinet in particular. For example, the protracted emergence of a single pitch from inaudibility at letter 'H' in Takemitsu's score (in performance actually much longer than the notation would suggest) is clearly related to a similar gesture that appears repeatedly in the *Abîme* (Ex. 85). Similarly, the sustained crescendo on what is actually the lowest note of a B♭ clarinet in extract (i) of Example 86 closely parallels the crescendo

Ex. 86 Comparison between Takemitsu, *Quatrain* and Messiaen, *Abîme des oiseaux*

(i)

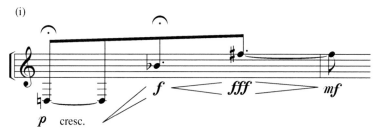

(ii)

(iii)

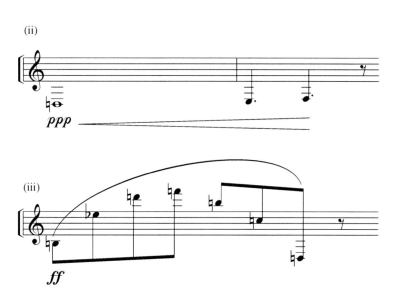

on precisely the same pitch in the quotation from the *Quatuor* shown in (ii); while the general character of extract (i), with its wide leaps between registers and ultimately strident dynamic level, bears comparison with the similar registral displacement of the melodic line, and sustained loudness, of the Messiaen extract shown in Example 86 (iii).

Like such closely coeval works as *Gitimalya* and *Marginalia*, *Quatrain* too has about it something of a transitional quality. Partly perhaps as a result of Takemitsu's intention to pay homage to Messiaen, much of the instrumental sonority has a rapturous mellifluousness which palpably looks forward to the composer's later orchestral manner. At least one reviewer of an early performance sensed that some sort of change was in the air; writing in the *New York Times*, Allen Hughes noted that '*Quatrain* is so pretty, so lush, so sumptuous in its melodic richness, vibrant colour and expansive aural spectrum that it was hard to believe'. Obviously per-plexed at how to categorise the novel stylistic direction the composer was so evidently taking, he commented: 'If Tōru Takemitsu's avant-garde standing is still intact among his peers, and if his *Quatrain* represents his present compositional practice fairly, we may have to revise our notions of what constitutes avant-gardism in music in the mid-1970s'.[21]

With hindsight, of course, it is easy for us to see that a simple revision of the definition of 'avant-gardism' was an inadequate response to the revolu-tion that was then going on, not just in Takemitsu's music, but in 'advanced' composition the world over. Although clearly he was unaware of the fact at the time, what Allen Hughes was witnessing at that New York performance was an important station on the road to Takemitsu's aban-donment of an 'avant-garde' idiom for ever. Only five years after the opti-mistic triumphalism of the Ōsaka World Fair, and the grandiose modernist statement Takemitsu had prepared for it, the composer's inter-est was beginning to focus on other priorities, as in the world of music at large the once self-assured, monolithic edifice of the 'international' avant-garde began to crumble. A new Takemitsu sound was beginning to emerge in response to the changed historical situation: texturally simpler, har-monically more opulent and consummate in its refinement of instrumen-tal sonority. Takemitsu's third and final period, the period of consolidation and 'Romantic' expression, begins here.

9 Descent into the pentagonal garden

The simplified style which characterised this new, 'third period' in Takemitsu's creative output was no adventitious development, but one whose roots can be traced in his work from the preceding years. In particular, the ground had long been prepared for the emergence of its more overt tonality by his engagement with a modal harmonic vocabulary which, though usually disguised somewhat by the dense textures of his 'pantonal' chromaticism, occasionally – as in the score of *Green* – had surfaced with surprising directness. There had also been sporadic excursions into conventional tonality in these years, such as the *Abiyoyo* quotation in *Wind Horse* and the Bach chorale in *Folios*; while outside the sphere of the composer's 'serious' work – in his film music, in the *a cappella* songs of *Uta*, or in the arrangements of pop 'standards' that formed *Twelve Songs for Guitar* (1977) – unapologetic tonal expression was flourishing shamelessly. The gradual emergence of the latter into the mainstream of Takemitsu's 'serious' composing activity was thus far from a sudden stylistic rupture, but more in the nature of an inevitability for which the soil had been carefully nurtured over a number of years.

While elements of his new style are certainly palpable in works such as *Quatrain*, in the author's opinion it is with the orchestral work *A Flock Descends into the Pentagonal Garden* (1977) that Takemitsu first gives clear and unambiguous expression to the new stylistic preoccupations with which he is henceforth to be concerned. Moreover, if one grants this score a key role in Takemitsu's stylistic transformation, then a particular line of descent for certain aspects of the 'late style' which emerged as a result begins to suggest itself. The present chapter concerns itself – albeit speculatively – with tracing the ancestry of these traits through three key works of the 1970s: *In an Autumn Garden* (1973/79), *Garden Rain* (1974) and *A Flock Descends into the Pentagonal Garden* itself.

The story of *In an Autumn Garden* begins in 1970, with the decision by the National Theatre of Japan to commission a series of new works by contemporary composers for that most venerable of traditional Japanese musical institutions, the *gagaku* ensemble of the Imperial Household. The first beneficiary of this new policy was Toshirō Mayuzumi, whose *Shōwa Tenpyō Raku* was performed in October 1970, and over the years that followed, a number of other distinguished composers were to contribute to this ongoing project: the Japanese musicians Toshio Hosokawa (*Tōkyō 1985*), Maki Ishii (*Momotarō Onitaiji*, 1988) and Toshi Ichinyangi (*Jitsugetsu Byōbu Issō-Kōkai*, 1989), as well as the Europeans Karlheinz Stockhausen (*Hikari*, 1977) and Jean-Claude Élois (*Kansō no Hono-o no Kata e*, 1983). Takemitsu, it would appear, also received a commission to provide a work for the series at the same time as Mayuzumi, but his own score was to have a rather more extended period of gestation. It was not until 30 October 1973, in fact, that his single movement *Shuteiga* – 'In an Autumn Garden' – received its National Theatre première, but even this proved to be far from the end of the story. Over the course of the next six years, Takemitsu would build five additional movements around the centrepiece of this original score, eventually producing *Shuteiga – Ichigu* ('In an Autumn Garden – Complete Version'), first heard at the National Theatre on 28 September 1979. With a total running time of fifty minutes, the full version must count among Takemitsu's most ambitious works, and certainly represents his most thorough investigation of the possibilities of traditional Japanese music: Poirier refers to it as 'probably the furthest removed from the West of any work he had written'.[1] The titles of the six movements – which Takemitsu initially conceived in English before supplying them with Japanese equivalents – are:

I. *Strophe*
II. *Echo I*
III. *Melisma*
IV. *In an Autumn Garden* (the original 1973 movement)
V. *Echo II*
VI. *Antistrophe*

The loose symmetry of this scheme is immediately apparent: Takemitsu was to recall it seven years later in the final version of *Gémeaux*, in which movements bearing the same titles as the outermost pair of *In an Autumn Garden* frame two inner movements ('Genesis' and 'Traces') in somewhat similar fashion. It is a symmetry also emphasised in the score in various ways, both by literal repetition and less exact forms of recollection. For example, the whole of the passage from letter 'F' to the end of letter 'G' in the final movement is a repeat of the material between the same rehearsal letters in the first movement; while at the end of the previous movement (*Echo II*), 'birdsong'-like interjections for *komabue*[2] and five *ryūteki* recall – without literally quoting – the similar bird sounds with which the equivalent movement in the arch-like scheme (*Echo I*) had begun.

Takemitsu employs the titles of the outermost movements in this arch-like scheme in their original, antique Greek senses: *Strophe* and

Antistrophe refer, respectively, to the music sung by the Chorus as it turns to the left to mount the stage, and when it turns to the right to depart, at the beginning and end of the ancient drama. Interestingly, the works comprising the traditional *kangen* and *bugaku* repertories of *gagaku* music are also subdivided into 'left' (*sahō*) and 'right' (*uhō*) groups, but Takemitsu here does not appear to be referring to this distinction. Rather he relates these Greek terms for promenading choral performance to the ancient conception of *gagaku* as 'a kind of strolling music for playing outdoors such as while strolling in a garden'.[3] To be sure, no such actual perambulation is undertaken by the musicians during a performance of *In an Autumn Garden*, but, nevertheless, this is another Takemitsu score in which the spatial distribution of the instrumentalists plays a crucial role, contributing to an overall 'spatial and temporal discrepancy of sound' which the composer obviously considers close to the spirit of the original outdoor style of performance. This spatialisation is already present in the 1973 version of the work, which is scored for a foreground ensemble of nine players (the 'Autumn Garden') and, upstage of them, an 'echo' ensemble of a further eight musicians (the 'Tree Spirits'). However, for the 1979 score Takemitsu added two more groups of 'Tree Spirits' to left and right at the rear of the auditorium, bringing the total number of players to twenty-nine. By means of this physical separation of the performing groups, he was able to offer a metaphorical interpretation of the work's title in the shape of another 'multiply-focused sound garden' of the type found in the orchestra of *Arc*; although, at the same time, he was not above offering more literal, anecdotal interpretations of the title too – in the form of the birdsongs already referred to, or the chimings of the wooden boards (*mokushō*) with which the work begins and ends, and which, according to Akiyama, create 'an echo similar to the chopping of a tree deep in a forest'.[4]

The arrangement of the two rows of musicians in the 1973 scoring – nine in the foreground, eight to the rear – is remarkably close to that of *The Dorian Horizon*, with its downstage group of eight 'harmonic pitches' supported in the distance by nine 'echoes'. The similarities to that earlier work do not end here either, for according to Akiyama – and very much in accord with the 'classical Greek' overtones suggested by the titles of the outer movements – Takemitsu composed the work 'mainly in the Grecian Dorian mode'[5] rather than in traditional *gagaku* scales. The accuracy of this observation would appear to be borne out by such passages as the haunting melody with which the fourth movement opens (Ex. 87), which uses all the pitches of the mode beginning on the supertonic of a D-major scale, i.e. of a 'Dorian' E minor.

At the same time, however, Takemitsu's writing here may not be so

Ex. 87 *In an Autumn Garden* IV, A/3–4

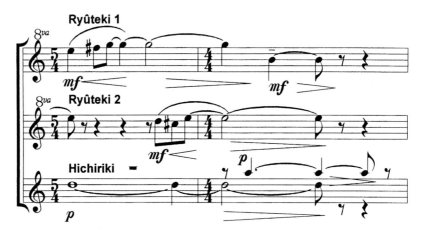

remote from traditional *gagaku* practice as Akiyama, or indeed maybe the composer himself, seems to think. *Gagaku* music uses two heptatonic scale-types, *ryō* and *ritsu*, which correspond more or less to the Mixolydian and Dorian modes of Western theory, and Takemitsu's 'E-Dorian' mode is identical with one of the three transpositions of the *ritsu* scale, *hyōjō*. While this congruence might not have displeased Takemitsu, who in this work was in part seeking to rediscover some of the origins of *gagaku* in Byzantium and the Middle East, it does nevertheless rather neatly illustrate *in nuce* one of the most striking features of *In an Autumn Garden*: the degree to which – despite the composer's best efforts to create a new musical language for *gagaku* – the old traditional idioms still managed to assert themselves in the finished composition, so intimately bound up were they with the performing techniques and indeed the very physical construction of the instrumental resources.

Much of Takemitsu's writing here, in truth, seems incapable of avoiding reference to orthodox *gagaku* models of performance. In a number of places, for instance, the *kakko* drum plays conventional accelerando patterns of the type known in traditional performance as *katarai*, while the patterns given to the *koto* during the repeated 'processional'-like passage at letter 'O' of the fourth movement are rhythmically identical to the type of thing this instrument would play in an orthodox setting. Heterophony, which the composer himself identified as a characteristic texture of *gagaku*,[6] is also widely used throughout the work, although admittedly the 'use of secondary melodic lines which ornament the primary melodic line'[7] may, as Akiyama asserts, equally well have derived from an observation of gamelan practice. More assuredly of authentic *gagaku* origin is the use of a particular kind of canonic writing, often in combination with hetero-phonic embellishment of the constituent parts, in which there is no attempt at a harmonious sounding result, but rather at the creation of a raucously dissonant web of voices: a type of texture which corresponds very closely to the kind of canonic performance in the traditional repertory for which the Japanese scholar Shigeo Kishibe coined the delightful neolo-gism 'chaophony'.[8] Passages from *In an Autumn Garden* such as the complex *senza misura* at letter 'D' of the second movement, or the canonic imitation of both a melodic line and its heterophonic embellishment at letter 'F' of the fourth, are good examples of the degree to which Takemitsu had imbibed the spirit of this 'chaophonic' style by the time he came to write his own work for the *gagaku* medium.

From the point of view of Takemitsu's own stylistic development, however, perhaps the most important of these aspects of traditional *gagaku* practice which contrived to assert themselves, despite the com-poser's efforts to the contrary, was the matter of the available pitch-materials. In this respect, different constituents of the instrumental ensemble afforded the composer varying degrees of freedom. For example, wind instruments such as the *hichiriki* and *ryūteki* were not only fully chromatic, but even allowed the composer the possibility of microtonal embellishment of his basic melodic lines. The plucked string instruments also permitted the possibility of bendings of pitch, and additionally Takemitsu prescribed an unorthodox tuning for the *koto* which enabled it to produce eleven out of the twelve pitch-classes of the total-chromatic (although, at the same time, the strings of the *biwa* are tuned according to the traditional pattern of rising fourths, F♯–B–E–A, known as *banshi-kichō*). The small mouth-organ known as the *shō*, however – whose deli-cate, 'metaphysical' sounds Takemitsu had already employed in his *Distance* – was totally intractable to any kind of extension of its basic gamut of limited pitch-materials. It could produce only the pitches of an A-major scale, plus one C♮ and one G♮; furthermore, the fingering of the pipes had been designed for optimum facility in the production of eleven standardised vertical types as shown in Example 88, which formed the har-monic basis of the traditional *gagaku* repertory.

In *Distance*, Takemitsu had ignored the traditional harmonic style with which the *shō* was associated, exploiting as best he could the limited gamut of pitches to produce more dissonant, freely chromatic vertical forms – even bringing the player's voice into play at one point as a means of extend-ing the instrument's chromatic possibilities. The *shō* writing of *In an Autumn Garden*, however, comes much closer to the traditional variety; on

Ex. 88 Standard chords of *shō*

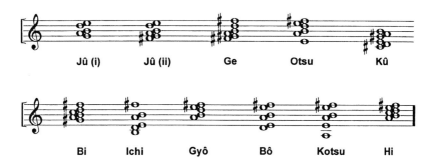

one or two occasions, in fact, the vertical forms Takemitsu assigns to this instrument are identical with forms found in Example 88 – for example, in the 'processional' passage of the fourth movement referred to above (letter 'O'-'P'), where the first and last chords of the *shō*'s repeated harmonic cycle correspond to the fourth (*otsu*) and seventh (*ichi*) of the chords in Example 88 respectively. And even when not limiting himself to the traditional harmonic vocabulary of the *shō*, Takemitsu here seems to accept the inherent limitations of the instrument, and build up similar-sounding modal clusters of his own, rather than attempt to go against its traditional function as he had done in *Distance*. Furthermore, this accommodation of the instrument's limitations somewhat circumscribes the pitches which Takemitsu is able to assign to the other instruments without creating a 'polymodal' texture. In this respect, it is revealing that in the most 'chromatic' passage of the work – the complex melismata of the third movement – the composer is obliged to eschew the harmonic support of the *shō* entirely.

Admittedly, a limited possibility exists for producing more chromatically dissonant forms by the simultaneous sounding of C♯ and C♮, or G♯ and G♮, and – as he had done in *Distance* – Takemitsu duly exploits this loophole in one or two places. For the most part, however, he not only contents himself with diatonic forms, but even models some of his harmonic types on transpositions of those contained within the instrument's traditional set of eleven. For example, in addition to the 'panpentatonic' chords on G and D found in the latter, the available pitches also permit the construction of other pentatonic verticalisations on pitches either side of this pair in the cycle of fifths – i.e. on C, A and E – all of which are duly exploited by Takemitsu in the course of the work.

The significance of such practices lies in the implication that, far from finding himself frustrated by the harmonic limitations of this instrument,

Takemitsu instead found the sounds it produced so satisfying that he was encouraged to construct his own harmonic forms on the same basic principles. And the wider significance of this discovery lies in the fact that very soon he would be constructing similar harmonic types in works for other, more conventional instrumental media – modal verticalisations which, it is true, had formed part of his basic harmonic vocabulary since the very earliest years, but which in recent times had seldom been presented in such undisguised clarity as they were shortly to be.

One such work for conventional Western instruments – many of whose features owe much to the example of *In an Autumn Garden* – appeared in the year following the first version of the latter. *Garden Rain* for brass ensemble takes its title from that of a *haiku* poem by an Australian schoolgirl, Susan Morrison, which appears in the preface to the score:

> Hours are leaves of life.
> And I am their gardener.
> Each hour falls down slow.

It is amusing to reflect how this unknown eleven-year-old unwittingly started something big by giving this evocative title to her work. Not only did it inspire Takemitsu to produce another work in the ongoing series of 'garden'-inspired pieces that had begun with *Arc* in the previous decade; Morrison's title also granted to *Garden Rain* the privilege of being (with the possible exception of the early tape piece *Water Music*) the first work in another series of Takemitsu compositions linked by a common extra-musical theme, and one which was to assume much greater importance in his works of the succeeding few years (as chapter 10 will reveal): the 'Waterscape' series. *Garden Rain* proclaims its membership of the latter in particular by the inclusion of a three-note motif that was to appear repeatedly in later works sharing an aquatic reference: the 'S–E–A' motif, which we have already encountered in the score of *Winter*. In Example 89, the motif is heard in the transposed form A♭–A–D, preceded by, and overlapping with, a statement of its own retrograde form.

Besides glancing forward to the 'waterscape' obsessions of the following decade, however, *Garden Rain* also looks backwards to *In an Autumn Garden* in certain respects, most obviously in the spatial disposition of its instrumental forces. Like the ensemble required by *In an Autumn Garden* in its first version, that of *Garden Rain* is divided into 'upstage' and 'downstage' groups, in this case each composed of five instrumentalists. This means, of course, that the work's on-stage layout recalls that of *The Dorian Horizon* as well, and once again there is also a common ground with the

Ex. 89 *Garden Rain*, p. 7

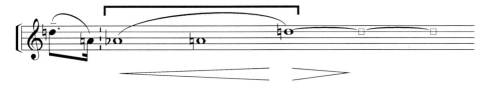

latter in the use of modality. Takemitsu is less explicit about the exact nature of this modal construction than he was regarding his 'Grecian Dorian mode' in *In an Autumn Garden*; but nevertheless one is able to gather that 'in this instance' he 'chose a mode with many possibilities – a mode that, beginning as a wide stream, will divide into many branches', and in which 'the perfect fifth, even if not always present in sound, is at the core of my musical perception'.[9] Certainly the modal basis of much of the musical material here is apparent enough at the surface level, both horizontally and vertically – in the latter dimension, most conspicuously perhaps in the closing bars of the work, which tend towards (without ever unambiguously stating) a 'panpentatonic' conclusion on a B final.

It is also perhaps feasible to suggest a direct *shō* influence on some aspects of the distinctive brass style of *Garden Rain*. Such a relationship would certainly not be without precedent: Takemitsu had, after all, explicitly acknowledged that the massed strings of *Arc* represented the 'most suitable instruments to express the continuous sounds of the *shō*',[10] and a similarity between the senza vibrato string chords of *The Dorian Horizon* and the sounds of the *shō* had also been commented on by Akiyama. A thoroughgoing attempt to analyse the pitch-material of *Garden Rain* in terms of subsets formed by 'partitioning' of the traditional repertory of *shō* chords has actually been attempted by one commentator on the work,[11] but it may be the case that the style of instrumental writing offers a more obvious reflection of such an influence. For much of the time, the brass instruments of *Garden Rain* are preoccupied with quiet, long-held chords, typically with very low bottom notes, notated by means of square-headed symbols whose durations are given by figures shown in boxes above them. These figures are to be understood only as relative to one another, with a unit value greater than 1″; in effect, therefore, the absolute durations of these chords in performance will be more or less a function of the instrumentalists' breath capacity, relating the style of execution to that of the *shō* whose power, Takemitsu believed, was 'inherent in its relationship with man's breathing'.[12] The static quality achieved here, a distinctive feature of *Garden Rain*'s sound-world, is in fact equally apparent in those sections of the work which, on paper at least, would rather tend to suggest a dense and complex polyrhythmic chaos formed from simultaneous irregular subdivisions of the beat; as Wilson observed, the overall effect of such rhythmic superimpositions is so complex 'that the ear tends to fuse it into a certain homogeneity creating a new sense of stagnation clearly related to the opening, sustained chords'.[13]

Garden Rain obviously recalls *In an Autumn Garden* also on account of the common metaphor shared by the two works' titles, but there is a suggestion in the later work that Takemitsu is beginning to apply this metaphor to his compositional process in a manner somewhat different from heretofore. Wilson mentions hearing the composer give a lecture at the Eastman School of Music in 1974, in which he compared the structure of *Garden Rain* to that of a Japanese rock garden.[14] If Wilson's memory is accurate, then Takemitsu's revelation is highly significant, for it represents an acknowledgement that the 'garden' metaphor is here being translated into musical equivalents other than, or at least additional to, those by means of which the composer had interpreted the image in such earlier works as *Arc*. In *Arc*, there had been an attempt at offering parallelisms between the 'time-cycles' of various components of a Japanese garden – rocks, grass, trees and sand – and the speeds of activity of various elements in the instrumental texture: in other words, the garden analogy operated largely by virtue of the *vertical* aspect of the music, in terms of Takemitsu's 'pan-focal', stratified treatment of the orchestra. Takemitsu's remarks about *Garden Rain*, however, suggest that in this case it is the overall form of the music that is modelled on a Japanese garden: the metaphor is now related to the *horizontal* aspect of the music, the actual contents of the piece as it unfolds in time, of which the term 'structure' is descriptive.

The importance of this change of emphasis resides in the fact that the latter application of the metaphor proved the more enduring of the two, and eventually became the norm in Takemitsu's third and final period. This in a way is hardly surprising: the dense stratifications of different textures by means of which the image is interpreted in such works as *Arc* belong emphatically to the 'avant-garde' style which Takemitsu was subsequently to abandon, and it was appropriate that in his simplified later manner the composer should prefer another interpretation of this evocative theme. Thus in works of later years such as *Fantasma/Cantos* for clarinet and orchestra (1991), which the composer claimed was inspired by viewing a Japanese 'tour' garden, the 'formal' interpretation of the 'garden' metaphor becomes the dominant model: it is as if the soloist, and vicariously the listener, were wandering through a series of fixed musical 'objects', some of which may be viewed in a different light, and some of which may be revisited – as, typically, at the end of the work, in which via a literal repetition of material the music usually arrives back where it began. Takemitsu himself appears not to have drawn attention to this inconsistency, or at least slight discrepancy, between his interpretation of 'garden form' in works of his middle and late periods, but it has not gone unnoticed by other commentators: Akimichi Takeda, for instance, observes that while in the earlier works 'landscape gardening' was taken as equivalent to 'pitch organisation', in later works (like *Fantasma/Cantos*), the latter concept has been completely replaced by the notion of a 'site for walking'.[15]

The 'garden' metaphor is evoked again in the title of *A Flock Descends into the Pentagonal Garden* for orchestra (1977), although at the same time this piece also belongs to another series of works which make common reference to an extra-musical theme: the series referred to by Takemitsu as 'Dream and Number'. The allusion to 'dream' refers to the circumstances of the work's inspiration: after seeing a photograph by Man Ray of the artist Marcel Duchamp, in which the latter's head had been shaved to leave a bald patch like a five-pointed star, Takemitsu dreamt of a flock of white birds, led by a black bird, descending into the 'pentagonal garden' of the title. Using this dream as a starting point, Takemitsu sought musical equivalents for its imagery via the mediation of an unusually rigorous precompositional process – an application of the science of 'Number'. The work's apparently cumbersome title is thus an accurate reflection of both its extra-musical inspiration and internal musical processes; yet, despite being carefully worked on in consultation with the composer Roger Reynolds, it has not been immune from ambiguous interpretations. In particular, at performances in Scotland and Australia – to the composer's surprise – audiences assumed it referred to a flock of sheep![16]

As suggested above, Takemitsu's translation of the contents of his initial dream into sound is achieved with a certain precision, even if of a somewhat idiosyncratic kind. The 'black bird' is represented by the central pitch of the pentatonic scale formed by the 'black notes' of a keyboard, F♯ – a note Takemitsu refers to as his 'favourite pitch . . . whose sound is like a mountain peak with surrounding vistas'[17] (a similitude apparently deriving from the central position this pitch occupies in the octave C–C). Moreover, Takemitsu also revealed that 'in German that pitch [i.e. F♯] is *Fis*, which sounds like the English "fix"; and with the intentional pun in mind, I use that F♯ as a fixed drone'.[18] The last part of this statement is interesting because Takemitsu here explicitly acknowledges a practice which has often been remarked upon by his commentators: the emphasis placed on specific pitch-classes by means of pedal points or drone-like devices. This emphasis may be achieved either by repeatedly attacking the same pitch-class throughout a section, or by means of a 'pedal point' in the more traditional sense of a sustained pitch; the insistence on F♯ in *A Flock Descends* involves both types of practice. Thus at letter 'M' of the score, where Takemitsu simply sets out a series of six chords which he has derived from the pentatonic scale by means of the 'magic square' referred to below, the 'fixity' of '*Fis*' in his precompositional scheme guarantees that this pitch appears in at least two octave registers, and sometimes three, in each subsequent chordal attack. Elsewhere in the piece, on the other hand, there are numerous references to this same pitch-class in the form of sustained pedal tones: as in the passage from letter 'I' to 'K', where F♯ – here stabilised in the octave above middle C – is sustained throughout.

Takemitsu's starting point for the musical realisation of the 'pentagonal garden' into which his 'black bird' descends is – unsurprisingly – the 'black note' pentatonic scale on F♯. 'In music the number five makes us think of the Orient and Africa', he commented; 'to explain it simply, it is the scale of the black keys of the piano'.[19] It is revealing that Takemitsu here speaks of 'the Orient' as if, like Africa, it represented some musical 'other'. Although by this time he had long been reconciled to traditional Japanese music, he still regarded it somewhat from the 'etic' standpoint of a composer primarily in the Western tradition, and thus did not elect to mention here – as he might well have done – that this pentatonic scale is also the *yō* scale of traditional Japanese music, 'light' counterpart to the 'dark' *in* scale which he had used in his very earliest compositions.[20] In *A Flock Descends*, Takemitsu refers to this scale primarily in a vertical sense: 'panpentatonic' superimpositions of the entire collection, of the kind usually heard only intermittently in his work to date, now assume the importance of fundamental referential sonorities, and additionally furnish the work with that specific signifier of final closure that was to become something of a trademark over the course of the next few years. Of frequent occurrence, too, are vertical forms based on the addition of extraneous pitches to pentatonic collections; Example 90 illustrates an extreme case, where the 'blacknote' collection within the bracket forms the core of a massive orchestral sonority whose pitches contain the total-chromatic. The passage where this event occurs, incidentally, provides a good example of a gesture typical of Takemitsu's musical rhetoric: a climax which – in contrast to the gradual accumulations of energy typical of Western music – takes a form described by one commentator as 'a sudden, brief outburst which immediately subsides'.[21] The manner in which this climax is preceded by a dramatic sounding of the double pedal point, C–C♯, in the bass prior to the unleashing of the full orchestra, is also highly typical of the composer.

Ex. 90 *A Flock Descends into the Pentagonal Garden*, F/3

One could speculate that the addition of all seven 'white notes' to the five black ones here is some kind of reflection of the 'flock of white birds' that follow the black one in Takemitsu's initial dream image. Whatever the actual derivation of the pitches in Example 90, however, it is unlikely that they were arbitrarily arrived at, for *A Flock Descends* – as hinted above, and explicitly acknowledged by the composer himself – is written according to an unusually rigorous 'system'. 'Sometimes I change my previous plan with my intuition', Takemitsu observed, 'but *A Flock Descends* is written with a very strict row. It is programmed, controlled.'[22] Takemitsu's account of this precompositional process, which appears in his monograph *Yume to Kazu* ('Dream and Number'), is actually the most candid explanation of his secret technical workings that he ever made public, and as such has been eagerly seized upon by scholars of his music: as Poirier has observed, it is not simply a matter of chance that this work and *Quatrain* are among the most commented upon of Takemitsu's entire œuvre.[23] For this very reason, I have decided that it would be supererogatory to add my own description to those already available, and the reader interested in finding out more about the 'magic squares' and other *arcana* by means of which Takemitsu derived the basic pitch-materials of *A Flock Descends* should turn to the appropriate sources.[24] At the same time, however, anyone who expects to find an exhaustive analysis of the work in question should be warned that they are likely to be disappointed by Takemitsu's description. While the composer certainly reveals how, retaining F♯ as a 'fixed pitch', he subjected the remaining notes of the black-note pentatonic scale to transposition operations by means of 'magic squares' to derive the basic harmonic fields of this work, many of the graphics and musical quotations with which he illustrates his argument seem to stand in a merely decorative relationship to the text, being referred to only obliquely or sometimes not at all. As a result, the reader's curiosity on a number of points still remains tantalisingly unsatisfied. For instance, one of Takemitsu's diagrams hints that, in addition to those used to derive the pitch-materials, there is another 'magic square' of numbers (marked 'rhythmic construction series'), the sum of whose rows and columns is always fifteen, which appears to be used to generate the durational values of the work from various pairs of figures whose sum is always five. Kuniharu Akiyama certainly takes the hint, observing of the work's rhythmic aspect that 'various shapes are derived from cells whose rhythmic construction is related to the number five: 3+2, 1+4, 2+3, 4+1 . . .';[25] but, since Takemitsu's text almost provocatively fails to make any explicit reference to this intriguing diagram, such observations are doomed, in the last analysis, to remain somewhat speculative in character.

These 'magic squares' of Takemitsu's constructional system may also constitute a secret reference to the 'garden' metaphor of his title. At all events, Poirier has suggested an intriguing analogy between the two: the distribution of stones in a traditional Japanese rock garden, he notes, is determined by the rhythm 7–5–3, which are also the central numerical values in a Taoist 'magic square' whose columns and rows all add up to fifteen – just like those in Takemitsu's own square of 'rhythmic construction series'.[26] At the same time, the 'garden' reference of Takemitsu's title is almost certainly interpreted musically in both senses Takemitsu more habitually attributes to it: referring both to the 'pan-focal' orchestral texture, and to the overall patterning of the work after the form of a Japanese garden. Admittedly, this latter suggestion appears to be contradicted to a certain degree by the composer's own remarks on the work, which imply a different structural model, and one whose linear, sectional nature seems at first sight incompatible with the idea of a rambling, circular stroll. It is a model not unlike the 'eleven steps without any special melodic scheme' of *November Steps*, but in this instance the number of '*dan*' in Takemitsu's scheme would appear to be thirteen: 'Each section of this piece has a special story: maybe, thirteen small sections, thirteen variations – not variations in the Western sense, rather, like a scroll painting. So when I composed this piece I made up a story, a picture, like a scroll painting.'[27]

The 'maybe' with which Takemitsu qualifies his description is apt, recalling Ohtake's remarks about the 'eleven ambiguously separated sections' of *November Steps*: it is indeed as difficult to arrive at any definitive partitioning of the later work as it was of the former (although, once again,

Takemitsu's score suggestively provides thirteen rehearsal letters, 'A'–'M').
Perhaps one should not be too surprised at such an outcome, if the work is
in fact patterned after the continuously unfolding sequence of 'boundless'
images in a Japanese *emaki*, as the composer claims. However, as suggested
above, this interpretation of the work's formal outline does not necessarily
militate against its simultaneous apprehension as an example of
Takemitsu's 'garden form' – the network of interpenetrating repetitions in
the score, both literal and less accurate, implies that this might not be inappropriate. That these two simultaneous interpretations of the same form
may not be incompatible is certainly suggested by the composer's remarks,
many years later, about *A Bird came down the Walk* (1994), a work for viola
and piano based on the same materials as those with which *A Flock
Descends* opens: here 'the bird theme goes walking through the motionless,
scroll painting like a landscape, a garden hushed and bright with
daylight'.[28]

Takemitsu's 'pentagonal garden' is also self-evidently in a direct line of
descent from the 'autumn garden' of the *gagaku* piece on which he was still
working, and it may be appropriate to conclude discussion of *A Flock
Descends* with some speculations on the degree to which the experience of
writing for *gagaku* may have influenced the style of the orchestral piece
and, by implication, the whole 'third-period' aesthetic of which it constitutes one of the earliest clear expressions. One such possible source of
influence may have been of a kind that operated on the composer's sub-
conscious, furnishing part of the dream-content which was the initial
impetus for *A Flock Descends*' composition: anyone who has attended a
performance of *In an Autumn Garden*, surrounded by the spatially separated instrumental groups, cannot but be reminded by this experience of
sitting in the midst of a 'triangular garden' of the five-sided one which
Takemitsu saw in his dream-vision. Without indulging in amateur
psychology, however, it is also possible to discover links between the two
works in the shape of more concrete, musical similarities. Most obviously,
the starting point for Takemitsu's 'magic-square' chords – the verticalisation of a pentatonic scale – is identical with the construction of five out of
the eleven standard vertical forms played by the *shō* in its conventional
context. Transpose the first chord of Example 88 down a semitone and you
have the 'black-note' pentatonic chord with which *A Flock Descends* opens;
orchestrate it for wind instruments, add further vertical forms of similar
construction, and you have the very passable simulacrum of *shō*-like
chords of the work's first few bars. Furthermore, add to this a melodic line,
the 'theme of the flock . . . based on the same pitches [as the accompanying
harmonic progression]',[29] assign it to solo oboe, and you have something

like the orchestral equivalent of a *hichiriki* melody to counterpoint this movement of ethereal harmonies. Or – as at letter 'M' of Takemitsu's score – colour the basic six 'magic-square' chords on which *A Flock Descends* is based with silvery, 'overtone'-like formations for muted trumpets and divided strings, add crescendo–diminuendo dynamic envelopes to the latter, and the orchestration as a whole begins to shimmer with the magic, celestial timbre of the *shō* itself.

It thus seems highly plausible that Takemitsu's experience with the limited harmonic range of the *shō* was one factor determining the more obvious preference for verticalised modal forms, and for 'panpentatonic' chords in particular, that is such a conspicuous feature of his later work. In this sense, his 'descent into the pentagonal garden' – apt metaphor, perhaps, for those who view his abandonment of avant-gardisme as some sort of decline in standard – may therefore have been prepared for by his experiences in the 'autumn garden' of his *gagaku* piece. Other aspects of his later style, too, such as the increased emphasis on *melos*, or the simplified textures with their reliance on instrumental doublings rather than complex layerings, may also owe their origins in part to the same creative stimulus. Yet it would be going too far to suggest that the experience of writing *In an Autumn Garden* alone was responsible for such a wholesale transformation of Takemitsu's style. The sources of Takemitsu's late manner were manifold; this chapter has only related the story of one, albeit important, element in the mix.

Another influence that was to become of especial importance in the succeeding years, for example, is already hinted at by the second work considered in this chapter: the extra-musical influence implied by the second half of the title *Garden Rain*. In 1978 Takemitsu returned to this theme, complementing the earlier work with a similar aquatic allusion in the title of *Waterways*, and in the subsequent decade this motif was to become something of an obsession with him, referred to again and again in a series of works which steered the former 'avant-garde' composer definitively in the direction of what he called his 'sea of tonality'. It is this route towards the consolidation of Takemitsu's 'third-period' manner that will be examined in chapter 10.

10   Towards the sea of tonality: the works of the 1980s

A Flock Descends marked a significant watershed in Takemitsu's work. Something of its musical language had already been glimpsed in earlier pieces, but these had not, in the end, announced the inauguration of a new simplicity in the composer's discourse: *Green* had been followed by *Asterism*, *Quatrain* by *Waves* and *Bryce*. After *A Flock Descends*, however – with the exception of the delayed première of the *Gémeaux* project – there was to be no turning back to the 'modernist' style with which Takemitsu had been preoccupied in the earlier part of the decade. This time, the work's glowing sensuality was to prove no temporary aberration from the true path, but instead embodied an aesthetic that would preoccupy Takemitsu for more or less the remainder of his career. His 'third period' had begun.

The 1980s were the years in which this new style was to be refined and consolidated. As Poirier has pointed out, they were years characterised by 'an identity such as results from a long sedimentation';[1] years, further-more, in which – for Poirier at least – Takemitsu's writing progressively takes on the character of the 'post-modernism' prevalent at the time.[2] Poirier does not explain precisely what he means by this problematic and much-abused term, and significantly the composer himself – as we shall see later – preferred to categorise his later manner as 'Romantic'; but nevertheless, one can certainly assert that Takemitsu's compositions from henceforth, at least relative to his own earlier work, would become 'post-avant-garde,' 'post-experimental' – in other words, would constitute his own response to the decline of modernism as the dominant aesthetic of new music.

Two consequences in particular flow from this decision by Takemitsu to dissociate himself from the modernist adventure. First, radical experi-mentation is mostly abandoned, and as a result during the 1980s Takemitsu's style acquires a certain stability, a consistent sound which was to become more or less normative for the remainder of his career. Secondly, while modernism had aspired to become the single interna-tional, collective language of advanced composition, the styles that now emerged from beneath its shadow were pluralist, individual and personal. At the height of his 'experimental' period, Takemitsu's career had appeared to run in tandem with the leading Western avant-garde musicians of his day. Now, however, as he followed more and more his own inclinations, Takemitsu's stylistic trajectory was henceforth to diverge irrevocably from that of his former Western colleagues.

Besides his confessions to being a 'Romantic', Takemitsu indirectly acknowledged the changed priorities of his later music via another keyword, or rather key phrase, that reflected a particular technical aspect of the new order. It was a phrase that was to occur repeatedly in the prefaces to the series of works whose titles refer to the imagery of rain: for example, that found in the score of *Rain Coming* reads:

> *Rain Coming* is one of a series of works by the composer inspired by the common theme of rain. The complete collection entitled 'Waterscape' includes other works . . . It was the composer's intention to create a series of works, which like their subject,[3] pass through various metamorphoses, culminating in a *sea of tonality* [my italics].[4]

Takemitsu's metaphor of the 'sea of tonality' here is provocatively ambiguous. On the one hand, he could simply be referring to aspects of individual works in this series – their tendency to move towards tonal resolutions, their 'pan-tonal' harmonic language. On the other hand, however, he could be suggesting that the 'Waterscape' cycle as a whole represents a journey towards the 'sea of tonality' – in other words, represents a vehicle for the wholesale transformation of his harmonic language into a more overtly tonal idiom. If the latter interpretation is correct – and the historical coincidence of the 'Waterscape' cycle with the consummation of Takemitsu's stylistic metamorphosis suggests that this may be a possibility – then this series of works is of particular importance for understanding the genesis of Takemitsu's 'third-period' manner. It is therefore with a discussion of the works comprising this cycle that the analytical matter of this chapter begins.

Waterscape

Takemitsu himself, as the above quotation indicates, identified the unifying feature of the 'Waterscape' series as the inspiration of rain, but nevertheless it may be more fruitful to think of the cycle as comprising all the works from this period whose titles contain some aquatic reference of whatever kind. This is certainly the view taken by Yukiko Sawabe, who sees the series as pointing in two directions, 'namely to the horizontal level of river, sea and ocean . . . and the vertical level of rain'.[5] And indeed, a more inclusive approach is not without support in Takemitsu's own description – at all events, his references to the 'various metamorphoses' undergone by rain on its journey to the 'sea of tonality' suggest that he, too, was aware of the 'horizontal' dimension of his subject. Thus more broadly defined, the area encompassed by this 'Waterscape' cycle is a large one. It begins in 1974, with a work which was described in the last chapter as belonging to Takemitsu's 'garden'-inspired works, but which is also simultaneously the first member of the 'Waterscape' series – a form of 'dual citizenship' that, as we shall see below, Takemitsu was to grant to a number of subsequent pieces. *Garden Rain* was followed by *Waves* and *Waterways*, and the following decade saw the addition of no fewer than twelve works to the Takemitsu canon with a watery reference in the title: *Toward the Sea* (1981) and its two rearrangements for larger forces; *Rain Tree* (1981); *Rain Coming, Rain Spell* and *Rain Tree Sketch* (1982); *Wavelength* (1984); the tape piece *The Sea is Still* (1986); *Rain Dreaming* (1986); *riverrun* and *I Hear the Water Dreaming* (1987). With the last piece, the composer seems to have brought the main corpus of 'aquatic' works to a close, but the theme is briefly invoked again in the titles of two works from the following decade: *Rain Tree Sketch II* (1992) and *Between Tides* (1993).

As was noted in the previous chapter, one of the ways in which *Garden Rain* proclaims its membership of this series is its incorporation, albeit in transposition, of the 'S–E–A' motif, formed from the pitch-classes equivalent to those three letters in German nomenclature (i.e. Es [E♭]–E–A). This 'three-note motif, consisting of a half-step and a perfect fourth',[6] was to assume special significance in the composer's works for a period of at least twenty years, appearing – as the representative selection of extracts quoted in Example 91 shows – both in works from the 'Waterscape' series, and in others whose titles contain no aquatic reference. Perhaps the latter apparent anomaly can best be explained by considering Takemitsu's own metaphorical extension to his key word's significance: the 'sea of tonality'. Interpreted in this sense, the appearances of the 'sea' motif in these works, written during a period of the composer's career when his interest in tonality was coming to the fore with the greatest clarity, seem perfectly appropriate. One might observe in passing, too, that the three letters comprising this musical tag, in retrograde (and Takemitsu was to submit his motif to the full range of 'serial' transformations), also form the musically viable letters of the composer's own family name: tAkEmitSu.

As noted above, one possible interpretation of the problematic term 'sea of tonality' might be to assume that it refers to the 'tonal' resolutions centred on a particular pitch or key towards which so many of these works gravitate – resolutions which may often employ fairly conventional harmonic indices of closure, such as the 'panpentatonic' scale verticalisation. One might also observe that the same 'tonal centre' serves as final in a

Ex. 91 Versions of S-E-A motif

(i) *Folios*, for solo guitar (1974)

(ii) *Quatrain* (1975), D/4 (fl.)

(iii) *A Flock Descends into the Pentagonal Garden* (1977), H/2 - 3 (vln. 1)

(iv) *Far Calls. Coming, Far!* (1980), O/8 (solo vln.)

(v) *Toward the Sea* (1980), p. 11 system 1 (guitar)

(vi) *A Way a Lone* (1981), bar 120 (vln. 1)

(vii) *Rain Tree* (1981), p. 12 bar 1 (vibr.)

(viii) *Dreamtime* (1981), B/7 (vln. 1+2)

(ix) *Rain Tree Sketch* (1982, solo pno.), bar 24

(x) *Rain Coming* (1982), D/5 (vln. 1)

(xi) *I Hear the Water Dreaming* (1987), K/4 (solo fl.)

(xii) *Paths* (solo trumpet, 1994), p. 4, system 6

number of different works from this period. Thus *Rain Tree, Rain Coming* and the string quartet *A Way a Lone* (1981) all end with strong suggestions of Db major – in the case of the *Rain Tree*, presented in the unambiguous form of a very quiet triad in that key, tremolando, for two marimbas. A closely related 'modal' Bb minor with flattened seventh is implied by the final Bb-minor-seventh chord of *Toward the Sea*, as well as by the 'panpentatonic' closure of *Dreamtime* (1981); *Garden Rain, Rain Spell* and *To the Edge of Dream* (1983) all end with affirmations of B♮ as their 'tonic'; while C♮ would appear to have something like a tonic significance at the end of *Far calls. Coming, far!* (1980), *Orion and Pleiades* (1984), *Twill by Twilight* (1988) and *A String Around Autumn* (1989) – even if in the last instance the effect of the final pentatonic collection is rather to suggest a modal 'A minor' by the placing of A♮ in the bass.

One notes additionally that the final 'tonal' arrival in these works is not necessarily simply an afterthought, but may be carefully prepared by the material preceding it. One such form of preparation takes the form of the establishment of some kind of long-term progression of significant pitches. Koozin, for example, has suggested that this is the case in *Rain Tree Sketch*: by isolating all occurrences of pitches lower than Eb^2, he derives a fairly convincing long-term 'bass progression' for the piece – particularly for its second half, from the climactic C♯ doubled in three octaves in bar 33^7 down to the Bb with which the work ends.[8] *Toward the Sea* for alto flute and guitar also appears to demonstrate evidence of such long-term thinking, here working in co-operation with harmonic devices to lead the work towards its ultimate tonal destination of Db major/Bb minor. This tonal area is hinted at throughout the piece by the use of the Bb-minor-seventh chord already referred to as a 'reference sonority', but it is also constantly thrown into relief by repeated reference to a secondary tonal area a major third higher – suggesting a 'rival' pair of tonic centres, F major/D minor, with particular emphasis on the note A. It is partly the tension generated between these two rival tonal areas, and its resolution at the end of the piece, that lends such a convincing air of finality to the last movement's closing bars (Ex. 92).

Here, against a transposition of the ubiquitous 'S–E–A' motif in the alto flute with a C♯ final, the guitar counterpoises first a verticalisation of the pentatonic scale on F (the 'rival' tonal area), and then a transposition of the same chord down a major third (i.e., on to the 'tonic'). In this context the guitar's third chord – whatever its actual theoretical derivation – sounds like an altered IV of C♯ major, and the ear accepts the flautist's lingering C♯, persisting as the harmony fades away, as conclusive. The final appearance of the 'referential' chord here, with its Bb root, might on paper

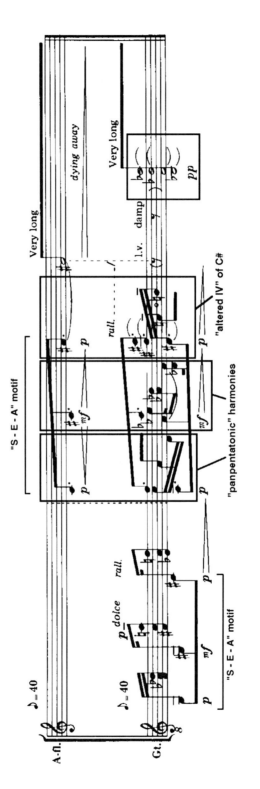

Ex. 92 *Toward the Sea* III, conclusion

appear to undermine this sense of finality; but in practice, the ear by this time has become so accustomed to its sonority that it perfectly fulfils the cadential role here demanded of it.

A secondary, and possibly more likely, meaning of Takemitsu's 'sea of tonality' is, however, suggested by his commentary on *Far calls. Coming, far!* where he speaks of the '"sea of tonality" from which many pantonal chords flow'.[9] The word 'pantonal' again suggests the theories of George Russell (rather than Réti), where it is used to describe the manner in which a totally chromatic music may be achieved by an accumulation of modally derived materials. Takemitsu's metaphor thus appears to be suggesting something like the reverse of this process: that the 'sea of tonality' is a matrix of possibilities from which the modally based harmonies of his music derive. Such modally based forms are certainly much more obvious at a foreground level in the composer's later music than had generally been the case in his middle years. The two 'panpentatonic' chords in the example from *Toward the Sea* quoted above are a case in point, as are the panpentatonic valedictions that, following the precedent of *A Flock Descends*, were to become almost a cliché of the composer's later style: *Dreamtime*, *Vers*, *l'arc-en-ciel*, *Palma*, and *A String Around Autumn* all end with this gesture. But the full range of other modal forms that Takemitsu had added to his harmonic vocabulary over the years is also exploited to the full in these later works, and very often in a 'bolder', much more exposed state than previously. In particular, the octatonic scale is used with such frequency that glib comparisons with Messiaen's music have, inevitably, sprung all too easily to the minds of Takemitsu's critics, as we shall see in the concluding chapter of this book.

The recurrence of harmonic devices already familiar from earlier works illustrates an important aspect of Takemitsu's 'third-period' style: it did not represent the abandonment of the technical preoccupations of former years, but rather the employment of proven techniques that Takemitsu had acquired over those years of 'long sedimentation' in the service of a rather different aesthetic vision. Thus, besides the harmonic language, various other elements of his later music wear a familiar aspect. In the sphere of 'formal' patterning, for example, repetition of whole 'blocks' of material – whether literal, or subjected to some kind of transformation – continues to be a trademark of the composer's discourse. Sometimes, too, the ordering of materials appears to project some kind of higher-level organisation, as in the case of *Rain Tree Sketch*, which temporarily resurrects the 'ABA' form common to several of Takemitsu's earliest works. Other types of formal organisation are also found; for example, something like the linear sequence of short sections which the composer had employed in *A Flock*

Descends is also suggested by his remarks on a chamber orchestra work written five years later: '*Rain Coming* is a variation of colours on the simple figure played mainly on the alto flute which appears at the beginning of the piece'.[10] Indeed, one notes similarities between Takemitsu's descriptions of the two works in the shape of a common reference to 'variations', and to the role of a solo instrument (oboe in *A Flock*, alto flute in *Rain Coming*) in delineating the beginning of formal sections. But while Takemitsu's less hesitant application of the term 'variation' in the later instance is to a certain extent borne out by the content of the score, in which the characteristic augmented-triad-arpeggio incipit of the 'theme' does recur at strategic points, the sections of *Rain Coming* are in the last analysis no more 'variations in the Western sense' than those of *A Flock Descends* had been. In fact, it is probably more profitable to think of the work as a sequence of sections in which the solo melody plays the role of occasional formal marker – a function that approximates more nearly to that of ritornello than of variation subject, and which was to become another favoured formal device of Takemitsu in later years.

However, despite the occasional presence of intentional formal schemata of the types outlined above – ternary form, 'picture-scroll' sequence – it would be inaccurate to give the impression that the material of most of Takemitsu's later scores is organised after these kinds of patternings. Much more frequently, the sequence of events is rather that of a free perambulation amongst the sound-objects of a musical 'garden', and the whole idea of an intermediary conceptualisation that is implied by the imposition of an abstract 'form' prior to the compositional process, into which the musical ideas are poured as into a mould, is refreshingly absent. To proceed in the latter manner would, indeed, be directly antithetical to the composer's own professed aesthetic intention, for – as he himself has eloquently expressed it – 'I gather sounds around me and mobilise them with the least force possible. The worst is to move them around like driving an automobile.'[11]

Another feature of earlier practice that Takemitsu was to retain in his final period is the self-borrowing and economical recycling of material that we have already observed in such works as *November Steps* and *Green*. The composer continued to 'rearrange' works, generally for larger forces: thus *A Way a Lone* for string quartet was to generate *A Way a Lone II* for string orchestra, and *Toward the Sea* was to give rise to subsequent rescorings for alto flute and harp (*Toward the Sea III*) and the same combination plus string orchestra (*Toward the Sea II*). At the same time, however, Takemitsu continued his established habit of purloining short fragments

Ex. 93 *Rain Tree Sketch*, bars 61–2

of pre-existent works to provide material for new ones – often lifting a bar
or two verbatim as if cut out with a scissors, replicating the kinds of internal repetition found in his scores at a higher level, one that operated
between self-contained works rather than *within* their confines. 1982
appears to have been a particularly busy year for the composer in this
respect: three works written in that year – *Rain Coming, Rain Tree Sketch*
and *Grass* for men's chorus – all share such overlappings of material. For
example, the closing gesture of *Rain Tree Sketch* (Ex. 93) turns up in
expanded form, and with only minor variations, in *Rain Coming* (Ex. 94).

In the case of the material shared between *Rain Tree Sketch* and *Grass*, the
repetition is combined with transposition – just as frequently occurs when
passages are repeated internally. Example 96, from the latter work, is clearly
a transposition at T^3 of the passage from *Rain Tree Sketch* quoted in
Example 95, although revoiced and with one pitch substitution in the final
chord – precisely the kinds of alterations to which, as we have seen, repeated
materials are routinely subjected within the context of individual pieces. (It
goes without saying that the sequence of composition suggested by this
description is purely for the sake of convenience, and that there is as always
no definitive means of determining which of these two variants was composed first.) Finally, yet a third passage from *Rain Tree Sketch* (not quoted
here) also leads a double life of this kind: bars 42–3 appear in a vertically
expanded and reworked version in *Rain Coming* (letter 'D', bars 2–3).

Ex. 94   *Rain Coming*, 'Q'/9

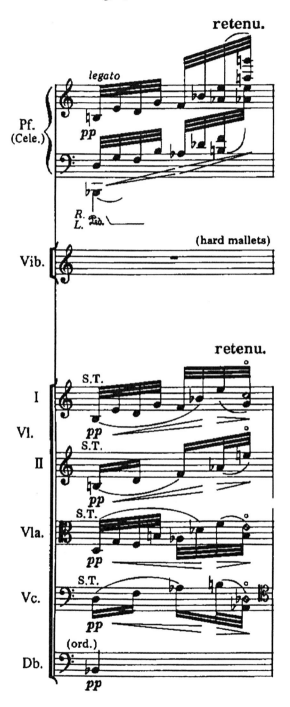

Ex. 95 *Rain Tree Sketch*, bars 25–6

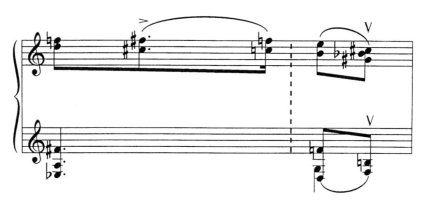

Ex. 96 *Grass*, bar 17

Ex. 97   *Rain Tree*, p. 10, systems 1–2

As far as their rhythmic aspect is concerned, the works of Takemitsu's
later period generally present a somewhat simplified picture by comparison with the works of his middle years, one that invites comparison rather
with the rhythmic devices of his 'first period': at all events, there are fewer
of the simultaneous subdivisions of the beat into different fractions that
had played such a significant role in creating the complex textures of his
'modernist' years. On the other hand, however, a full range of rhythmic
devices of familiar aspect continue to appear. The upwardly mobile
'iambic' pattern which had constituted such a characteristic *topos* of
Takemitsu style from the very earliest works, for instance, was still part of
the composer's habitual mode of utterance in the 1980s, as Example 97
demonstrates. This simultaneously illustrates another recurrent feature of
Takemitsu's melodic construction, and one especially associated with the
products of his maturer years: the emergence of themes in a kind of additive, incremental fashion, or exposition *in statu nascendi* – a procedure he
may have arrived at from a study of Alban Berg's music, which, as we shall
see, was to assert an increasingly apparent influence over the composer
during the later part of his career.

   One or two of the rhythmic experiments of Takemitsu's avant-garde
years were, however, retained in the later style. The type of 'spatial' or 'proportional' notation used in such scores as *Bryce* and *Waves*, for instance, is
revived in parts of *Rain Spell* (1982) for flute, clarinet, harp, piano and
vibraphone, where all players are instructed to play from the full score,

Ex. 98 *Rain Tree Sketch*, bar 40

suggesting the necessity for a high degree of awareness by each player of the material given to the others. 'Mobile' writing involving the repetition of materials independently of tempo – of the type once characterised by the composer as 'heterocyclic' – is also still found occasionally in Takemitsu's later work. Furthermore, it may be legitimate to extend Takemitsu's concept of 'heterocyclicity' to include a type of writing which likewise consists of the simultaneous repetition of melodic cycles of dissimilar lengths, but which takes place within the confines of an orthodox metrical context. Example 98, from *Rain Tree Sketch*, provides an illustration. Here the right hand has an ostinato of ten even semiquavers, the left hand one of eight semiquavers, and – as Koozin points out – 'since patterns in the upper and lower scores are of unequal length, the patterns overlap irregularly'.[12]

A similar, but slightly different situation obtains in the case of the ostinato repetitions in Example 99, from *Rain Tree*. The repeating patterns for the two marimbas are melodically and rhythmically identical, and differ only in the irregular placing of the *sforzandi* accents; the discrepancies between the cycles of repetition of the two parts arise from discrepancies between the number of repetitions of *whole bars* of each deviant accentuation. Here the economy of the notation, the ambiguity as to the placing of the downbeat created by the offbeat accents, the choice of instrumentation and, of course, the repetition itself all suggest an acquaintance with another contemporary music for 'mallet instruments' from across the Pacific – a rather ironic choice of model, perhaps, when one considers Takemitsu's later disparaging comments on 'minimalist pieces' that 'drift from the cosmic to the cosmetic'.[13]

Ex. 99 *Rain Tree*, p. 13, system 4

As for the timbral world of these later pieces, one is not greatly surprised to discover that the spirit of bold exploration of new instrumental possibilities that had characterised Takemitsu's music of the early 1970s is mostly absent. However, the composer did not simply revert to the more restrained and conventional instrumental idiom of his works from the 1950s. Instead, the preoccupation with sonority which he had begun to cultivate during his years of experimentation still expressed itself in two ways. On the one hand, Takemitsu continued to refine his skill in the handling of instrumental colour, particularly by means of imaginative and unusual combinations and doublings of instruments, eventually acquiring a mastery of rapturously beautiful tone shadings that was unsurpassed amongst composers of his generation. And on the other hand, many of the fruits of the years of experimentation with timbral possibilities became assimilated into the 'common practice' of the relatively stabilised instrumental language that served this new aesthetic vision. The writing for alto flute in *Toward the Sea*, for example, continues to make use of multiphonic trills and other 'extended' devices, such as the instruction at one point gradually to bring in an octave harmonic by overblowing; while quarter-tone scordatura of five of the harpist's strings in *Rain Spell* is used to give a characteristically 'twangy', *koto*-like sonority to the writing, enabling the instrument to play glissandi and 'Æolian rustlings' on what – to a Western listener at least – sound rather like octatonic or whole-tone scales with wrong notes.

Finally, the exploitation of the theatrical aspect of performance – another aspect of Takemitsu's 'second-period' works that had seemed so quintessentially of its time – is not entirely absent from these later scores either. At least, in *Rain Tree* Takemitsu contrives to create a little drama, even if this is achieved without calling on the aid of visible human performers at all. Each of the three percussion soloists is lit from above with a spotlight, and detailed instructions are given in the score as to when these lights are to be switched on and off. The elaborate 'lightshow' which results, in combination with the scattered, 'raindrop' sounds of tuned percussions, is almost certainly intended as a picturesque reflection of the image conjured by the work's title, which is taken from a novel by Kenzaburo Ōe, and refers to a type of Hawaiian tree observed by the author:

> It has been named the 'rain tree'; for its abundant foliage continues to let fall rain drops collected from last night's shower until well after the following midday. Its hundreds of thousands of tiny leaves – finger-like – store up moisture while other trees dry up at once. What an ingenious tree, isn't it?[14]

Other 'themed' series of compositions

Though by far the most extensive, the 'Waterscape' project was by no means the only series of works from this period linked by a common extra-musical reference. Various other contemporaneous scores may be grouped according to their preoccupations with a number of such shared 'themes' – some of these explicitly acknowledged by the composer, others referred to only in the secondary literature. Into the first category, for instance, falls the theme which Takemitsu refers to as 'Dream and Number' (the title, also, of a 1987 collection of essays on his work), where 'Dream' represents the undefined and 'Number' the antagonistic, conscious desire for form. These preoccupations had already been reflected in two works from the 1970s: *Quatrain*, with its insistence on the number 4, emphasising 'number', and *A Flock Descends* – simultaneously dream-inspired and rigorously controlled by the number 5 – representing an equilibrium of the two forces. In the five works from the 1980s representing this particular obsession, however, it is to 'Dream' alone that the title makes reference – suggesting the existence of a 'dreamscape' series to parallel and complement the 'waterscape' cycle.

In a sense, this overt reference to 'dream' was only making explicit something that had been present in Takemitsu's music since the very earliest years: at least since the time of his acquaintance with the poet Takiguchi, the composer had been under the spell of the methods and aesthetics of surrealism, and much of his work – whether it explicitly relates to 'dream' or not – is 'composed as if fragments were thrown together somewhat unstructured, as in dreams'.[15] It is hardly surprising, therefore, that after a visit (with Berio) to Groot Eylandt in 1980 as part of an event sponsored by Eurovision, Takemitsu should decide to bestow the name of the old Aboriginal myth of the *Dreamtime* on his 1981 composition for the Nederlands Dans Theater, and speak of a desire to build therein 'an imaginary music scene';[16] in reality, he was doing no more than acknowledge a preoccupation and a method of construction which had consistently informed his music for several years previously.

This link between his 'dream' preoccupation and the surrealist movement is explicitly acknowledged in Takemitsu's next work in this series, *To the Edge of Dream* for guitar and orchestra (1983), which owes its inspiration to the weirdly oneiric images of the Belgian artist Paul Delvaux (1897–1994). Here Takemitsu creates an appropriately 'nocturnal' ambience by instructing the strings to play muted throughout, except in two short passages – thereby lending to the typically sonorous, *Requiem*-like string interludes an even more intense *film noir* quality than they usually possess. He also, perhaps, hints at his 'nocturnal' subject in the enigmatic closing bars of the work, in which a series of chiming B♮s – the pitch towards which the work is gravitating – are each harmonised with a different chord, rather like the famous 'chimes at midnight' of Verdi's *Falstaff.*

While the titles of these two works refer to 'dream' alone, those of the other three works comprising Takemitsu's 'dreamscape' cycle at this period refer simultaneously to one of his other recurrent extra-musical preoccupations – thereby granting these works membership of more than one 'themed' cycle. The title of *Dream/Window* (1985), for instance, alludes simultaneously to Takemitsu's 'garden' metaphor, although this is not readily apparent from the English title, whose Japanese original contains a piece of untranslatable word-play. For the two Chinese ideograms which spell these words in Japanese, in a different reading, also spell the name of [Soseki] Musō (1275–1351), a Buddhist priest who had been a legendary master of the formal art of the Japanese garden. This 'garden' metaphor is perhaps realised here in the same 'vertical' sense of a stratified instrumental texture that had been the case in works from an earlier period such as *Arc for piano and orchestra*: certainly the unconventional seating of instrumentalists to achieve a spatial effect suggests another of the preoccupations of Takemitsu's experimental period that was retained in the more conservative idiom of his later years. In fact, the arrangement of the orchestral apparatus suggests striking parallels with the 'symmetrical' disposition of forces in *November Steps*, written some eighteen years previously. As in the earlier work, percussion and strings are placed to left and right, with brass and woodwinds in between, while in front of these – in the position occupied by the two harps of *November Steps* – is an ensemble of two harps, celesta and guitar, and at the very front of the stage, a soloistic group of flute, clarinet and string quartet – in precisely the position where the *biwa* and *shakuhachi* players of the 1967 work had been.

The spatial dimension is not the only aspect of this work to recall the experimentations of a more adventurous epoch, for the means whereby some of the basic pitch-materials of the work are generated also recall some of Takemitsu's earlier flirtations with serial organisation. Certainly the first of the two sets of 'raw materials' from which the composer fashioned the piece – and which he describes, with typical idiosyncrasy, as 'harmonic pitch 1'[17] – suggests a continuing interest in dodecaphonic method, containing as it does all twelve pitch-classes (Ex. 100). To be sure, it does not present them as an ordered set, but rather in the form of four trichords, and thus implies a rather different attitude to such material from that found in 'classical' serialism, or indeed in Takemitsu's own

Ex. 100   *Dream/Window,* 'harmonic pitch 1'

earlier practice. Nevertheless, the internal construction of this 'harmonic pitch' indicates that the care Takemitsu bestowed on the shaping of twelve-note series at an earlier period is still active in this less rigorous context. The collection is both symmetrical and 'hexachordally combinatorial': the trichord pairs a/d and b/c are in inversion relationship to one another, so that the whole of the second hexachord becomes a retrograde inversion of the first, and the pitch content of this second hexachord thereby yields a transposed inversion of the diatonic collection, [0,2,4,5,7,9], implied by the first.

The two other 'dream' pieces from this period also possess 'dual citizenship' in terms of Takemitsu's recurrent thematic preoccupations, both being simultaneously members of the 'waterscape' series. *Rain Dreaming* (1986) was written in response to a commission for a work for solo harpsichord for the Aliénor Awards held in Augusta. It is the composer's sole work for this instrument outside his film music, and one of its most striking properties is the fact that it demonstrates – by their very absence – all the qualities which otherwise lend such a supreme expressivity to his keyboard works. The absence of a sustaining pedal in particular deprives the writing of those resonance effects and shadings into silence which are so characteristic a feature of his piano music, while the almost total absence of dynamics from the *Urtext*-like score makes one all the more conscious of the scrupulousness with which Takemitsu usually notates every level and nuance of pianistic attack. As a result of these intrinsic limitations of the instrument, Takemitsu is constrained to offer much more of a 'note-by-note' discourse than is generally the case, and – perhaps in honour of the historical associations with which this instrument is invested – it is a discourse that is also more rigorously motivic and contrapuntal than usual, with particular emphasis on a three-note idea comprising a falling major second followed by rising perfect fifth.

The other work from the 1980s whose title conflates the same pair of references is *I Hear the Water Dreaming* (1987) for flute and orchestra, the last of Takemitsu's works from this period to incorporate a 'dream' allusion. Like the alto flute in *Rain Coming,* the solo flute here punctuates the form

Ex. 101   *I Hear the Water Dreaming*, 'C'/3–4

with a ritornello-like thematic marker, again generating a structure which is episodic and 'strophic' in character. This theme – of which a version for oboe is quoted in the upper system of Example 101 – is of considerable interest for a number of reasons. Not only does its incipit contain two typical Takemitsu gestures (the emergence out of 'silence', followed by a rising 'zig-zag' formula); it also projects, horizontally, a pitch-collection that is particularly favoured by the composer elsewhere as a vertical sonority, the set [0,2,3,4,6,8] (heard here in inversion), a subset of the ubiquitous '7-33' collection.

Although this derivation of horizontal, melodic materials from harmonic collections (and vice versa) is a standard procedure of twentieth-century composition, it is one not regularly favoured by Takemitsu, and it is therefore surprising to discover that the score of *Water Dreaming* offers quite a rich variety of applications of this device. But what is most striking about Example 101, of course, is the fact that the theme is here accompanied by its own inversion in rhythmic unison, thereby generating a 'mirror-image' structure analogous, on the vertical plane, to Takemitsu's palindromic constructions in the horizontal dimension – and one that is dramatically impressive visually, at that.

That both *Rain Dreaming* and *Water Dreaming* should share a preoccupation with 'dream' and 'water' is perhaps apt enough, considering that the two ideas did not stand so far apart in Takemitsu's mind, coalescing, for example, in the title of an essay by the French novelist Gaston Bachelard (1884–1962) he much admired, *L'Eau et les rêves*. They also converge in another work of twentieth-century literature of which Takemitsu was especially fond, whose narrative purports to represent a dreaming state, and is suffused by aquatic imagery: James Joyce's *Finnegans Wake*. *Far calls. Coming, far!* for violin and orchestra (1980), the first of Takemitsu's works to take its title from Joyce's novel, can thus be understood, as the composer puts it, as the 'confluence of the two series'[18] of water and dream; but it can also be understood, although the composer did not express it thus, as the first member of another thematic series: what Funayama has aptly described as the 'Finnegans Wake Triptych',[19] of which the other two members are *A Way a Lone* for string quartet (1981) and *riverrun* for piano and orchestra (1987).

Joyce's notoriously difficult final novel, from which these titles are quotations, might seem an unlikely source of inspiration for a composer such as Takemitsu, and not simply on account of the formidable problems it presents for a would-be Japanese reader. Euro- and logo-centric, Joyce's densely layered, multilingual complexity appears to lie at the opposite pole from Takemitsu's anti-academic aesthetics, and it is therefore no surprise to learn that the composer's reading of the work is a highly personal one. Indeed, precisely because 'it is so difficult for me to comprehend this almost unreadable novel in the original language' Takemitsu had 'no choice but to form my own image with the help of translation into Japanese and other literary commentaries'.[20] Although Poirier notes that the potential for word-play that exists in Japanese might have predisposed Takemitsu towards this aspect of Joyce's work,[21] the latter appears to figure less significantly in this 'image' of Takemitsu's than does the 'beautiful sound' of the language itself, as well as the imagery of dream and water already alluded to. It is also possible that *Finnegans Wake* may have appealed to Takemitsu on account of its incomplete opening and closing sentences: like those of the composer's own *Requiem*, the 'beginning and ending' of Joyce's book 'remain unclear'. Certainly all three of Takemitsu's titles derive from the very beginning or the very end of Joyce's narrative: *Far calls. Coming, far!* from its closing lines, *riverrun* and *A Way a Lone* from, respectively, its opening and closing sentences.

Far calls. Coming, far! Takemitsu noted, 'is, according to Mr Masayoshi Oshawa, the song Anna Rivia [*sic!*] (the Liffey) sings on joining Father Sea',[22] and elsewhere the composer explained more precisely how this watery self-annihilation was interpreted in musical terms. 'Father Sea' is of course, on one level, represented by Takemitsu's omnipresent 'S–E–A' motif, which is here further expanded by the addition of a series of rising thirds to create a characteristic pattern and its inversion, as shown in Example 102.

Takemitsu evidently liked this expanded version of his motif, for the

Ex. 102 Six-note idea and inversion, *Far calls. Coming, far!*

S   E   A

variant forms from both *Dreamtime* and *Paths* quoted in Example 91 make
use of precisely the same device of upward extension and, transposed, map
on to Example 102 exactly. According to the composer, this interest
stemmed from the tonal implications these piled-up thirds impart to the
original three-note idea: 'The A-major and D♭-major triads in the ascending pattern have a very bright sound when compared to the darker inversion, which, descending from A♭, had two minor triads, G–D–B♭ and
B♭–G♭–E♭. Using these patterns I set the "sea of tonality" from which many
pantonal chords flow.'[23] These remarks might lead the reader to expect
that Takemitsu uses these cascading thirds to derive vertical forms of
triadic construction with strongly tonal implications; after all, the illustration from *I Hear the Water Dreaming* proves that he could, on occasion, use
the same pitch-materials as source for both horizontal and vertical collections. It comes as something of a surprise, therefore, to discover that he
does not choose to exploit the obvious harmonic potential of the theme in
this fashion, but rather continues to adhere to his fairly standard procedure of treating 'theme' and 'harmony' as separate categories, each operating according to its own compositional rationale. Nevertheless, the
horizontal harmonic effect of these chains of thirds is palpable enough at
the aural level, and while this to a certain extent vindicates Takemitsu's
remarks about 'pantonal' chords, it also means that passages occur which
bear a striking resemblance to another classic of the twentieth-century
violin repertory, and one which uses very similar basic materials: Alban
Berg's Concerto. The resemblance is hardly fortuitous: since Berg's basic

Ex. 103 Comparison between materials from *Far calls. Coming, far!* and Berg, *Violin Concerto*, op. 24

Berg, *Violin Concerto*, P⁰

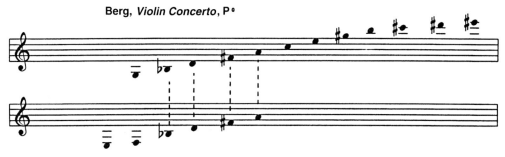

Takemitsu, S-E-A motif, transposed

Ex. 104 Comparison between materials from *Far calls. Coming, far!* and Berg, *Violin Concerto*, op. 24

Berg, R9

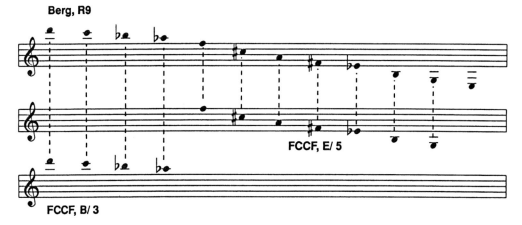

FCCF, E/ 5

FCCF, B/ 3

series, like Takemitsu's motif, contains chains of rising intervals of a third, alternately major and minor, it follows that a transposition of the latter will in part map on to the former, as Example 103 demonstrates.

One can in fact pursue the comparison further, for in certain instances Takemitsu extends the descending form of his theme downwards by the addition of three more intervals of a third, yielding a version which maps exactly on to seven notes of the retrograde of Berg's series. Furthermore, the four-note descent through the whole-tone scale at the beginning of the latter – inverse of the Bach *Es ist genug* tag – also has an exact counterpart at one point in Takemitsu's score, as shown in the third staff of Example 104. If this last comparison seems a little far-fetched, one has only to listen

Ex. 105 Comparison between Takemitsu, *A Way a Lone* and Berg, *Lyric Suite*

to the closing bars of both works, where in Takemitsu's case a muted horn, bassoon and harp descend through five notes of a whole-tone scale, in Berg's a muted horn through four. Takemitsu's indebtedness to Berg's example here surfaces to a level at which immediate aural comparisons become unavoidable.

One could argue that these references to Berg's model stem from the common preoccupation of both works with the symbolic 'self-extinction' of the soloist in some grander whole – Eternity, Father Sea. Less easy to explain, however, are the similarities which exist between the next member of the 'Joyce' triptych, *A Way a Lone*, and another Berg score: similarities nevertheless so striking that the *New York Times* critic could not fail to notice that 'the work's mood is constantly evocative of Berg's *Lyric Suite*'.[24] At one point in the score, in fact, this approximation to Berg once again almost takes the form of direct thematic quotation: in inversion, Takemitsu's 'S–E–A' motif is intervallically identical with the incipit of the twelve-note theme with which the second movement of the *Lyric Suite* opens, and the tie across the beat to a flowing semiquaver rhythm is also very similar in both cases (Ex. 105).

Besides such specific thematic similarities, there is a more general kinship between the two works: a sombre intensity created in both instances by the use of an expressive harmonic vocabulary, a variety of techniques of string playing, and a richly contrapuntal and thematic

Ex. 106   *A Way a Lone*, bars 8–9

texture. This last feature suggests at least one possible explanation for the emulation of Berg's example: the desire to create a musical language more appropriate to the 'seriousness' with which the string quartet medium – like the harpsichord of *Rain Dreaming* – has historically been invested. Certainly, *A Way a Lone* contains a few of the rare instances of genuinely contrapuntal writing in Takemitsu's music, such as the passages at bars 130 and 161, where all four instruments are given clear independent lines. Much of it is also more closely argued from tersely motivic ideas than is usually the case, amongst which, unsurprisingly, the 'S–E–A' motif and its various transformations loom large, again reflecting the origins of the title in Anna Livia Plurabelle's watery metamorphosis. One particular manner of using this idea is worth singling out for especial mention: the form shown in Example 106, in which an inversion of the 'S–E–A' tag is followed by a 'consequent' consisting of a new three-note idea, formed from a falling minor sixth plus rising semitone. Heard always at the same pitch relative to its 'antecedent', and appearing nowhere else, the idea lends to the five statements of this particular thematic pairing a certain stability and consistency which has the effect of foregrounding them as points of repose in the overall scheme: they become – on analogy with Takemitsu's 'referential' harmonies – 'referential thematic statements'.

A Way a Lone possesses at least one vertical 'referential sonority' as well, conspicuously identifiable as such because three of its statements – in bars 75, 88 and 141 – appear in the same guise of a sustained harmony with a crescendo–diminuendo envelope. The harmony here, [0,2,4,5,8], is also of interest because of its strong aural resemblance to another chord coincidentally quoted in Berg's *Lyric Suite*: a chord which is also the most famous 'reference sonority' in the whole literature, the opening chord of Wagner's *Tristan* ([0,2,5,8]). With its one added pitch, the 'superset' Takemitsu uses here sounds like a 'chromatically enhanced' version of the Wagnerian sonority, but elsewhere Takemitsu proved he was not embarrassed to quote the original harmony unembellished, and (on three occasions at least) at its original pitch: in *I Hear the Water Dreaming* (fourth bar of letter 'G'), *Tree Line* (second bar of letter 'F') and *Les yeux clos II* (bar 8).

Ex. 107 *Grass*, bar 15

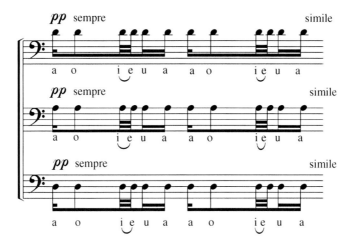

While 'garden form' may be abundantly present in works of this decade, the 'garden series' was referred to only twice in the titles chosen by Takemitsu in the 1980s: directly in the case of *A Minneapolis Garden* for tape (1986), more cryptically – as we have seen – in that of *Dream/Window*. Nevertheless, at least two of the elements from which a formal Japanese garden is composed were to provide sources for the titles of other works from this period. To the series which had been inaugurated with *Music of Tree* in 1961, and had continued with *Green* and *Eucalypts*, Takemitsu added further titles containing an arboreal reference in the shape of the 'dual citizen' work *Rain Tree* and *Tree Line* for chamber orchestra (1988). And in the title of a work from 1982, Takemitsu alluded to what, in the 1975 essay quoted at the beginning of chapter 5, had stood as symbolic opposite to the qualities 'trees' were said to embody: *Grass*, for male chorus.

Apart from *Wind Horse*, *Grass* constitutes Takemitsu's only 'serious' *a cappella* vocal work. Written for the Harvard Glee Club, it makes considerable technical demands on the performers, and although ostensibly a setting of a Shuntarō Tanikawa poem in English translation, in reality much of it consists of various wordless vocalisations and *bocca chiusa* effects, including a passage which suggests that the influence of Takemitsu's encounter with Stockhausen, a decade previously, might still be lingering. At all events, as the men's voices run through the whole gamut of vowel sounds on monotones, colouring them with variant harmonic spectra, the listener cannot but be reminded of the similar effects obtained in Stockhausen's *Stimmung* (Ex. 107).

Ex. 108 *Star-Isle*, bars 1–2

Tree Line was also written for a virtuoso ensemble, the London Sinfonietta, one at least of whose soloists is put under the spotlight at one point, when the flautist is requested to 'counter improvisation to the strings as bird's calling, not periodical with many spaces [*sic*]' – an instruction which demonstrates that the use of poetic verbal instructions as stimuli for improvisation, which had figured so largely in earlier works such as *Waves*, could also form part of the composer's vocabulary in the very different aesthetic climate of the late 1980s. The passage where this occurs is one of three in the score of *Tree Line* whose remarkably similar character serves an important function in the formal articulation of the work: in each of these sections (rehearsal letters 'B'–'C'; 'C'/7–'E' and 'H'–'I'), an essentially static background harmony is projected by means of such devices as long pedal notes, ostinati and 'aleatorically' repeated mobile materials, against which materials such as the flute solo appear in the guise of more 'foreground' events. It is perhaps these sections that Takemitsu is alluding to in the preface to the score when he notes that 'the music proceeds like a tapestry woven around D♮ and B♭ in various modes, along with its main line of tonal variation'; certainly, whatever this statement may mean, those two pitches – plus F♯ – are conspicuously present as multiple pedal points, or drones, in the three sections. Takemitsu's programme notes, like his remarks about *A Flock Descends*, thus provide further explicit corroboration of his interest in drone-like pedal points, and indeed one of the pitches used – the 'fixed pitch' F♯ – is of course common to both works.

The last of Takemitsu's 'themed' series of compositions to be considered here is the 'star' series, inaugurated with *Asterism* in 1967 and augmented in the following decade by the addition of *Cassiopeia* (1971) and the first part of *Gémeaux* (1971–86). This series was to receive two additions in the course of the 1980s. For a performance by the orchestra of Waseda University in Tōkyō to celebrate the university's centennial, Takemitsu wrote *Star-Isle* (1982), fulfilling the commission by using the same device which had generated the Bryce and 'S–E–A' themes. By turning the viable letters of the institution's title into their equivalent note-names, he arrived at the four-note cell with which the work opens, and which subsequently provides so much of its thematic content: w–As[= A♭]–E–D–A (Ex. 108).

The other work of the 1980s to reflect Takemitsu's 'sidereal' obsession in reality consists of two scores, both dating from 1984: *Orion* for cello and piano, and *Orion and Pleiades* for cello and orchestra. The former is a good example of the new instrumentalism of Takemitsu's later style, to which more attention will be given at the end of this chapter; the focus of interest lies very much with the long, rather *Requiem*-like extended *melos* of the cello line which, according to Ohtake, 'gradually becomes more defined, as in Orion's belt',[25] and although a reminiscence of Takemitsu's more 'experimental' years occasionally surfaces in passages of microtonal inflection, these function as expressive ornamentations to the essentially chromatic solo part, rather than as intrinsic features of the musical discourse. There are also one or two strong suggestions of a Messiaen influence, for example in the subsidiary theme which first appears in the piano at bar 34, with its characteristic five-note figure followed by a descending tritone final. Interestingly, as this idea is repeated in the course of the movement, the intervallic relationship between the second part of the theme and the first fluctuates, varying from a minor tenth above (Ex. 109a) to a perfect eleventh above (Ex. 109b) or a semitone lower (Ex. 109c). It is as though the tritone final were treated as an independent unit and transposed globally relative to the rest of the theme – a process analogous, on the horizontal level, to the wholesale transposition of segments of harmony by a different intervallic factor from the remainder which we have already observed in a vertical context.

Another of the idiosyncratic devices of Takemitsu's quirky compositional method is illustrated by the passage from *Orion* quoted in Example 110. His own remarks about 'throwing together' fragments 'as if in a dream' are peculiarly apposite here, for the material on the upper staff simply 'pastes together' two chord pairs heard already in completely separate contexts (both of which take the form of the composer's characteristic 'rising anacrusis' gesture). Moreover, the passage again illustrates Takemitsu's indifference to the logic of ordered succession: the order in which the chord pairings appear here is the reverse of that in which they have previously been heard – 'B' comes from bar 7, and 'A' from bar 3.

Takemitsu orchestrated the chamber original of *Orion* to form the first movement of *Orion and Pleiades*, adding two new movements to represent 'the aggregate nature of the constellation of the same name' and contrast it 'to the straighter line of *Orion*'.[26] While the first movement of the new

Ex. 109(a) *Orion*, bar 34

Ex. 109(b) *Orion*, bar 54

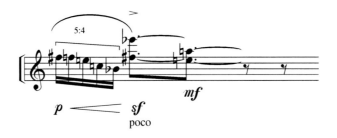

Ex. 109(c) *Orion*, bars 68–9

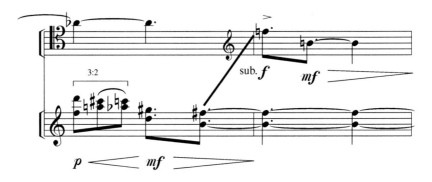

work consists of a fairly straightforward rescoring of *Orion*, however, the 'intermezzo' second movement '*and*' – in reality not the brief interlude its title might suggest – already contains in its second bar a chord that cannot be played by a pianist's two hands, pointing to a direct conception for orchestra. Clearly orchestral rather than pianistic in conception, too, is the passage beginning at letter 'D', in which a constant harmonic backdrop is

Ex. 110 *Orion*, bar 36

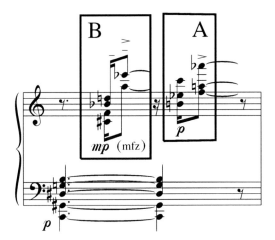

provided by the harp glissandi running through the pitches of a '6–20' ([0,1,4,5,7,9]) collection – a usage which suggests that the latter hexachord might on occasion be sufficiently 'scalar' in its effect to be nominated as an 'eighth mode of limited transposition' to complement Messiaen's other seven (Ex. 111).

The third and final movement, *Pleiades*, is another of Takemitsu's 'ritornello-like' conceptions, in which the opening material recurs at strategic points. Material from the original *Orion* movement also recurs for the first time here in the newly composed movements: bar 2 derives from bar 45 of *Orion*, the theme quoted in Example 109 turns up several times in the course of the movement (although only once with its characteristic tritone final), and the cello's cadenza is a reprise of its equivalent in the first movement. Alongside these reworkings, however, there are passages of new material, such as the oboe theme heard at letter 'G' (Ex. 112), which is representative of a thematic type found in a number of Takemitsu's scores from this period: similar examples may be located at letter 'C' of *Vers, l'arc-en-ciel*, *Palma* and letter 'L' of *To the Edge of Dream*. Recalling, ironically enough, the kind of 'Oriental' or 'Arabesque' *melos* to be found in certain Debussy scores, this theme constitutes another good example of the new instrumental style of Takemitsu's later work, to which attention must shortly be turned; although the continuing incorporation of certain 'extended' techniques – the characteristic 'N–O' patterns – indicates that lessons learned from the encounters with Bartolozzi's textbook and with musicians such as Heinz Holliger in the previous decade have not been entirely forgotten.

Ex. 111 *Orion and Pleiades* II D

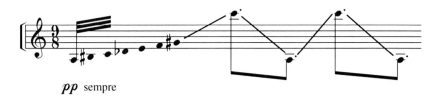

pp sempre

A new instrumental language

As suggested by Example 112, a new type of solo instrumental writing was beginning to emerge in Takemitsu's work over the course of these years – expansive and lyrical, with a greatly reduced role for the 'extended' techniques that had characterised his instrumental style of the previous decade. There was a convenient synchronism between this development and the fruits of Takemitsu's burgeoning international status – for now, commissioned to provide works for such glossy mainstream 'classical' soloists as John Williams, Julian Bream and Nobuko Imai in addition to his own circle of stalwart interpreters, Takemitsu was in a position to write for them without the least trace of stylistic disparity. Moreover, as other commentators have observed, the types of instruments in which Takemitsu was interested themselves underwent change as a result of this new interest in *melos* and the sustained line. Poirier, for instance, notes that – with one exception – there were to be no more works for traditional instruments after 1979, a phenomenon he directly attributes to the composer's increasing number of international commissions, and the difficulties involved in exporting specialist traditional musicians to fulfil them.[27] Narazaki, however, who also remarks upon Takemitsu's changed instrumental preferences, relates the phenomenon rather more to exclusively musical imperatives: 'the change in the selection of instrumental soloists', she believes, 'is related to the change in Takemitsu's style'.[28] In particular, she notes, the abandonment of such 'non-sustaining' instruments as piano, percussion and marimba in favour of instruments 'whose strong point is the production of sustained rather than short sounds' is, for her, 'an indicator of the degree to which the composer's textures have become dominated by song-like writing'.[29]

Some of the works reflecting this new lyricism have already been referred to in discussing the composer's 'themed' series; it remains to describe a few other works involving solo instrumental parts which do not appear to fall within any of the categories outlined. Two such pieces

Ex. 112 *Orion and Pleiades*, III/G

appeared in 1983, both owing their titles to a four-part series of linked verses which the Japanese poet Makoto Ōoka (already encountered as the source of the text for *Coral Island*) produced in collaboration with his English colleague Thomas Fitzsimmons. The title of their collective sequence – *Rocking Mirror Daybreak* – was bestowed by Takemitsu on a work for the two violinists Ani and Ida Kavafian; while a line from one of Ōoka's own contributions to the cycle, *In the Shadow*, served Takemitsu as the extravagant title of a test piece for violin and piano which he supplied for the Committee of the Second International Competition of Japan, Violin Division: *From far beyond Chrysanthemums and November Fog.*

Takemitsu would appear to have taken the 'shadowy' imagery of Ōoka's verses as a source of inspiration for the basic *materia musica* of *From Far beyond*. Like *Dream/Window*, this is one of the few Takemitsu scores regarding whose construction the composer gave specific hints, and – again like that earlier work – the compositional means described hint at a lingering application of techniques that might be described as *quasi*-serial. Admittedly, the composer's disclosure of a six-note set and its 'shadow' in the preface to the score mystifies as much as it reveals when one examines the actual surface details of the music, but nevertheless, it is once again possible to make a number of observations about the internal construction of this material *per se*. For instance, the 'shadow' hexachord is clearly so called because it functions as the chromatic complement of the initial

Ex. 113 *From far beyond Chrysanthemums and November Fog*, basic idea and its 'shadow'

six-note set (presumably rather as the black notes on the piano function as 'shadow' to the white ones). It is also the inversion of the first hexachord, and since both pitch-collections project a set much favoured by Takemitsu elsewhere – [0,2,3,4,6,8], a subset of the ubiquitous '7-33' collection – the net result of combining the two hexachords would be to produce a twelve-note series which once again is internally symmetrical on the one hand, and on the other projects materials favoured by Takemitsu in non-serial contexts (Ex. 113).

Nevertheless, despite Takemitsu's claim that 'the structure of the work is concise', with one or two exceptions few of the actual pitch-materials prove tractable to analysis in terms of the materials he presents as their underlying basis. Occasionally in this work, however – as in others by Takemitsu – one comes across passages which bear striking resemblances to one another, even though there would appear to be little or no obvious relationship between them in terms of pitch-content. To describe this more diffuse variety of kinship, it is perhaps appropriate to invoke something like the 'paradigmatic' analysis favoured by a certain type of musical scholar, and list the common features of those passages which are connected in spirit rather than according to the letter of the score. For example, any form of analysis which took absolute identity of pitch-content as its point of departure would be hard pressed to describe the relationship between the three passages illustrated in Example 114; yet the eye (and ear) immediately perceive in them convergences of a number of recurrent preoccupations:

(1) Each contains a 'rocking' ostinato figure on the interval of a diminished fourth.
(2) Each combines the figure with a drone-like, sustained pitch.
(3) These elements, combined together, always project a [0,1,4] pitch-collection, either in original or inverted form.
(4) One of the pitches is always an open string of the violin. In the case of the example from bar 6, it is one of the notes of the ostinato figure (A♮); in the other examples, it is the sustained pitch against which the ostinato is counterpointed (D♮ or A♮).

Ex. 114 Relationships in terms of common features, *From far beyond Chrysanthemums and November Fog*

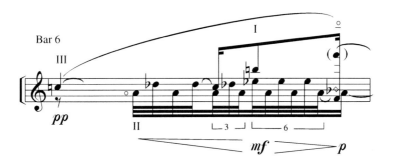

The next exemplar of Takemitsu's new instrumental manner to be considered, *Vers, l'arc-en-ciel, Palma* for guitar, *oboe d'amore* and orchestra (1984), was written to showcase the artistry of no less glamorous a figure than John Williams. His partner on the concert platform is entrusted the task of introducing the successive sections of the work with a recurrent theme, a function akin to that of the oboe in *A Flock Descends*; and, as with the latter work, the result is another form comprising a set of linked segments whose 'strophic' character may perhaps be alluded to in the 'verse' of Takemitsu's somewhat enigmatic title. Perhaps the 'rainbow' is also figured symbolically towards the close of the piece in the interjections for piccolo (Ex. 115), which, it will be observed – and somewhat unusually for Takemitsu at this period – are all cheekily 'palindromic' in construction.

Ex. 115   *Vers, l'arc-en-ciel, Palma,* letter 'P'

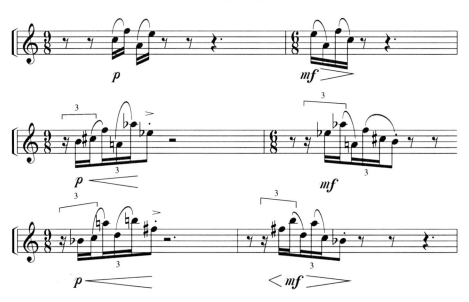

In honour of its dedicatee, the Catalonian artist Joan Miró (1893–1983), the score also contains another of Takemitsu's 'quotations' from an external source: a Catalan folksong, *La filadora,* here granted the appropriate two sharps of its D-major key signature when it appears towards the close of the work. The piece as a whole, indeed, has a decidedly tonal, or (to echo Takemitsu's preferred description) 'pantonal', flavour, in which a prominent role is assumed by what was becoming one of the composer's favourite harmonic devices: the 'panpentatonic' verticalisation [0,2,4,7,9]. Here it not only functions, as in so much 'late' Takemitsu, as signifier of final closure, but is also raised to the status of 'referential sonority' throughout the work, typically voiced in such a manner as to emphasise its relationship both with the cycle of fourths/fifths, and the quartally tuned open strings of the guitar, which in themselves of course also project a pentatonic collection. The latter relationship can clearly be seen from Example 116: Takemitsu's reference chord 'A' is a transposition up a perfect fourth of the first six pitches of 'B', which comprise those of the lowest five strings of the guitar, plus a doubling at the octave below of the uppermost B♮.

The anacrustic gesture with which *Vers, l'arc-en-ciel, Palma* opens itself contains a horizontal statement of four out of five pitch-classes of this 'reference sonority', with the remaining A♮ appearing at the top of the fourth chord in the bar (Ex. 117). Moreover, the stacked-up fourths interpolated

Ex. 116 *Vers, l'arc-en-ciel, Palma*: reference chord (A) and its derivation from open strings of guitar (B)

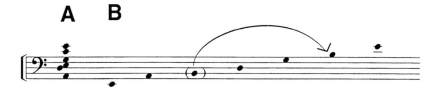

Ex. 117 *Vers, l'arc-en-ciel, Palma*, bars 1–2

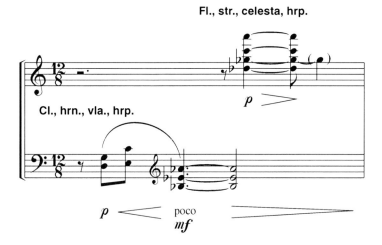

between these two segments of the harmony also constitute a statement of the same 'panpentatonic' collection at transposition T^6 – the phrase as a whole thereby projecting Messiaen's 'seventh mode of limited transposition'.

The rising-fourth incipit here may furthermore be intended to offer a distant foretaste of the work's major 'structural downbeat', the *Filadora* quotation shown in Example 118. As this example also suggests, there is evidence that in this case Takemitsu's very act of quotation may in itself be a 'quotation', and that the idea of using a folksong at this point might have been borrowed from the same model that is suggested by the work's pentatonic conclusion, as well as by a number of features of *Far calls* discussed above: Berg's *Violin Concerto*. Certainly, if one transposes Berg's theme into the same key as Takemitsu's, as in Example 118(ii), a number of thematic similarities emerge: the second phrase of Berg's theme contains both

Ex. 118 Comparison between themes from *Vers, l'arc-en-ciel, Palma* and Berg, *Violin Concerto*

(i) Takemitsu, *Vers, l'arc-en-ciel, Palma*,   0/2-5

(ii) Berg, *Violin Concerto*, II, bars 207-11 (transposed)

complete ('A1') and partial ('A2') statements of the segment labelled 'A' in Takemitsu's melody, and the falling-third figures at 'B' are also strikingly similar.

Vers, l'arc-en-ciel, Palma also contains fleeting reference to a rising octatonic arpeggio idea which is – although not explicitly acknowledged by the composer as such – like the 'S–E–A' theme a recurrent motif in a number of works from this period, as Example 119 shows.

Entre-temps (1986) for oboe and string quartet also owes its inspiration to an extra-musical source, in this case verse by that colourful figure from the French 'Dada' movement, Tristan Tzara (1896–1963). The work's origins thus have an affinity of sorts with those 'surrealist' influences that had operated on the composer since his very earliest years, and the piece

Ex. 119   Motivic type recurring in various late period works

(i) *Vers, l'arc-en-ciel, Palma* **(1984),**
bar 9, vln. + cl.

(ii) *I Hear the Water Dreaming* **(1987),**
L / 5

(iii) *Tree Line* **(1988), A / 2**

could perhaps be counted as an unacknowledged member of Takemitsu's 'dream' series; certainly his remarks that 'the piece is structured like a dream'[30] would suggest as much. However, while this remark might suggest a rather haphazard method of construction, Takemitsu elsewhere notes that its 'different episodes make their own way in the dark towards the morning twilight in the external form', and this suggestion that the work gravitates towards some kind of 'awakening' is perhaps borne out by a passage near the end (bars 126–9), where the strings repeat a one-bar ostinato four times against the oboe's independent materials. The sense of stasis projected by this ostinato – like that produced by the 'chaconne' at the end of *Poem II* in *Coral Island* – creates a sense of arrival for the listener, functioning as signifier for the work's imminent closure, which follows only a few bars later.

Extra-musical reference – to the eponymous painting by Paul Klee – also informs the title of *All in Twilight*, a set of four guitar pieces which Takemitsu wrote for another prestigious soloist, Julian Bream, in 1988. It is interesting to compare this work with Takemitsu's previous essay for solo guitar from thirteen years earlier, *Folios*; while, as described in the last

Ex. 120 Motivic type recurring in various late period works

(i) *A Flock Descends*
into the Pentagonal Garden (1977), E/9 (cl.)

(ii) *To the Edge of Dream*
(1983), Z/2 (solo guitar)

(iii) *Rocking Mirror Daybreak*
(1983), IV, bar 19, vln. 1

(iv) *All in Twilight*
(1988, solo guitar), II, bar 26

(v) *A String Around Autumn*
(1989), I/4 (solo vla.)

chapter, a certain 'A-minor' presence does indeed permeate *Folios* (most obviously in the shape of its Bach quotation), the tonal references of *All in Twilight* are much more overt. The last movement in particular, unequivocably centred around Ab major, with its chromatically descending bass lines at times even conveys a certain 'pop-like' unctuousness, suggestive of a crossover from Takemitsu's own arrangements of pop standards for this instrument.

All in Twilight also makes brief reference to another of the unacknowledged recurrent themes in Takemitsu's work of this period. Like Example 119, this is another octatonic idea, contrived from a three-note cell and its transposition at T^6 in such a manner as to suggest two dominant sevenths, a tritone apart (Ex. 120).

As Example 120 also shows, the motif figures additionally in the last of the works to be considered here, *A String Around Autumn* for viola and orchestra, written for Nobuko Imai and premièred by her at the 'Festival

Ex. 121 *A String Around Autumn*: basic scale

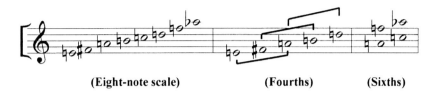

(Eight-note scale)   (Fourths)   (Sixths)

Ex. 122 Loosely related thematic types, *A String Around Autumn*

d'Automne à Paris' in 1989. Chosen because it conflates the twin ideas of this 'autumnal' festival and the 'string' soloist, the evocative title – again taken from the poetry of Makoto Ōoka – also, explained Takemitsu, refers to a musical analogue for the 'string' in the shape of an 'irregular eight-note scale which generates the work's melodic material'.[31] According to the composer, this 'nonce scale' derives from the conflation of two pitch-collections: a pentatonic scale on D, and a major–minor chord on F, elements derived respectively from overlapping perfect fourths and minor sixths, as illustrated in Example 121.

The presence of the first of these collections, at least, is readily detectable in the shape of the pentatonic and quartal basis of much of the thematic material, as can be seen from the selection of types shown in Example 122; despite their surface diversity, all these forms contain elements built up from various transpositions of this collection, or from a variant version built from overlapping perfect fifths.

Ex. 123 *A String Around Autumn*, J/1–2

At the opposite extreme from such loosely related thematic types, however, the score also contains a more stable pentatonic theme – a 'referential idea', in a sense, rather like the one already quoted from *A Way a Lone*. At each of its five appearances, this theme not only takes on the melodic shape shown in Example 123, but is also always accompanied by the same basic harmonic progression: a 'panpentatonic' ([0,2,4,7,9]) chord verticalising all the pitches contained in the first part of the thematic material in a 'minor' voicing, followed by a superset of the same harmony, [0,2,3,5,7,9] – this pair related in such a fashion that the pitch representing the '0' of the latter is a minor third higher than its counterpart in the former. Closer examination of the chord pair reveals the hidden presence of the whole of Takemitsu's eight-note scale as well, at transposition T^{11}: a 'D♭ pentatonic' scale in the first chord, followed by the pitches of an 'E-minor' triad in the violas and cellos in the second.

The particular unfolding of the essential pentatonic materials of *A String Around Autumn* shown in the viola part of Example 123 – whose characteristic three-note incipit interestingly recalls that of the *gagaku* classic *Etenraku* – in fact constitutes the basic 'theme' of the work. It also turns up again in *Visions* for orchestra, a work from the 1990s. But to describe this, and other works from the same period, it will be necessary to begin a new chapter: the last in this part of the book describing Takemitsu's music from a technical perspective, devoted to the final five years of the composer's life.

11 Beyond the far calls: the final years

By the year of his sixtieth birthday, 1990, Takemitsu's reputation as the senior Japanese composer of his generation had become an established feature of the international music scene. The prestigious circumstances of the *Visions* première – by the Chicago Symphony Orchestra, under Daniel Barenboim – typify the level at which his music was now accepted in the West. So too does the stream of high-profile engagements, awards and commissions that continued to fill his diary over the next few years. From the perspective of Western reception, in fact, it now rather seemed as if contemporary Japanese music *were* Tōru Takemitsu.

All this hectic activity, however, came to a sudden halt in the summer of 1995 with Takemitsu's collapse and admission into hospital. Even here, deprived of the opportunity for any other kind of work, he methodically kept a diary and devised a fantasy cookbook of outlandish recipes, charmingly illustrated with meticulous pencil sketches, both of which have recently been published in Japan.[1] Released from this spell of incarceration, his enthusiasm for all aspects of his creative life re-emerged unabated, but the reprieve proved short-lived. Takemitsu was readmitted to hospital, and there, on the afternoon of 20 February 1996, died of cancer, aged sixty-five – listening in his final hours, by some uncanny synchronistic coincidence, to a radio broadcast of the Bach work he loved above all others: the *St Matthew Passion.*

As the generous tributes that appeared in the world's obituary columns soon demonstrated, his premature death shocked the international artistic community. It also left one or two tasks on which he was working at the time of his death tragically incomplete. Most sadly of all, perhaps, it deprived the world of the opportunity to hear Takemitsu's first venture into the operatic medium; the première had been scheduled to take place in Lyon in the autumn of 1998, with the Swiss film director Daniel Schmidt in charge of production. Takemitsu had written a book on 'Making an Opera' a few years earlier in collaboration with his Nobel laureate friend, the novelist Kenzaburo Ōe,[2] but in the event the task of providing a text for Takemitsu's Lyon project fell to a rather more unlikely choice: Barry Gifford (1946–), the American 'beat generation' writer best known as the creator of *Wild at Heart: the Story of Sailor and Lula,* on which the screenplay of David Lynch's 1990 film is based.[3] His collaboration with

Takemitsu had advanced at least as far as the completion of a libretto, *La Madrugada* ('Dawn' or 'Daybreak'), which has apparently appeared in print (although it was unobtainable at the time of writing). It would seem, however, that Gifford's scenario is a story about whales – a subject dear to Takemitsu's heart too, as the next chapter will reveal more fully.

Takemitsu's composing activity in the previous decade had begun with *Far calls. Coming, far!* whose Joycean title had been rendered into Japanese by the composer as *Tōi Yobigoe no Kanata e!* In 1992, Takemitsu used this name again as the title for another of the collections of essays which he periodically published, but when literally retranslated back into English – as, for example, in Schott's catalogue of the composer's work – this title comes out somewhat differently from what Joyce originally wrote: *Beyond the Far Calls*. Inaccurate retranslation though it may be, the phrase might nevertheless conveniently stand as a symbol of Takemitsu's considerable composing output in these last few years: beyond Takemitsu's own 'Far Calls' of a decade earlier, post-'sea of tonality', post-transitional, maybe even (in the context of Takemitsu's own music, at least) 'post-post-modern'. It will be the task of this, the final chapter in this book to deal with specifically musical matters, to describe a few points of this 'late-period style' – of the works written when the composer had progressed a long way beyond the beginnings of a new language which pieces such as *Far calls* had embodied.

The works of the final years

In essence, Takemitsu's compositions of the 1990s are characterised by a continuation of the same basic 'third-period' style which had informed his music since the later part of the 1970s. As suggested above, however, there are certain senses in which they may also be thought of as constituting a special category within that basic overall definition. On the one hand, specific new preoccupations emerge in some of these works, which will be examined below. On the other, many of the typical features of the com-poser's 'third period' are exaggerated in these pieces, to a degree where it might be legitimate to speak of a specific 'late style' in which Takemitsu gives full rein to the 'Romanticism' towards which his music had been tending for over a decade. One has the suspicion at times, indeed, that the composer no longer cared what his critics thought, but as his life drew to a close, was allowing the latent tendency of his music towards a certain 'expressionism' (and even sentimentality) to flourish unashamedly.

In specifically musical terms, this 'exaggeration' of third-period style results, for example, in even more overt tonal references: for the most part, this is music that dwells unapologetically in the 'sea of tonality'. Thus Takemitsu no longer feels it necessary to end with anything as exotic as a panpentatonic verticalisation: a plain major triad will serve his purpose equally well, as at the Db-major close of *And then I knew 'twas Wind* (1992); or a common chord with some added pitches floating above like Messiaen's 'added resonances', as in *How slow the Wind* (1991), which ends in the same key. One also comes across passages written unequivocally within the parameters of classical tonality for extended periods: one such occurrence is the G-minor opening of the section marked 'Slightly Slower' (bar 42ff) in *Equinox* for solo guitar (1993). Despite such minor-key incursions, however, the overall impression gained from the freer use of tonality, and especially of major keys, in Takemitsu's late period is that the music wears a more genial, sunnier aspect than heretofore. It is almost as if, paradoxically, the '*Lento* composer' were discarding that trademark melancholy, the 'Takemitsu tone', that had characterised his music from his earliest years, precisely at the moment when his physical health was deteriorating and one might have expected his thoughts to take on an even darker hue than usual. Referring to its mysterious 'epilogue' with cascading woodwind sounds and a kind of 'clock-chime' effect for two *Almglocken*, Oliver Knussen once remarked to the audience before a performance of *How slow the Wind* that many of the composer's works seemed to 'end with a smile'. One could almost extend this metaphor to apply to the composer's career as a whole: just when it seemed he ought to be writing his own *Requiem,* Takemitsu was appending to the body of his creative work an 'epilogue' of decidedly positive outlook.

In addition to this more abundant use of tonal reference, a second characteristically 'counter-modernistic' tendency of Takemitsu's later music was its increased emphasis on *melos*. Admittedly, this was an aspect of music in which he had been interested since his very earliest work: according to Sukeyasu Shiba, it was his habit to sing musical ideas in the process of creating them,[4] while as early as 1975 the composer himself had observed that 'I probably belong to a type of composer of songs who keeps thinking about melody; I am old fashioned'.[5] Nevertheless, this 'thinking about melody' – often of a pronouncedly tonal flavour – came to occupy the foreground of his music much more palpably in the final years. The title of what was to be, in effect, the composer's 'swansong' – *Air* for solo flute (1995), his last completed score – contains an appropriate allusion to this preoccupation, referring not to the performer's breath but to the antique English equivalent of 'aria' (as in *Londonderry Air,* which the composer had arranged for guitar eighteen years previously). A similarly revealing allusion is also found in the second halves of the titles of

Fantasma/Cantos (1991), *Fantasma/Cantos II* (1994) and *Spectral Canticle* (1995), works for orchestra with, respectively, clarinet, trombone and violin plus guitar. It is illuminating, indeed, to compare the writing for the trombone in the second-named work with that of *Gémeaux*, written in the early 1970s: the model is no longer the tradition of avant-garde virtuosity embodied in the soloist for whom the earlier work was written, Vinko Globokar, but rather the suavely vocal trombone style of Jack Teagarden, a Dixieland musician whose records Takemitsu recalled his father playing in his childhood years.[6] Takemitsu was to admit to even more unlikely models than this, however, for the outpouring of song that characterised the close of his life. In the last interview he gave (with the pianist Noriko Ogawa for the BBC), the former 'avant-garde' musician was heard to assert that 'since the music of today is for some reason over-forgetful of song, learning from things of the past like Brahms – not turning back to the past, but creating new things – is, I think, very important for composers'.[7]

Both tonality and melody had, of course, long been employed with unambiguous directness in Takemitsu's 'lighter' works, such as his film or theatre scores or pop-song arrangements. There is thus often a sense, in these later works, that the barrier between the composer's 'serious' work and such peripheral activities has become at least permeable, if not on occasion abolished altogether. Such an impression is, in one instance at least, an accurate reflection of the truth: music written for the cinema *is* being admitted into the concert room without any attempt at makeover. In 1992 Takemitsu, whose *November Steps* had been written to commemorate the 125th anniversary of the New York Philharmonic Society, was asked to provide a new work to mark the 150th anniversary of that institution. The result was *Family Tree – Musical Verses for Young People* (1992), for narrator and orchestra to a text by Shuntarō Tanikawa: music which in its sumptuous luxuriousness stands as a revealing index of the degree to which Takemitsu's aesthetics had changed in the twenty-five years since the *November Steps* première. Much of the work – which has subsequently been presented by the NHK as a television drama – sounds, with its soaring string lines and functional harmonic accompaniments, like film music, and in fact this superficial impression on the listener's part turns out, in the final bars, to be literally true: the accordion melody which appears near the close is taken from a score which Takemitsu provided for Jim Jarmusch's *Night on the Planet*, but which was subsequently rejected by the director. The very use of the accordion here, of course, suggests a blurring of the boundaries between Takemitsu's film and concert work – although the composer had already used it once before in a 'serious' context, in a work entitled *Cross Talk* for two bandoneons and tape (1968).

Ex. 124 *Dream/Window*, 'harmonic pitch' 2

A further characteristic of Takemitsu's music of the 1990s is the degree to which the process of stabilisation, or normalisation, of musical language observed in the works of the 1980s has been pursued to a point at which there appears to be a certain interchangeability between one work and the next: they tend to sound, to quote Oliver Knussen, as if 'all cut from the same gently hedonistic roll'.[8] Although, as Knussen himself observes, Takemitsu himself thought otherwise and regarded each new piece as 'something very different', one can understand the listener's perplexity – especially when so many works from this period, as we shall soon see, audibly share thematic materials. Perhaps the wisest course for the confused listener might be to suspend entirely Western expectations of a self-contained musical discourse, proper to each individual work, and instead regard each piece as a tour around another musical 'garden', many of whose contents are drawn from the same basic repertory of musical 'paradigms' as those of coeval Takemitsu works. Certainly, the composer's own remarks about gardens suggest that he regarded their permeability to the outside world as one of their most appealing features; the garden, he claimed in a film interview towards the end of his life,[9] does not reject things from outside itself, and Takemitsu's musical 'gardens' are able to accommodate 'things outside themselves' too: fragments of other pieces by Takemitsu, even fragments of pieces by other composers.

Thus – to speak of self-quotation first – *Quotation of Dream – Say sea, take me!* for two pianos and orchestra (1991) refers back to material already employed in *Dream/Window*: in addition to the 'harmonic pitch 1', quoted in the previous chapter, also using 'harmonic pitch 2', a characteristic 'zig-zagging' figure (Ex. 124).

More confusingly, *How slow the Wind*, *And then I knew 'twas Wind* and *Archipelago S.* for twenty-one players (1993) are all interrelated by means of shared thematic materials. The first half of the principal melodic idea of *How slow the Wind* (Ex. 125a) appears again in *And then I knew 'twas Wind* (Ex. 125b), and its second phrase in *Archipelago S.* (Ex. 125c); while the first phrase of Example 125c, though not identical with its counterpart in the other works, shares with them its basic circular shape and final falling

Ex. 125 Comparison between themes from Takemitsu works of the 1990s

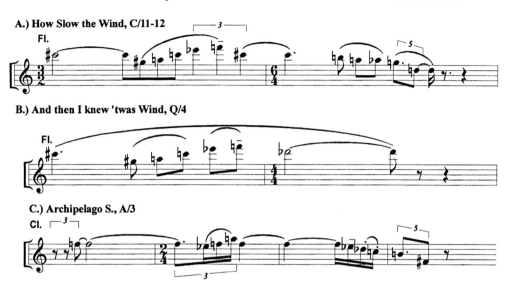

A.) **How Slow the Wind, C/11-12**

B.) **And then I knew 'twas Wind, Q/4**

C.) **Archipelago S., A/3**

third. Perhaps too, in the case of *How slow the Wind* and *And then I knew 'twas Wind*, whose titles are taken from the poetry of Emily Dickinson, the shared motivic material was intended to reflect the reference to 'wind' in both quotations – although at the same time, Takemitsu clearly did not fail to take into account the fact that the verse from which the first title is taken continues 'how slow the sea'. The relevant 'S–E–A' motif thus also appears in this work, at one point in minims as an accompaniment to a statement of the theme of Example 125a.

There is also a second, less obvious, motivic idea which recurs repeatedly in a number of scores from the 1990s, and which is particularly prominent in *Between Tides* (1993): Example 126 gives a number of instances of its occurrence.

In addition to such self-reference, however, there are also in these late works of Takemitsu one or two quotations from external sources, of the kind that had occasionally been found in works from early years. Without a doubt the most spectacular of these borrowings – more shocking for the listener even than the *Abiyoyo* interpolations in *Wind Horse* – are those to be found in *Quotation of Dream*, a work which appropriates substantial passages of Debussy's *La Mer* wholesale, as well as reworking materials from the latter work in the context of Takemitsu's own original composition. At the opposite extreme of subtlety from this 'schizo-eclectic'[10] confection, however, the viola part of *And then I knew 'twas Wind* incorporates

Ex. 126 Comparison between themes from Takemitsu works of the 1990s

a brief allusion to Debussy's *Sonata for flute, viola and harp* – a quote so well concealed that Takemitsu was obliged to draw attention to its provenance through a note in the printed score. On the other hand, of course, the entire instrumentation of this work is itself a 'quotation' from Debussy's *Sonata* – and an unmistakable one at that.

As these occasional uses of quotation illustrate, Takemitsu's final scores continue to embody many of the preoccupations familiar from his earlier work. Thus, to take another example, Takemitsu continues to explore the 'garden' metaphor as a pattern for overall formal organisation, explicitly drawing attention to this in his remarks on *Fantasma/Cantos* and in the title of *Spirit Garden*, an orchestral work dating from 1994. *Spirit Garden* also demonstrates that Takemitsu's interest in dodecaphonic construction was by no means dead, even at this late stage in his career: not only is it in part based upon a twelve-note series, but Takemitsu for the first time in his programme notes explicitly acknowledged this fact: 'The work is based on a twelve-note row from which three chords each of four notes are generated. These chords, accompanied by changes in tone colour . . . are an ever-present undercurrent, vibrating at the fundamental, from which a musical garden is composed.'[11]

As our examinations of the manner in which Takemitsu uses twelve-note materials in *Sacrifice* and *Dream/Window* have already shown, this treatment of the series as a resource from which harmonic materials may be fashioned, rather than as a definitive linear ordering principle, is highly typical of the composer. In the case of *Spirit Garden*, as Miyuki Shiraishi explains in her liner notes for the recording,[12] the harmonic materials are

Ex. 127 Basic chords of *Spirit Garden*

obtained by extrapolating pitches from the basic series by means of skips of regular size, in a manner that suggests a new interest in late Takemitsu for the kind of numerological 'constructivism' that also fascinated the composer of *Lulu* in his final years. Here, by selecting in turn pitches 1-4-7-10, 2-5-8-11 and 3-6-9-12 from the ordered twelve-note set A–B♭–E–E♭–D–A♭–G–F♯–C–B–C♯–F, Takemitsu arrives at the three four-note forms shown in Example 127.

One notes that this whole process has somehow been engineered to result in a derivative series whose internal construction once again reveals certain symmetries, and which also contains harmonic materials favoured by the composer in other contexts. In this instance, the second and third chords stand in inversion relationship to one another, while each chord consists of an augmented triad plus one extraneous pitch – these three extraneous pitches in turn forming the augmented triad needed to complete the chromatic collection. There is thus a strong affinity between these materials and the type of series already encountered in *Hika*, based on the division of the total-chromatic into four augmented triads, or in other words into two statements of Takemitsu's favoured '6-20' collection. A similar type of construction is used to generate the basic pitch-materials of *And then I knew 'twas Wind*, which are again based upon two '6-20' hexachords: F–G♯–A–C–C♯–E and D♯–F♯–G–B♭–B♮–D. In this case, however, the manner in which this division of the total-chromatic is handled is far from serial. First, Takemitsu does not use his hexachords as a definitive ordering principle, but instead appears to take delight in deriving as many permutations as possible of the pitches of the first of the two six-note sets quoted above, as for example in the opening bars. Secondly, while there is continued reference to the pitches of this primary hexachord throughout the work, its chromatic complement is never heard in full at any point, but rather used simply as a resource from which pitches are selected to add varied harmonic colour to the pitches of the first hexachord – in a manner which recalls Takemitsu's remarks about the six pitches and their 'shadow' in *From far beyond Chrysanthemums and November Fog*. Takemitsu thus successfully avoids the harmonic 'sameness' that might otherwise result from the consistent use of the '6-20' collection (and which is such a

Ex. 128 *And then I knew 'twas Wind*, O/9–10

conspicuous feature of certain dodecaphonic works by other composers constructed on the basis of that form); moreover, his chosen method allows him such freedom that he is able to quote the *Leitmotiv* of *How slow the Wind* in parallel major thirds, and still remain faithful to his basic constructional premises. The pitches of the resultant phrase all lie within the primary hexachord, with the exception of the additional 'colouring' of two pitches drawn from its chromatic complement, shown in brackets in Example 128.

In addition to such quasi-'serial' practices, one or two other preoccupations of Takemitsu's more adventurous years continued to resurface from time to time in his later works. For example, spatialisation of the instrumental ensemble – and indeed a theatricalisation of the performative act that was probably the most dramatic Takemitsu ever attempted – both reappear to spectacular effect in *From me flows what you call Time* (1990), a work for orchestra and five percussionists, who operate distant bells distributed throughout the auditorium by means of lengths of coloured tape. A spatial dimension is also present in *Ceremonial – An Autumn Ode* for *shō* and orchestra (1992) – the sole work of Takemitsu's later years to use a traditional Japanese instrument – where three duos of flutes and oboes are placed to the left and right of the stage, and behind the audience. Such an arrangement recalls the distribution of forces of *In an Autumn Garden*, a work from which Takemitsu actually quotes here, using the beautiful Dorian theme already cited in Example 87 as a principal thematic source.[13] The stage layout of *Archipelago S.*, written in the following year for performance by the London Sinfonietta at Snape Maltings, also recalls that of *In an Autumn Garden*; though in this instance, the twenty-one players required for performance – grouped into five 'islands' of which two (the twin clarinet soloists) are placed to the rear of the auditorium – really do place the work's listeners in the midst of a 'pentagonal garden' of sound.

It is easy to see – especially from such examples as the exquisite off-stage chiming effects of *From me flows what you call Time* – how these spatial interests could survive Takemitsu's conversion to his later, more 'audience-friendly' manner after so many of the more abrasive experiments of his middle years had been abandoned. For similar reasons, the composer's emphasis on the importance of instrumental colour was another quality that remained a consistent feature of his music. For the most part, it is true, his last works had rather less use than heretofore for the kind of extended instrumental techniques that had characterised the work of his more experimental years – though they were far from dispensed with entirely, as such effects as the harpist's tuning-key glissandi in *And then I knew*, or the scordatura of the guitar in *Equinox* (1993) indicate. On the other hand, however, the composer's skill in a more conventional form of timbral expertise – the achievement of rapturous orchestral sonorities by means of the skilful blending of instrumental colours – reaches in these last works its apogee. In an interview given as late as 1988, the composer had expressed a wish 'to study . . . orchestration with someone else';[14] faced with the staggering orchestral competence of these late works, fruit of a lifetime's practical experience in the film studio and concert hall, one can only assume Takemitsu was here being either ironic, or fanatically modest.

In addition to this ultimate refinement of ensemble scoring, the late works continue to demonstrate the composer's skill in writing for solo instruments, and, as in the past, often reflect Takemitsu's personal association with particular instrumental artists. For example, the solo percussion parts of *From me flows what you call Time* were conceived for the Canadian ensemble Nexus, and *Ceremonial* was written for the young Japanese *shō* soloist Mayumi Miyata. For Nobuko Imai, the violist who had premièred *A String Around Autumn*, Takemitsu went on to write *A Bird came down the Walk* for viola and piano, basing it on the oboe theme and opening chord progression of *A Flock Descends into the Pentagonal Garden* – the theme explicitly identified by the composer as representing the 'flock' in the earlier work thus symbolising the 'bird' of the latter.[15] The soloist who had commissioned Takemitsu's first work for guitar – Kiyoshi Shōmura – also received a further gift in the 1990s in the shape of *Equinox*, a work which, like *Vers, l'arc-en-ciel, Palma*, draws its inspiration from the work of Joan Miró. (The Catalan artist was also to suggest the title for a commission from the BBC which remained incomplete at the time of Takemitsu's death: *Comme la sculpture de Miró*). And Shōmura was to be further honoured two years later as the dedicatee of *Rosedale*, the second movement of the solo guitar piece *In the Woods* (1995), whose remaining two movements likewise bear dedications to performers who had become intimately associated with Takemitsu's guitar music: John Williams (the

Ex. 129 *Les yeux clos*, p. 2, system 1, bar 2

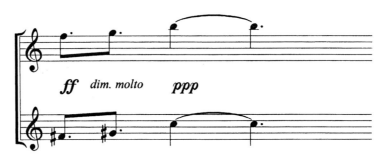

first movement, *Wainscot Pond*) and Julian Bream (the final movement, *Muir Woods*).

But alongside such expressions of gratitude for living contemporaries, with the passing of the years and the death of many of his most revered colleagues, Takemitsu's scores were increasingly to be prefaced by dedicatory remarks of an altogether more sombre hue. Reverence for the dead is of course a prominent feature of Japanese culture, and it is therefore hardly surprising that a Japanese composer – especially one of such a melancholy cast of mind as the '*Lento* composer' – should reflect this general preoccupation by producing several works of memorial or funerary character. It might be appropriate, therefore, to end the discussion of Takemitsu's music by considering another 'series' of works linked by a common 'theme': a theme to which the composer never drew explicit attention, but which nevertheless was to prove more insistent than any other, occupying him – it could be argued – for nearly forty years of his creative life.

Epitaphs

The more recent part of this creative history begins in 1979, with the death of Takemitsu's long-serving mentor, Shūzo Takiguchi. In memory of Takiguchi, Takemitsu wrote a short piano piece which took its title from a monochrome lithograph by Odilon Redon (1840–1916) he had seen in a Chicago Art Gallery eleven years earlier: *Les yeux clos*. The mysterious 'closed eyes' of the female figure depicted by the French symbolist artist thus also become those of the Japanese surrealist poet, sealed now forever in the dream of death. There are perhaps hidden references to Takiguchi, too, on a more purely musical level. At least, as Noriko Ohtake has pointed out, one of the principal thematic ideas of *Les yeux clos* – a striking three-note motif, powerfully stated in parallel major sevenths (Ex. 129) – is iden-

Ex. 130 *Les yeux clos II*, bar 1

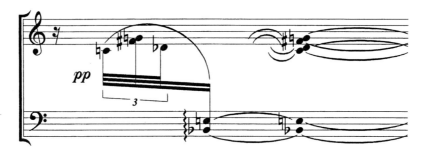

tical with the uppermost voice of the sequence of block chords from *Uninterrupted Rest* quoted in chapter 4, Example 25, when they reappear in retrograde later in the movement. Since *Uninterrupted Rest* takes its title directly from a verse by Takiguchi, Takemitsu is possibly encoding here a cryptic signature of *Les yeux clos'* dedicatee.

Redon produced three versions of his lithographic image, two in mono-chrome and one in colour, and Takemitsu was to emulate this three-part scheme by the addition of two subsequent works to his 1979 original. The first, another 'monochromatic' essay for piano solo, was *Les yeux clos II*, written in response to a commission from Peter Serkin in 1988. While it does not quote directly from its eponym, this later work nevertheless pro-claims its kinship to the original *Les yeux clos* by the inclusion of a three-note motif closely related to Example 129: first heard in the form A–B–F, it consists in effect of a reordered inversion of the same basic [0,2,6] collection as the above. For whatever reason, *Les yeux clos II* also makes repeated use of a short octatonic idea that was subsequently to reappear as a con-stant feature of a work written in the following year, *A String Around Autumn* (Ex. 130).

The third instalment of Takemitsu's Redon triptych – analogue to the artist's 'colour' version of the lithograph – was the second movement of *Visions* (1990): entitled simply *Les yeux clos*, it is an orchestral version of the 1979 piano work. Unlike the translation of *Orion* to the orchestral medium that forms the first movement of *Orion and Pleiades*, however, it is much more than simply an 'orchestration' of the original. Takemitsu here effects substantive alterations to the musical text in the process of reworking: in particular, he adds barlines and makes considerable rhythmic changes, subjects materials to transposition and reordering, adds new material in some places and in others omits material from the original. Of particular interest is the manner in which certain elements of this orchestral rewriting attempt to imitate some of the effects of the piano version: sustaining pitches beyond their original notated durations to replicate resonance effects and create new melodies, differing voice-leadings or sustained harmonies. This is especially telling at the end of the work, where the performance direction of the piano original – 'let ring throughout the piece' – is simulated by the use of an off-stage bass trumpet doubled on stage by bass flute, harps and celesta, eloquently revealing the degree to which the decay of sound in time, and the illusion of space created by such resonance, were intimately linked in the composer's mind.

Nostalghia for violin and string orchestra (1987), the next of Takemitsu's musical memorials to appear, derives its title – and its Italianate spelling – from a 1983 Italian–Soviet co-production by the Russian film director Andrei Tarkovsky (1932–86), to whose memory it is dedicated. Written for yet another high-profile soloist, Yehudi Menuhin, it possesses a distinctly more overt funerary character than either of the pieces described above – a quality that in part derives from a number of characteristics it shares with the much earlier *Requiem for Strings*. Most obvious is the very use of the string orchestra in itself; the work's extremely slow opening tempo, and instruction 'Calm and mournful, entirely rubato' also suggest an affinity with the *Requiem*, as does the manner in which the work begins with a single pitch, C♯, emerging out of the 'stream of sound'. But Takemitsu additionally appropriates more specific musical symbols of mourning from his earlier *déploration*: most obviously, he again favours harmonic forms built up from superimpositions of triads, and specifically of augmented triads, which yield verticalisations of the '6-20' form and its subsets, strongly recalling the type of sonority quoted above in Example 13 (chapter 4). For all that, this is a work from Takemitsu's 'third period', and in consequence the harmonic language is at times much more straightforwardly 'tonal' than that of the *Requiem*. For example, the first two chords accompanying the main theme when it is introduced by the solo violin at bar 5 – a C-minor triad and F-minor seventh in second inversion – constitute harmonic types which it is unlikely that the composer would have permitted himself to use in so direct a manner in 1957.

Augmented-triad superimpositions also appear at one point in Takemitsu's next musical elegy, *Twill by Twilight* for orchestra (1988), written to mourn the loss of the American composer Morton Feldman (1926–87). The passage in question, Example 131, actually provides an exemplary illustration of the relationship between the augmented triad, the '6-20' collection, and Messiaen's third mode of limited transposition – eloquently revealing the degree to which Takemitsu was consciously aware

Ex. 131 *Twill by Twilight*, 'G'/9

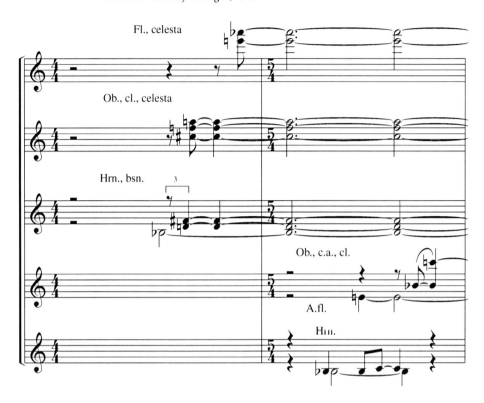

of their connection. Here, Takemitsu places two augmented triads above one another in the first bar to generate a '6-20' hexachord, and then adds the pitches of a third augmented triad – E, A♭, C – to produce a full vertical statement of the pitches of 'Mode III³', with two notes – B♭ and C – doubled at the octave. Attention should also be drawn to the characteristic 'rocking' figure played by the horns and woodwind in the second bar of this example. Repeated as an ostinato in the opening bars of the work, it subsequently reappears on no fewer than eight occasions, thus acquiring something of the role assumed by the oboe and alto flute themes in delineating sections in, respectively, *A Flock Descends* and *Rain Coming* – in other words, again functioning after the fashion of a ritornello.

Like *Asterism*, *Twill by Twilight* derives its enigmatic title – perhaps Takemitsu's own attempt at a kind of Joycean word-play – from one of the more obscure entries in the English dictionary. 'Twill' is a type of woven material, and besides referring to the manner in which Takemitsu's own 'ritornello' theme weaves its way through the piece, the choice of this word is also perhaps an affectionate allusion to Feldman's fascination with carpets. Interestingly enough, the same metaphor that Takemitsu indirectly suggests here had already been applied to his later music six years before *Twill* was composed: writing in 1982, Dana Richard Wilson observed that the composer's more recent works could be likened 'to a Persian tapestry, while the earlier [i.e. 'pointillist'] works are like the paintings of Seurat or Pissarro'.[16] However, while Takemitsu's title might hint at a shared interest with Feldman, his own 'textures' are very different from the sparse, ascetic lines of the American composer's work. Much of the harmonic and instrumental language of *Twill*, indeed, might best be described as lushly impressionistic – nowhere more so, perhaps, than in the passages at E/4-5 and L/5-6, where, over a pedal C♮ (the 'tonal centre' with which the work will conclude) pairs of massively scored chords swell and recede, interwoven with cascades of figuration for flutes and celesta and harp glissandi, and underpinned by crescendo–diminuendo patterns for percussion. The effect as a whole is rather as if these two climactic bars had strayed here from the orgiastic finale of Ravel's *Daphnis and Chloë* – a rare instance of a palpable influence of that other great 'French impressionist' master on Takemitsu. The latter, it is true, had certainly known Ravel's music since his earliest days, since he recalled performing it on his rented Pleyel piano;[17] but in general – apart from isolated instances such as the above – there is little evidence of its influence in the composer's mature music.

The deaths of the Japanese-American sculptor Isamu Noguchi (1904–88) and the artistic director of the London Sinfonietta Michael Vyner (*d.* 1989) were the next to be commemorated by Takemitsu. For Noguchi, the composer wrote *Itinerant* for solo flute, first performed by Paula Robison in 1989; while alongside numerous tributes by other composers, Michael Vyner was to be honoured with two works by Takemitsu. One of these, *Litany* for piano (1990), has already been remarked upon in the discussion of the composer's 'début' composition *Lento in Due Movimenti*, of which it is a 'recomposition from memory'. The other, *My Way of Life* (1990), which Vyner had commissioned for the Leeds Festival before his death, is for the unique combination of baritone solo, chorus and orchestra, sung to a text by Ryūichi Tamura in English translation. It is a vastly different work from the only remotely comparable previous offering of Takemitsu, *Coral Island* for soprano and orchestra, which dates from the period of the composer's intensest engagement with modernist gesture. In contrast to the angular, dissonant vocal line of *Coral Island*, the solo part of *My Way of Life* is suave, slow moving and melodic; generally undemonstrative and syllabic, it forms an effective foil to the more pas-

Ex. 132 *Rain Tree Sketch II*, opening

sionate outbursts of the chorus, which clearly reflect the skill Takemitsu had acquired in handling this medium in the *a cappella* songs of *Uta*. Takemitsu's plans for a first opera were curtailed by his untimely death, but it may be that in *My Way of Life* we have a reasonably approximate image of what parts of that projected opera might have sounded like.

The following few years – those immediately preceding Takemitsu's own death – were to take their toll on some of his most esteemed colleagues in the international composing community. John Cage and Olivier Messiaen both died in 1992, to be followed two years later by Witold Lutosławski, and while Takemitsu did not leave a musical tribute for Cage, he was to commemorate the deaths of both of these other leading musicians. For Messiaen he wrote *Rain Tree Sketch II* for piano (1992), another comparatively late addition to the 'Waterscape' series. Given the circumstances of its dedication, it is highly appropriate that in this work Takemitsu should make his usual frequent references to Messiaen's modal system – although at the same time it is rather ironic that the opening bars of the piece (Ex. 132), which certainly sound as if they ought to derive from one of the Messiaen scales, are in fact not based on any of the 'modes of limited transposition' at all, but rather on one of the scales of George Russell's system, the harmonic major or 'Lydian Diminished' (here used at the same transposition as in the 'upbeat' figure from *Coral Island* quoted earlier, D–E–F♯–G–A–B♭–C♯).

Marked 'Celestially Light', this opening material recalls at least the general atmosphere of the earlier *Rain Tree Sketch*, even if the two works bear no obvious thematic relationship to one another: like its namesake,

Ex. 133 *Paths*, p. 6 system 4

the second *Rain Tree Sketch* is a study in brittle sonorities and high tessi-
tura, to such a degree that pitches in the bottom register, when they do
appear, acquire the status of major events. The music thus has no real 'bass
line' for the most part, only isolated pedal notes; and significantly, all of
these isolated bass events in *Rain Tree Sketch II* consist of the pitch D♮ –
clearly the 'tonal centre' of the work, as the material quoted in Example
132 implies.

Lutosławski's memorial was to take a form unique in Takemitsu's
output: *Paths* for solo trumpet, written for performance by Håkan
Hardenberger at the Warsaw Autumn Festival in 1994. The work displays
an unusually tight motivic organisation, weaving its extended melodic
lines out of a number of short generative cells – amongst which the S–E–A
motif, extended upwards by means of piled-up thirds as in *Far calls*, is here
making what is possibly its farewell appearance in Takemitsu's music.
Though unusual, such a technique had by no means been without precedent in Takemitsu's work, and at one point at least, the melodic construction of *Paths* closely echoes one of the processes used to generate the
melodic line of *Distance de Fée* forty-three years earlier. In a similar
fashion to that illustrated by Example 8, the passage quoted in Example
133 uses statements of two motivic forms, overlapping one another via the
use of common pivotal pitches, to generate a series of 'sequential' statements, each one a minor third higher than that previous to it.

Paths was to be the last in Takemitsu's series of musical epitaphs: less
than eighteen months after its première the composer himself had passed
away. Yet at the same time, the list of Takemitsu's musical *tombeaux* does
not in a sense end here; nor, indeed, as suggested at the very beginning of
this section, did it begin with *Les yeux clos* either. For, over twenty years
before composing *Les yeux clos*, Takemitsu had written the first of his
musical memorials, *Requiem for Strings*, in memory of Fumio Hayasaka.
And by later hinting that he himself might be a second dedicatee for this
piece, Takemitsu effectively bequeathed his own *Requiem* to the musical

world when he died in 1996. Certainly it would appear to be in this sense that the *Requiem* has been received since the composer's death, to judge by the numerous commemorative performances of it – as *Requiem* for both Hayasaka and Takemitsu, simultaneously first and last in the sequence of Takemitsu's musical memorials.

12   Swimming in the ocean that has no West or East

By choosing a scenario about whales for his abortive opera project, Takemitsu was reflecting a preoccupation that had long been dear to his heart. More than once in his final years – for example in a letter sent to Peter Serkin a few days before his death – he expressed a wish to 'get a more healthy body as a whale' and 'swim in the ocean that has no west and no east'.[1] Takemitsu's choice of words here evokes more than simply his whimsical intention to be reincarnated as a whale; it is also poetically suggestive of his lifelong quest as an artist for a kind of cultural transcendence, an internationalism of outlook. In this final chapter, I propose to discuss the degree to which Takemitsu may have been successful in the realisation of more general, aesthetic goals of this sort, and thus try to arrive at some kind of critical assessment of his status as a composer.

It is important at the outset of any such discussion to draw attention to the precise wording of Takemitsu's wish: he wishes to swim in an ocean that has *neither* West *nor* East, not in one that somehow links the two. One still comes across the misunderstanding that Takemitsu saw himself in some way as a bridge between these two cultures, perhaps because the early success of *November Steps* left some listeners with the indelible impression that his life's work was devoted to reconciling the differences between the symphony orchestra and the *shakuhachi*. Takemitsu himself, however, explicitly denied any such intention; as he once expressed it: 'It would not be so difficult to adopt traditional Japanese music into Western music or to blend both. I am not, however, interested in either of these possibilities'.[2] Rather, as his 'whale' metaphor illustrates, Takemitsu regarded his role as assisting at the birth of a culture that transcended such polarities, that was truly global and internationalist. Such a role, and indeed such an image of birth, are explicitly suggested by another of the composer's favourite metaphors, borrowed from the American architect and sociologist Richard Buckminster Fuller (1895–1983). 'There is no doubt, as Buckminster Fuller pointed out', explained Takemitsu, 'that from the early twentieth century . . . the various countries and cultures of the world have begun a journey toward the geographic and historic unity of peoples. And now all of us, individually and collectively, share in incubating that vast universal cultural egg.'[3]

Yet, despite such utopian visions of a cultural future that was global and pluralist, Takemitsu was at the same time keenly aware of the cultural contradictions of the present, and in particular of his own ambivalent identity as a Japanese composer working within a Western musical tradition. This was an inescapable fact of his geographical and historical position: as one commentator aptly puts it, 'it is unavoidable that any Japanese professional musician, who composes or performs in the realm of Western art music, has to confront the problem of how to identify himself as a Japanese'.[4] The history of Takemitsu's artistic development is therefore in part the history of precisely such a confrontation: beginning, in its earliest phase, with almost total rejection of all things Japanese, passing through a period of experimental confrontation of the two traditions, and finally arriving at a more thoughtful integration of Japanese elements within a fundamentally Western composing style, in mature works 'where the two cultures are no longer separately identifiable'.[5] In this sense, therefore, it is legitimate to consider Takemitsu as one of the many heirs of Shūji Izawa in his quest for what was to prove the 'holy grail' of subsequent generations of Japanese musicians: the resolution of the 'double structure' in the Japanese psyche, the assimilation of native Japanese and Western traditions into some sort of unity. And, in turn, it is also legitimate to consider to what extent he may have succeeded or failed in that problematic task.

The general consensus of opinion would appear to be that Takemitsu scored a singular success in this matter – discovering a personal symbiosis of the two cultures which deserves to be ranked as one of his most significant artistic achievements, and whose elegance certainly far surpasses that of the solutions adopted by previous generations of Japanese composers. Thus Koozin, for example, observes that 'strongly identifying himself both as a Japanese and as a composer in the Western sense, Takemitsu projects in his music a maturity of personal expression which transcends the hybrid styles of previous Japanese composers',[6] achieving such transcendence of 'earlier efforts to blend Eastern and Western idioms through a subtle balance of opposing features'.[7] The invidious comparisons with earlier Japanese composers here, which might at first sight seem merely gratuitously uncharitable, are in fact of crucial significance: it is by placing Takemitsu's own methods in opposition to those adopted by his forebears that we are able to gain a fuller insight into the distinct character of his own preferred solutions, and the possible reasons for their superior degree of success. The salient observation that emerges from any such comparison, of course, is that Takemitsu avoids the temptation of opting for the most obvious and superficial form of East–West 'hybridisation', the appropriation of actual Japanese scales and melodies, of the kind practised in particular by the 'nationalist' musicians of the *minzokushugi* school.

Apart from the early experiments with modalism under Kiyose's tutelage –
of which some vestigial traces perhaps remain in the mode-based harmonic idiom of his work in general – Takemitsu's music for the most part
almost pointedly eschews this kind of anecdotal 'Japanese' reference. 'I
don't like to use Japanese tunes as material', the composer once expressly
indicated; 'No power . . . no development. Japanese tunes are like Fuji –
beautiful but perfectly eternal.'[8] Their absence in his music, indeed, is
made almost ironically apparent by the fact that Takemitsu has no qualms
about using popular music from other cultures, such as the African and
Catalan songs in *Wind Horse* and *Vers, l'arc-en-ciel, Palma*, although there
is at least one major exception to this self-imposed veto: one of the songs of
Uta is an arrangement of *Sakura* (Cherry Blossom) – not merely a
Japanese folksong, but in effect the unofficial second national anthem!

This exception apart, however, the 'Japanese' input in Takemitsu's case –
by contrast with the more 'concrete' style of Japanese allusion favoured by
his predecessors – tends to take the form of a set of 'abstract', ideological
preoccupations, which inform certain aesthetic or philosophical aspects of
a sound-world that is fundamentally twentieth century and Western in
substance. But if Takemitsu thus used 'an international musical vocabulary to express an indigenous Japanese aesthetic goal'[9], there was at the
same time something in the nature of that 'international musical vocabulary' itself, at that particular moment in its historical development, which
facilitated the process by meeting him somewhere along the way. For
another important aspect of Takemitsu's achievement was his discovery of
several points of congruence between certain aspects of his own native
culture – at least, as he interpreted them – and the contemporary preoccupations of a number of 'advanced' musicians in the West. These areas of
overlap included: the common ground between Takemitsu's 'garden' form
– in both its horizontal sense of a non-directed, rambling process, and its
vertical one of a 'panfocal' instrumentation – and the interest of Western
musicians in 'mobile' or indeterminate forms and stratified instrumentation; the spatialisation and theatricalisation of instrumental performance
in both traditional Japanese and Western contemporary music; the concepts of the 'stream and sound' and *ma*, which relate to John Cage's philosophy of silence; a secondary meaning of *ma* which Takemitsu applies to the
simultaneity of tempi in *nō* music, and which relates to similar polymetri-
cal organisations in the West; the common interest of both traditions in
microtones; and the preference of both traditions for the complexity of the
individual sound-event over the syntactical relationships between sound-
events, for that heightened awareness of the possibilities of timbre which,
for Takemitsu, is expressed by the Japanese term *sawari*.

Of these, the points relating to *ma* and *sawari* would appear to merit deeper discussion – not least because they introduce specific technical terms from Japanese aesthetics which demand further elucidation. The first of these terms, *ma*, is notoriously difficult to pin down, particularly in the senses in which Takemitsu uses it. Its literal meaning, that of an 'interval', or 'space', in both the spatial and temporal senses of these words, is clear enough, but when questioned as to its deeper significance, Takemitsu's own response seemed to be to withdraw into a kind of inscrutable silence which was an example of *ma* in itself. '*Ma* is not only a concept in time; it is at the same time very spatial, a spatial thing, I believe. *Ma* is perhaps . . . oh, *ma* is a very philosophical term'.[10] In the absence of any clearer definition, then, one is forced to turn to the secondary literature for elucidation of this problematic term. Koozin, for example, glosses *ma* as 'an expressive force which fills the void between objects separated in time and space',[11] relating it specifically to those shadings into 'silence' that characterise Takemitsu's piano music. Since these lack a clear point of termination, 'one is more likely to hear the silence arising toward the end of such a figure as a direct outgrowth of the previous sound-event. In this sense, the sound-event draws silence into the piece as an active rather than a passive element . . . The moment of waiting for sound to become silence is imbued with *ma*.'[12]

However, Kenjiro Miyamoto offers a slightly different and, to my view, certainly more fruitful definition of this term. First, he clears up the confusion created by Takemitsu's use of the word in two differing senses, distinguishing as 'the *ma* of *nō*' the specific meaning attached to the word when Takemitsu applies it to *nō* music, where it refers to simultaneity of tempi.[13] (It will be observed that the present author follows Miyamoto's precedent in the last but one paragraph.) Secondly, he suggests that when Takemitsu uses the term *ma* with reference to traditional Japanese music in general, the concept implies for him 'the temporally unquantifiable, metaphysical continuum of silence that, in Japanese music, is consciously integrated between the notes played'.[14] This so-called 'silence' is, in reality, 'in no wise something void, but rather is filled with the numberless tones or noises of space',[15] and it is the function of the 'notes played' to contrast with and render perceptible this underlying continuum: to 'enliven the countless sounds of silence through music',[16] or in Takemitsu's words, '*ma o ikasu*' ('enliven the *ma*').

Thus defined, Takemitsu's understanding of *ma* obviously approximates not only to his own conception of the 'stream of sound', but also to John Cage's aesthetics of 'silence' as a space teeming with sonic events rather than a mere void – a less than surprising congruence, perhaps, when one considers Cage's own 'Eastern' philosophical orientation. But it is rather less easy to explain some of the other correspondences between 'East' and 'West' referred to above simply as the result of the hankering of certain disillusioned post-war Westerners after the 'mysterious East'. In many cases there really does appear to be a quite fortuitous and, for Takemitsu, highly fortunate coincidence between traditional Eastern and contemporary Western aesthetics, as in the matter of the common interest which both share in the complexities of timbre. In the West, an increasing interest in tone-colour on the part of musicians is observable from the latter half of the nineteenth century onwards, developing in tandem with improvements in instrument manufacture and performance techniques, and a better understanding of the physical complexities of sound-production – tendencies which ultimately converge in the post-war period with the development of electro-acoustic media and the possibility of offering listeners self-sufficient discourses conducted in terms of the timbral quality of sound-events alone. In the East – and specifically in the case of indigenous Japanese music, according to Takemitsu – an acute sensitivity to the timbral quality of individual sound-events has long been a distinctive feature of traditional aesthetics. 'The Japanese', Takemitsu claimed, 'are a people who have been endowed with a keen receptivity towards timbre from ages past'[17] – a gift which, the composer believed, expressed itself in a traditional music whose 'sensitivity to tone quality is unparalleled'.[18]

One aspect of traditional Japanese music which, in Takemitsu's view, particularly vindicates such claims is 'the aesthetic concept of *sawari*'.[19] Like *ma*, this is another key word in Takemitsu's aesthetic vocabulary. Deriving from the verb *sawaru*, 'to touch', it traditionally refers to a playing technique associated in particular with such instruments as the *biwa* or *shamisen*, whereby as a result of the instrument's construction and the mode of attack a complex sound is produced, with a pronounced 'noise' component. In Takemitsu's view, this method of production suggests a sound-ideal radically different from that of European music, with its emphasis on purity of 'the note': the *sawari* effect, by contrast, 'aims at the production of noises from our everyday lives, rather than musical sounds'.[20] Moreover, by so doing, it produces sounds which approximate ever more closely to the ambient 'noise' of the 'stream of sound', or indeed of *ma*, linking Takemitsu's two most important aesthetic ideas in a complex reciprocal relationship. 'As each note is refined and emphasised in isolation, the significance of the scale to which it belongs becomes of less importance, and thus the sound approximates to a condition that resembles silence, since it is no longer distinguishable from natural noises, which, though full of concrete tones, as a whole represent "silence"'.[21]

Furthermore, as these remarks about the decreasing significance of notes as members of 'scales' indicate, Takemitsu was well aware that a shift of focus towards the tone-quality of individual, isolated sounds tends to be made at the expense of a focus on the relationships *between* sounds considered only in terms of their conventionalised abstractions as discrete 'pitches' – the area with which Western music is traditionally concerned. 'We speak of the essential elements in Western music – rhythm, melody and harmony. Japanese music considers the quality of sound rather than melody.'[22] This shift of attention away from syntactical relationships towards individuated sound-events is another aspect of traditional Japanese practice that has certain parallels with modern Western composition: from the atomised fragmentation of syntax in Webernian and post-Webernian *pointillisme*, through the deliberate avoidance of any imposed structures in Cage's chance procedures, to the wholly timbre-based arguments found in certain electro-acoustic compositions. Moreover, this aspect of Takemitsu's aesthetics can also assume crucial importance as a means of understanding exactly why the level on which 'East' and 'West' meet in his work produces more artistically satisfying results than those granted to Japanese musicians of the preceding generation. For, while the general consensus of critical opinion does indeed seem to suggest that Takemitsu's predecessors 'attempted to graft Oriental elements on to Western forms with little success in creating a true synthesis',[23] it might at first sight appear that such unsupported assessments reflect nothing more profound than the dictates of changing fashion. Takemitsu's aesthetics of timbre, however, can provide the starting point for an enquiry into the basis of such assessments on a deeper level, one which suggests that there may indeed be an important qualitative difference between his own means of incorporating traditional Japanese elements, and those attempted by his forebears.

Such an enquiry might best be initiated by considering Takemitsu's own distinction between 'portable' and 'non-portable' musics. 'Music with two different faces probably has appeared in the world', the composer believed; 'one is transportable in form, the other is a music which it is impossible to move from the particular land and time in which it dwells'.[24] Western music exemplifies the former type, in which 'the art of music is systemised symbolically so that it becomes transportable, something anyone can play'; by contrast, non-Western music 'cannot be transported to another land', for if this were attempted 'its contours would be changed'.[25]

Takemitsu himself was granted a very literal and graphic illustration of the 'non-portability' of traditional Japanese music when he travelled to New York for the première of *November Steps*: the *biwa* and *shakuhachi* soloists, afraid that their delicate instruments would crack up in the cold, dry climate, were obliged to resort to such expedients as wrapping them in lettuce leaves and wet cloths to protect them from the atmosphere. This experience in turn seems to have suggested to Takemitsu a conception of the uniqueness of timbral phenomena far more sophisticated than the standard Western one. The latter takes into account only the quantifiable physical characteristics of the acoustic phenomena, whereas Takemitsu realised that timbre was also the product of all the circumambient local factors by means of which the listener's perception of these 'objective' physical events was mediated. 'Sound and its aspects vary according to a range of conditions', he was later to write; 'those of the atmosphere, its breadth, dryness, moisture, the weather and so on . . . In itself the concept [of timbre] can of course be described in physical terms, but the case of timbre is an individual one, in that the abstraction of the touch or feel of timbre as it permeates a particular climate and is refined as it passes through time is not possible.'[26]

In contrast with locally circumscribed traditional genres, Western music, in its quest for 'universality', has developed instruments which – unlike the vulnerable *biwa* and *shakuhachi* – are 'functional and easier to use', but at the same time 'a great deal that is valuable has been cut away in the process'.[27] Specifically, Takemitsu believed, this 'process of modernisation and functionalisation in Western music' resulted in the loss of precisely 'those miscellaneous sounds – noises, if you will'[28] that make the sounds of traditional music so rich and distinctive in comparison – in other words, robbed such music of the power of *sawari*. Moreover, in addition to this reliance on technically more consistent instrumental mechanisms, Western music's quest for 'portability' also manifests itself, as the quotation from Takemitsu in the previous paragraph indicates, in the fact that it is 'systemised symbolically': in other words, represented in conventionalised notation, enabling it 'to be interpreted by others who do not belong to the same culture'.[29] And – although he does not appear to make the connection explicit at any point – this convergence of its content with what can be represented by the symbols of its notational system is also responsible for another property of Western music remarked upon by Takemitsu: its ability to withstand 'arrangement', of transference to other musical media. Since the essential content of Western music consists of the syntactical relationships between abstracted idealisations of sound-phenomena, represented as notes in a score, it follows that its essence is able to survive even when those same abstracted idealisations are mediated by the timbrally quite different sound-phenomena of another instrument or ensemble. Or as Takemitsu expresses it (admittedly selecting some rather extreme examples to make his point): 'In the fugal technique of Johann Sebastian Bach, structure is very important. When played by any instrument, that musical structure remains essential and will not be destroyed. In my case it is quite different.'[30]

'Quite different' because, in Takemitsu's case, the essence of music is not to be found in the artificial conceptualisations of relationships between 'notes', but rather in the unfathomable complexity of sound itself which, being 'the real music in my compositions, cannot be arranged'.[31] Admittedly there is a divergence here between Takemitsu's theoretical stance and his own practice, for of course he did on a number of occasions 'arrange' his own music for alternative media, for example by orchestrating *Orion* to produce the first movement of *Orion and Pleiades*. But in fairness, it should be pointed out that such 'arrangements' are almost always 'additive' rather than 'subtractive', and that it would be difficult to imagine anyone undertaking the reverse process, for example by attempting a 'piano reduction' of *November Steps*. Even in the case of the texturally simpler later scores, such a transcription would assuredly involve the loss of most of Takemitsu's 'real music' from the timbrally impoverished final result.

What Takemitsu holds true for his own music must of necessity also hold true for any music whose essence is defined by the timbral quality of individual sounds rather than their syntactic connection. And since Takemitsu emphatically believes this to be the case with traditional Japanese music, it follows logically enough that the latter music, like his own, admits of no 'arrangement'. This, of course, is because not only its timbral sophistication, but almost all the features that are the lifeblood of traditional musics, are lost when the attempt is made to accommodate such sounds within the inadequate symbols of Western staff notation. The problem is a familiar one for ethnomusicologists, and seems also to have been faced by Japanese musicians as early as 1888, when the first attempts were made by the teachers at the Tōkyō Music School to record traditional music in Western notation: as Akira Tamba notes, the attempt proved a setback 'because traditional Japanese music is based on different techniques from those found in Western notated music, such as attacks sliding from the note above, fluctuations of pitch, temporal fluctuations, very large *vibrato* and irregular, diverse instrumental noises which classical Western notation is powerless to transcribe'.[32] Takemitsu too was aware of the loss sustained by traditional music when 'transcribed' in this fashion, though he expressed the point rather more flamboyantly: 'The subtlety of traditional music', he observed, 'is not something describable through notation. On the contrary, many things would be lost if we tried to designate it systematically with symbols. If one slides down the narrow trough of description, a unique fragrance has been lost by the time one reaches the bottom.'[33]

And this brings us to the crucial point towards which this whole argument has been tending: that those predecessors of Takemitsu who attempted to import traditional Japanese music directly into their own works via the intermediary of Western musical notation were inevitably doomed to create only bland, impoverished reflections of their models, deprived of virtually all those features which had given vitality to the original. In their efforts to assimilate such manifestly 'non-portable' musics via these inadequate means, they were erroneously confounding the actual sound-substance of this music with the types of relationship that could be represented by Western notation, and were doomed therefore to enjoy only limited success as a result.

By contrast, Takemitsu's relative success stemmed from the fact that, eschewing such a naïvely 'mimetic' approach, he rather 'adopted the concepts of Japanese traditional music and succeeded in applying them in Western musical contexts'.[34] In particular, by reinventing its timbral liveliness on his own terms within the context of a modern Western instrumental technique, he discovered an especially fortunate coincidence with the Western tradition at that stage in its development. As suggested by his own observations about the relationship between sounds and their functions, too, this focus on the timbral quality of individual sound-events was made at the expense of their roles as signifiers within a larger structural system: he believed that 'the task of the composer should begin with the recognition of the more basic sounds themselves rather than with concern about their function',[35] since 'when sounds are possessed by ideas instead of having their own identity, music suffers'.[36] As a result, the perceptual priorities of his music are in harmony not only with those of traditional Japanese music, but also with those of certain prominent schools of modern compositional thought in the West. In particular, since the complexity of timbral phenomena defies the kind of rigid determination which the composer is able to exercise over the relationships between pitches in a more 'note-based' compositional method, the decision to focus on them of necessity involves a certain abdication of compositional control which accords well with the thinking of certain Western composers of the recent past. John Cage, for example, would heartily have ascribed to Takemitsu's famous dictum that the worst thing a composer can do is to move sounds around 'like driving an automobile'.

Criticisms

However, precisely those qualities of Takemitsu's music that endeared him to composers like Cage were at the same time responsible for some of the most damning criticism of his music from other quarters. In particular, the composer's emphasis on the 'basic sounds themselves' rather than the relationships between them rendered him vulnerable to the frequent charge, especially from commentators of more traditionally 'Western' orientation, that his music lacked 'structural rigour'. For instance, after the opening concert of the *Spirit Garden* event – a major retrospective of the composer's work held at London's South Bank Centre in 1998 – the *Times* critic John Allison commented: 'Takemitsu's fundamental fascination was with tone colour, and too often in his work sonority seems to take precedence over substance' – contrasting his work unfavourably with another item in the same concert by Ravel, whose 'sonorities are infinitely more varied and carry narrative weight'.[37] Anyone who has read thus far will recognise that the qualities Allison here dismisses pejoratively – preference for 'sound' over 'substance' (i.e. presumably 'discourse') or lack of 'narrative weight' – are precisely those qualities that Takemitsu consciously cultivated as the expression of complex and passionately held aesthetic convictions. Of course, this does not mean that they must of necessity be to everyone's taste; but at the same time, it is misguided to suggest that they are simply the result of technical shortcomings on the composer's part, that a composer of more rigorous training such as Ravel had somehow overcome.

Indeed, the fact that Takemitsu's relative lack of interest in structural organisation was no unconscious failing on his part, but rather a consciously pursued policy, is a point repeatedly borne out by his own writings. Rather than considering his own 'dream-like', rhapsodic method of construction as in any way shameful, Takemitsu instead singled out the kinds of highly deterministic construction favoured in contemporary Western music for his scorn: 'The technique of constructing sounds through mathematical formulas is trivial . . . The work of inventing and constructing music really holds no interest for me.'[38] In particular, the twelve-note method, he believed, 'may be the result of necessity, but it represents some very dangerous aspects. The mathematical and geometrical pursuit of sound apparent in this technique is purely an intellectual art.'[39]

Ex. 134 *Les yeux clos*, p. 4, system 2, bar 4

Moreover, in addition to these express comments from the composer's writings, Takemitsu's music itself provides evidence of the degree to which he held constructional processes to be merely 'trivial'. On the one hand, the occasional presence of such passages as the twelve-note canon by retrograde in bars 29–31 of *Music of Tree*, to which attention has been drawn in chapter 5, p. 74, indicates that he possessed formidable reserves of compositional artifice, upon which he could draw when necessary. But on the other hand, the fact that he never chooses to pursue the consequences of any such artful construction for more than a few bars proves that such matters were in themselves of little interest to him. A further example will perhaps illustrate this point even more dramatically. In the piano version of *Les yeux clos*, there occurs a short passage of quasi-'isorhythmic' writing in which two patterns with differing rhythmic cycles are played against each other (Ex. 134). In the left hand, a pattern of five quintuplets is repeated twice, each time a minor third lower (and with slight variations); in the right hand, a pattern lasting four quintuplet beats is repeated three times, each a whole-tone lower.

One can imagine the craftsman-like pride many Western composers might have taken in such a construction: some, like Messiaen, might even be moved to draw attention to what was going on by means of a note in the score. It comes as something of a surprise, therefore, to discover that when Takemitsu came to orchestrate this passage in the first movement of *Visions*, he so altered it as to destroy this little conceit entirely. Far from taking pride in his erudition, he considered it disposable: the work done really was 'trivial' for him in comparison with the necessity of producing a strong orchestral sonority at this point.

While the habit of pillorying Takemitsu for his music's lack of formal organisation seems to be very much a Western one, there is another criticism that one encounters in both Japan and the West: that the sensuousness of Takemitsu's harmonic and instrumental language can too often overstep the bounds of good taste and become cloying. 'Can one have too much beauty?' rhetorically demanded another harsh commentator on the London *Spirit Garden* event, Paul Driver, complaining of Takemitsu's 'swooningly beautiful voicing of chords and textures'.[40] The music which falls foul of critical opinion in this respect is mostly that of the last two decades or so of the composer's career, and the question might therefore legitimately be posed as to whether this 'third period' represents a decline in standard by comparison with the more ascetically abrasive manner of the composer's middle years. Again, the answer to this question is to a certain extent a matter of the listener's own criteria of taste, but it may nevertheless be worthwhile putting forward a few points in Takemitsu's defence. For example, it is important to note that the stylistic conversion which Takemitsu underwent in the mid- to late 1970s was not an isolated, solitary aberration from the true faith, but rather reflected a general trend which was shared by a number of the composer's colleagues in the international 'avant-garde' composing community. From Penderecki's spectacular 'change of direction' to the more thoughtful reintegration of tonality in the music of the later Ligeti, there were few modernist composers not in some way affected by the change of the prevailing *Zeitgeist* over the course of the last quarter of the twentieth century. If therefore Takemitsu stands indicted of deserting the field of battle on which the ongoing march of musical modernism was being played out, it has to be admitted that most of his former 'avant-garde' colleagues have by now also fled from the barricades – and that not a few of them did so at around the same time as Takemitsu himself.

The change in Takemitsu's musical language can thus be viewed as the composer's own personal response to this change in the aesthetic climate, and as such, it may represent another significant artistic achievement – especially when one considers how much less successfully most of Takemitsu's former colleagues in the Japanese avant-garde have fared in negotiating this particular historical problem. Moreover, it is the author's belief that despite the radically different sound-world these later pieces inhabit, in them Takemitsu still remained faithful to some of the most basic tenets of his aesthetic philosophy. The preoccupation with actual sound-materials rather than abstract discourse, for example, is still the guiding principle of these works, even if dressed in more glamorous garb than heretofore. Furthermore, there is a sense in which these final works grant free rein to a kind of political philosophy of self-expression that had been constant since the earliest days of the composer's career. Takemitsu's own preferred term for this later music was 'Romantic' – as he once remarked to Boulez, 'my music is very Romantic'[41] – or perhaps 'neo-Romantic' ('looking at recent trends, people are categorising these things, calling them neoromanticism and so on').[42] And, as he saw it, the general artistic movement which his later works reflected closely paralleled certain roughly contemporary developments in the political sphere: the 'resurgence of the Romantic feeling' typified by the political and social movements in Eastern Europe.[43]

What associates these two unlikely tendencies in Takemitsu's mind – the rise of 'Romanticism' in art, and the collapse of state Communism – is the fact that he views both as motivated by the same groundswell of popular desire for self-expression. 'Worldwide, there is a trend for everyone – the general lay public, the non-artistic public – to want to express themselves, and perhaps artists are at the forefront . . . they are triggering this . . . So this is what I was trying to express by the term "Romanticism", although it may not be the appropriate one.'[44] Given that Takemitsu's interlocutor in the dialogues from which these quotes are taken is a die-hard modernist, Takemitsu is perhaps understandably a little coy about spelling out precisely what the artistic equivalent to the denial of self-expression in the Communist world might have been. But it is not too difficult for any observer of 'serious' composition in the West to fill in the blanks, and supply suitable musical analogues, at least, for the totalitarian régimes that sparked the kinds of political reaction to which Takemitsu refers. Takemitsu's adoption of a 'Romantic' idiom in opposition to these constraints, then, reflects a profoundly held belief in personal expressive freedom; and, as such, far from representing a decline in artistic standards in later life, actually constitutes the reaffirmation of a faith that he had espoused since his very earliest years – the belief that 'music is song and song is love', for example, as he had expressed it as early as 1956.

A further frequent criticism of Takemitsu's music, once again levelled at his later scores in particular, is that their *materia musica* is too often, and too obviously, derivative. To quote Paul Driver once again, 'Takemitsu . . . seems to have produced his scores by strolling in the great garden of 20th-century orchestral composition, picking and choosing a flower of Messiaen harmony here, a Debussyan melodic tendril there'.[45] The comparison with the former composer in particular is one which springs readily enough to many listeners' minds – especially of course on account of Takemitsu's frequent reference to that most 'Messiaenic'-sounding of all harmonic materials, the octatonic scale or 'second mode of limited transposition'. Admittedly the French composer did not have some sort of exclusive patent on this scale, and composers such as Rimsky-Korsakov, Scriabin, Stravinsky and Bartók had all made extensive use of it before him; but while they contrived to do so without in the least sounding like Messiaenic precursors, Takemitsu somehow seems unable to avoid very often sounding like one of his closest disciples. Furthermore, since Takemitsu does not use the octatonic scale with anything like the rigorous consistency of Messiaen – preferring instead to move freely between different transpositions of the mode and other harmonic materials – there must be still further points of contact to create this impression of similarity between the two composers: the typical homophonic writing with an often modal upper line 'coloured' by underlying chords, for example, or the general surface sensuousness of both composers' music.

In fairness to Takemitsu, however, it should be pointed out that, despite the superficial resemblance his music often bears to Messiaen's, there are profound differences of approach between the two composers. Messiaen, despite his obvious spirituality, interest in Oriental musics, reverence for nature and outstanding sensitivity to harmonic and instrumental colour, was at the same time essentially a 'constructivist', whose music involves the rigorous application of melodic, rhythmic and harmonic *schemata* to generate materials. There is a kind of geometric quality to such musical abstractions, as the title of *Liturgie de cristal* suggests: the rhythms, though fluid, are conceived in terms of arithmetical multiples of a unit pulse, and this implicit, grid-like metrical background is paralleled, vertically, by the regularly spaced co-ordinates of the 'modes of limited transposition'. Furthermore, having set in motion a musical process of the kind found in *Liturgie*, Messiaen is content to allow the musical mechanism to run its course without further compositional intervention. In sum, while Messiaen has often been laxly described as a 'mystic', it would be more correct to amend this definition, as Robert Sherlaw Johnson has done, to Messiaen's own preferred title of 'theologian':[46] his encyclopaedic works, with their catalogues of bird- and plain-song and the artful 'constructions' of their isorhythmic and isomelodic cycles, are like the great *summæ* of the medieval Church Fathers, replete with convoluted theological arguments.

Takemitsu, by contrast, although sharing certain aspects of Messiaen's spiritual vision, could not by any stretch of the imagination be described as a 'constructivist'. The manner in which he treats the most obvious of his borrowings from Messiaen's 'technique musicale' bears witness to this: the modes are used for the most part simply as a resource from which to draw richly aromatic harmonic progressions, without any consistent underlying rationale; while on the few occasions where Takemitsu employs some kind of 'isorhythmic' construction, he seems to have no interest in pursuing the workings of the process for more than a few bars, and may even – as in the case of Example 134 from *Les yeux clos* – subsequently destroy it altogether. Furthermore, Messiaen's rhythmic system based on multiplications of a constant unit-pulse is mostly in complete contrast to Takemitsu's fluidity of tactus, 'endlessly oscillating' like the music of the *nō* drama, and obscured by the frequent subdivisions of the beat into various uneven factors, often simultaneously. In brief, while Messiaen's rich sonorities are used as fundamental units to present syntactical constructions of a precise, implacable rigour, Takemitsu – less interested, as we have seen, in the syntactical dimension of music than in the stuff of sound itself – uses certain of the precision mechanisms of Messiaen's technique only as another means of generating sonorities which he considers interesting *per se*. If Messiaen is the 'theologian', offering a commentary on his spiritual beliefs in terms of rigidly pursued and often descriptive 'arguments' of an architectural solidity, Takemitsu is simply giving meaning to the 'stream of sound' around him, and in consequence reflecting something of the chaotic and ineluctable fluidity of that medium. One is reminded here of a similar distinction which Roland Barthes once drew between the Western theologian and the writer of Japanese *haiku*. 'Description, a Western genre', Barthes observed, 'has its spiritual equivalent in contemplation, the methodical inventory of the attributive forms of the divinity or of the episodes of evangelical narrative.' The *haiku*, however, 'articulated around a metaphysics without subject and without god, corresponds to the Buddhist *mu*, to the Zen *satori*, which is not at all an illuminative descent of God, but "awakening to the fact", apprehension of the thing as event and not as substance'.[47]

However, when one turns one's attention to some of the other references which Takemitsu makes to Western predecessors – such as those to Alban Berg's *Violin Concerto* in *Far calls* – it becomes less easy to exonerate the composer from the charge of direct imitation. In such instances, it is probably wiser to allow the composer himself to appear in the capacity of his own advocate – especially since the defence he advances seems to be so intimately bound up with traditional 'Eastern' attitudes to matters of originality and invention that it would be difficult to imagine a Westerner offering it without embarrassment. 'As a composer – not an inventor – I don't need patents. Things I think of must have been thought of by others already . . . Therefore, I think I don't mind if things are not always my own.'[48]

Conclusions

Ever and again over the course of this chapter, the discussion has returned
to the same central point: that the focus of Takemitsu's interest as listener
and composer was the sound-quality of the individual event, not the relationships between such events that constitute the traditional 'discourse' of
Western music. Whether attempting to explain his philosophy of traditional Japanese music, or the relative absence of intentionally imposed
syntax in the composer's own work, it has repeatedly been necessary to
draw attention to this system of priorities to clarify the underlying basis of
his aesthetic thinking. It has also been necessary to emphasise this same
basic philosophical orientation when dealing with some of the most frequent criticisms levelled at the composer's work – that it lacks formal
direction, that it is too obviously derivative of Messiaen.

Precisely this same aspect of Takemitsu's aesthetic philosophy, whose
results can be so irritating to certain Western critics, is also problematic for
the commentator who would attempt an explication of the composer's
music with the tools of Western analytic theory. As a natural consequence
of the priority which Takemitsu assigns to the crafting of sounds as audible
phenomena, rather than to their subordination within some preconceived
constructional scheme, the composer's own 'modes of musical thoughts
follow the natural inclination of sounds',[49] and the final results therefore
tend to become impermeable to anything resembling exhaustive analysis
by traditional methods. To be sure – and despite Takemitsu's claim to have
'no pre-compositional assumptions'[50] – analysis can uncover some of
Takemitsu's basic generative strategies, and even on occasion tentatively
suggest certain higher-level ordering principles: the bulk of this book,
indeed, has been preoccupied with doing precisely that. But, as Bernard
Rands has pointed out, sooner or later there always comes a point in this
work of analysis at which 'certain assumptions, initially prompted by the
surface characteristics of the music, seem less certain'.[51] The trail seems to
be lost, ambiguity and arbitrary manipulations of the material conceal all
trace of whatever 'pre-compositional assumptions' the composer may
have started from – and one finds oneself at 'the ends of the fertile land'.
Takemitsu himself, referring to the limitations of analytic method when
applied to the works of other composers, might equally well have been
talking about the kinds of obstacles faced by the analyst bent on discovering the secrets of his own music. 'When we analyse a piece of music', he
observed, 'we often find some mysterious element that cannot be
explained. If this element is the most attractive or moving aspect of the
piece, the mystery deepens.'[52]

The approach to Takemitsu's music adopted in the preceding chapters has intentionally avoided trying to explain this 'mysterious element', this *residuum* consisting of the composer's free, perhaps unconscious, imaginative decisions and arbitrary manipulations of material. One cannot quit the subject of the composer's music, however, without at least making the reader aware of both the size and importance of this area, and suggesting what alternative methodologies might be appropriate for mapping this vast territory. One possible strategy for future Takemitsu scholars, for example – assuming they are fluent Japanese readers – might be to examine the composer's sketchbooks: the few samples that have so far appeared in print suggest that this exercise might yield some fascinating insights into Takemitsu's thought processes. Alternatively, there already exist examples of analytic approaches which would appear to have more success than conventional methods in explaining some of the more enigmatic aspects of the composer's work. I am thinking here of such studies as those by Ting-Lien Wu of *Bryce*[53] and by Jeong Woo Jin of *Rain Tree*.[54] The former score in particular is, as Wu observes, 'to a musician thinking only in terms of Western pitch, form and texture . . . quite bewildering'.[55] Wu therefore advises that 'we take another approach'; arguing that in *Bryce* 'the hierarchical pitch structure, which is the predominant character of Western traditional music, is less active than Eastern articulative aspects',[56] he suggests that each successive section may be considered a magnification of a single, microscopic germinal gesture: a single sound-event, acoustically divisible into beginning, middle and end. Jin's approach to *Rain Tree* likewise focuses on 'macroscopic' features rather than pitch-relationships, in this case not the articulative 'envelope' of sections but rather the manner in which they are distinguished by 'textural forces and timbral metamorphosis'.[57] Whether one agrees with their findings or not, both of these scholars are certainly to be credited for attempting to find a way beyond the impasse that conventional, pitch-based analysis finds itself confronted with when applied to music of this kind.

Ultimately, however, to pore over the composer's scores desperately seeking some constructional rationale may be to miss the point entirely. Takemitsu's music is clearly not written for the gratification of future analysts. Prioritising 'sound' over 'note-by-note' discourse, it departs capriciously at every step of the way from whatever pre-compositional ideas may have formed the composer's starting point. It is important to remember here the emphatically non-academic stance adopted by Takemitsu throughout his career: he never attended music college, nor did he accept any academic appointment. As a result, he did not consider the production of scores that would serve as textual documentations of a discursive process to be an important aspect of his vocation, in the manner which – one suspects – many more academically trained composers may have done. His music is designed primarily to be listened to rather than 'read': 'In the case of my music, there is no meaning in it if it does not have concrete figures as sounds actually created by instruments. With only the logic of written scores, sounds do not have any real existence as sounds.'[58] Takemitsu appears to have cared even less for the logic of written explanations to his scores, which he considered not merely irrelevant but actually harmful. 'If I put explanations in a concert pamphlet', he argued, 'the act of understanding the music through the eyes would be emphasised, and this might ruin the act of understanding the music with the ears'.[59] As a life-long outsider to academia, Takemitsu did not identify his audience exclusively with the 'new music' community of musically literate specialists to whom, one suspects, the music of many of his contemporaries was at least half-addressed, particularly in the West. The ideal 'target audience' for Takemitsu's work, by contrast, was always one of attentive, sensitive listeners.

And the signs are that this audience is responding. While Takemitsu's music may frustrate the academic analyst, and offend the taste of the professional critic, it nevertheless appears to be charming an audience that embraces a much broader constituency of listeners than the usual élite of new music admirers. The 1998 *Spirit Garden* Festival, for example, which so disappointed critics such as Allison and Driver, attracted an average audience attendance of 58 per cent – an exceptionally high figure for a 'contemporary music' series. Inviting its listeners to approach its sound-world directly without the mediation of pages of complex theoretical explication, Takemitsu's music affords them an accessibility that, perhaps, they feel is denied them by the music of the more rigorously 'intellectual' of his contemporaries. Possibly, too, by speaking of 'trees', 'gardens', 'wind' and 'water', it satisfies a deep thirst for reference to 'natural' subject-matter which for years Western modernism had rigidly proscribed – and which even now, indeed, was only being readmitted to the West because stamped with the legitimising seal of 'Eastern' cultural difference.

And perhaps Takemitsu offers his audience something more profound still. By electing to concentrate on sound itself, and in particular timbre, rather than syntax, Takemitsu was emphasising a quality of music so complex that, by comparison, the simple arithmetical procedures of most consciously applied systems of compositional control really do seem trivial. In the course of its complex evolution, as Takemitsu well knew, a single sound could supply vast amounts of information at a rate no rationalising mind could ever hope to follow. As he put it, 'In the process of their creation [i.e. the sounds of traditional music], theoretical thinking is destroyed. A single strum of the strings, or even one pluck is too complex, too complete in itself to admit any theory.'[60] In the face of such music, a Western theoretical training thus becomes a positive impediment to understanding: the listener must begin a process of re-education, learn anew to hear sounds in themselves rather than as components in a system of order.

The consequences of such a process of learning may be profound. In the classic Western conception of music as 'discourse', sounds only serve to bear significance as 'pitches' (or 'durations') in relationship to one another. This relativistic, self-contained system rather resembles the modern Western conception of language as a system of signs defined by their opposition to other signs, not by their reference to 'things' in themselves. By contrast, music which focuses on the ineluctable riches of timbre requires that the listener attempt to suspend the organising faculty in favour of a direct perception of the actual reality of sound-phenomena, an awareness of the boundless complexity of real events unhindered by the distracting simplifications of conceptualisation and analysis. A reference to a specific instance of the removal of such intermediary conceptualisation in Takemitsu's music, at the macrostructural level, may perhaps serve to clarify this point. Especially during his early years, Takemitsu appears occasionally to have organised his works according to some large-scale structural scheme such as ABA or 'arch' form. More often than not, however – particularly in his later music – there is no such overall formal patterning. A whole layer of intermediary conceptualisation is thus abolished: the totality of sound-events within the piece itself becomes the 'form', and the listener is invited to contemplate them directly without reference to any higher-level ordering. This absence of imposed 'form' replicates, at a higher structural level, the avoidance of imposed syntax at the microstructural level: in both cases the effect is the same, to remove the obstacles placed between events and their perception by the act of organising the former into some distracting conceptual 'system'.

By inviting us to cultivate a clear, direct apprehension of sound-phenomena as events in themselves, rather than fascinating the rational mind with complex organisations of quantities for which those sounds function as 'signifiers', Takemitsu is perhaps also granting us a certain intuitive experience of that kind of direct perception of phenomena, unmediated by the categorisations of language, which is the goal of his native religious traditions – the Buddhist *mu*, the Zen *satori*, the 'apprehension of the thing as event and not as substance'. In his more effusive moments, indeed, Takemitsu seemed to suggest precisely something of this sort. 'Of *shakuhachi* music it has been said, "Ichion Jōbutsu" – "With one sound one becomes the Buddha" . . . suggesting that the universe is explored in a single sound . . . So, with some exaggeration, I might say God dwells in a single sound.'[61] Of course, these aesthetic aspects of Takemitsu's music are not his exclusive property, but are shared by many other musics as well – traditional Japanese, for example, as the above quotation indicates. And it must also be admitted that Takemitsu's practice can depart remarkably from his theory in this respect – as in the case of his later works' insistence on one of the most time-honoured formulae of 'note-by-note' discourse of all, the melodic line. Nevertheless, as Western music enters a new millennium, and seeks some kind of 'philosophy of postmodern music' to supplant the old, it may be that Takemitsu's insistence on the primacy of sound over structural organisation may prove to have been prophetic. Alongside the part he played in hatching the 'universal egg'; alongside the relative finesse with which he negotiated the general loss of faith in modernism; alongside his lifelong efforts to abolish barriers between 'high' and 'low' culture – this specific achievement may yet, perhaps, prove to have been his most significant contribution to musical history.

Notes

Introduction

1 Yōko Narazaki, *Takemitsu Tōru to Miyoshi Akira no Sakkyoku-Yoshiki: Muchōsei to Ongun-Sakahō o Megutte* [The Compositional Styles of Tōru Takemitsu and Akira Miyoshi: Their Use of Atonality and Tone-Cluster Methods], Tōkyō: Ongaku no Tomo Sha, 1993, p. 86.

2 Jun-ichi Konuma, *Takemitsu Tōru – Oto, Kotoba, Imēji* [Tōru Takemitsu – Sound, Word, Image], Tōkyō: Seido Sha, 1999, p. 31.

3 Yukiko Sawabe, 'Alpträume und Träume: Der japanische Komponist Tōru Takemitsu', *MusikTexte* 59 (June 1995), 50.

4 Kenjiro Miyamoto, *Klang im Osten, Klang im Westen: Der Komponist Tōru Takemitsu und die Rezeption europäischer Musik in Japan*, Saarbrücken: Pfau, 1996, p. 53.

5 Takashi Funayama, *Takemitsu Tōru – Hibiki no Umi e* [Tōru Takemitsu – Towards the Sea of Sound], Tōkyō: Ongaku no Tomo Sha, 1998, p. 45.

6 Miyuki Shiraishi, 'Umi kara, Futatabi Ame tonari: Takemitsu Sakuhin – Shuhō no Hensen o Todoru' [From the Sea comes Rain Once Again: Tracking the Changes of Technique in Takemitsu's Work], *Ongaku Geijutsu* 54/5 (May 1996), 49.

7 See my 'Up the Garden Path: Takemitsu, Serialism and the Limits of Analysis', in *A Way a Lone*, Tōkyō: Academia Musica, 2001 (in preparation)

1 Pre-history: how Western music came to Japan

1 G. B. Sansom, *The Western World and Japan*, London: Cresset, 1950, p. 264.

2 G. B. Sansom, *Japan: a Short Cultural History*, Rutland, Vermont: Tuttle, 1979, p. 468.

3 Arnold J. Toynbee, *Civilization on Trial*, Oxford University Press, 1948, p. 194.

4 Apparently in honour of 'Herod the Great, the Edomite King of Judaea'. Cf. Arnold J. Toynbee, *The World and the West*, Oxford University Press, 1952, p. 87.

5 Toynbee, *Civilization on Trial*, p. 193.

6 *Ibid.*, p. 188.

7 *Ibid.*, p. 195.

8 Eta Harich-Schneider, *A History of Japanese Music*, Oxford University Press, 1973, p. 545.

9 Alain Poirier, *Tōru Takemitsu*, Paris: Editions TUM/Michel de Maule, 1996, p. 15.

10 Hidekazu Yoshida, 'Über die Musikentwicklung Japans in den letzten hundert

Jahren' in *Aspekte der neuen Musik (Professor Hans Heinz Stuckenschmidt zum 65. Geburtstag)*, Kassel: Bärenreiter, 1968, p. 98.

11 *Ibid.*

12 Miyamoto, *Klang im Osten*, p. 11.

13 Kōichi Nomura, 'Occidental Music', in *Japanese Music and Drama in the Meiji Era*, compiled and edited by Toyotaka Komiya, translated and adapted by Edward G. Seidensticker, Tōkyō: Ōbun Sha, 1956, p. 456.

14 *Ibid.*, p. 460.

15 *Ibid.*, p. 466. Nomura's work contains a translation of the complete text of Izawa's Study Plan (pp. 464ff), from which the quotations in the preceding lines have been taken.

16 Ikuma Dan, *Nihonjin to Seiyō-Ongaku: Ibunka to no Shukkai* [The Japanese and Western Music: Encounters with an Alien Culture], Tōkyō: Nippon Hōsō Shuppan Kyōkai, 1997, p. 83. *Gagaku* is the traditional court music of Japan, a highly sophisticated ensemble music; while the word here translated as 'popular song' (*zokugaku*) has the literal meaning 'worldly music' and is perhaps the nearest Japanese equivalent to 'U-Musik'.

17 Cf. Judith Ann Herd, 'The Neonationalist Movement: Origins of Japanese Contemporary Music', *Perspectives of New Music* 27/2 (1989), p. 118.

18 Nomura, 'Occidental Music', p. 493.

19 *Nippon Hōsō Kyōkai*, the Japanese state broadcasting corporation.

20 Harich-Schneider, *A History of Japanese Music*, p. 544.

21 Tōru Takemitsu, *Ongaku no Yohaku kara* [From the Space Left in Music], Tōkyō: Shinchō Sha, 1980, p. 148. Quoted in Noriko Ohtake, *Creative Sources for the Music of Tōru Takemitsu*, Aldershot: Scolar Press, 1993, p. 6.

22 Akira Ueno, 'Zwischen den Ufern: die Beziehung zwischen Tradition und zeitgenössischer Musik in Japan', *MusikTexte* 59 (June 1995), p. 45.

23 Herd, 'The Neonationalist Movement', p. 119.

24 Carl Dahlhaus (trans. Mary Whittall), *Between Romanticism and Modernism: Four Studies in the Music of the Later Nineteenth Century*, Berkeley, California: University of California Press, 1980, p. 87.

25 William P. Malm, *Tradition and Modernization in Japanese Culture*, ed. Donald H. Shively, Princeton University Press, 1971, p. 300.

26 Robin J. Heifetz, 'East–West Synthesis in Japanese Composition 1950–1970', *Journal of Musicology* 3 (1984), p. 445.

27 Herd, 'The Neonationalist Movement', p. 119.

2 Music and 'pre-music': Takemitsu's early years

1 End-blown, vertical Japanese flute.

2 Kuniharu Akiyama, biographical sketch of the composer, in Tōru Takemitsu, *Oto, Chinmoku to Hakariareru Hodoni* [Sound, Measuring with Silence], Tōkyō: Shinchō Sha, 1971, p. 211.

3 Tōru Takemitsu and Seiji Ozawa, *Ongaku* [Music], Tōkyō: Shinchō Sha, 1981, p. 21.

4 'The Inheritance', dir. Masaki Kobayashi, 1962.

5 'The Man Who Left his Will on Film', dir. Nagisa Ōshima, 1970.

6 'Summer Sister', dir. Nagisa Ōshima, 1972.

7 A zither-like instrument with thirteen strings, plucked with ivory picks attached to the player's fingers.

8 Tōru Takemitsu, 'Contemporary Music in Japan', *Perspectives of New Music* 27/2 (1989), p. 200.

9 *Ibid.*, p. 199.

10 *Ibid.* Years later, in a moving re-encounter, a shy, elderly man who had keenly followed the composer's career over the years finally plucked up the courage to introduce himself to Takemitsu in a Tōkyō restaurant – as that same young officer cadet who, with his wind-up gramophone, had unwittingly been so instrumental in setting that career in motion.

11 Takemitsu, quoted in Hitaru Kataoka, *Nipponjin to Kansei* [The Japanese and Sensitivity], Tōkyō: Ongaku no Tomo Sha, 1979, pp. 58–9. Translation from Sawako Taniyama, 'The Development of Tōru Takemitsu's Musical Philosophy', *Kōbe Joshi Tanki Daigaku Ronkō* 37 (Oct. 1991), p. 73.

12 Tōru Takemitsu (with Tania Cronin and Hilary Tann), 'Afterword', *Perspectives of New Music* 27/2 (1989), p. 207.

13 Takemitsu, 'Contemporary Music in Japan', p. 200.

14 Takemitsu, 'Afterword', p. 207.

15 See Eiko Kasaba, 'Notes sur la réception de la musique de Messiaen au Japon', *Revue internationale de musique française* 30 (November 1989), p. 94.

16 Conversation with Louis Dandrel in Takemitsu, *Ongaku no Yohaku kara*, p. 151. The original version appeared in *Le monde de la musique* (Nov. 1978), p. 1521.

17 Takemitsu, 'Afterword', p. 207.

18 Suzuki was to remain a close associate of Takemitsu until 1958, after which he gave up composition.

19 Cf. Takemitsu, *Oto, Chinmoku*, p. 212.

20 Tōru Takemitsu, *Ongaku o Yobimasu Mono* [Awakening of Music], Tōkyō: Shinchō Sha, 1985, p. 96.

21 Olivier Messiaen, trans. Kishio Hirao, *Waga Ongaku Gohō*, Tōkyō: Kyōiku Shuppan Kabushiki Gaisha, 1954.

22 Takemitsu and Ozawa, *Ongaku*, p. 139.

23 'Ongaku izen de aru' – 'It's pre- (or "before") music.' The reviewer responsible was the leading Japanese music critic of the day, Ginji Yamane (1906–82); the newspaper the *Tōto Shinbun*.

24 Takemitsu and Ozawa, *Ongaku*, pp. 144–5.

25 The score has now been published by Schott Japan (SJ 1123).

26 The honorific Japanese term for 'teacher'.

27 Tōru Takemitsu (trans. and ed. Yoshiko Kakudo and Glenn Glasow), *Confronting Silence: Selected Writings*, Berkeley, California: Fallen Leaf Press, 1995, p. 117.

28 Kuniharu Akiyama, *Nihon no Sakkyokukatachi* [Japanese Composers], Tōkyō: Ongaku no Tomo Sha, 1978–9, p. 258.

29 Timothy Koozin, 'The Solo Piano Works of Tōru Takemitsu: a Linear/Set-Theoretical Analysis', Ph.D. dissertation, University of Cincinnati (1988), p. 20.

30 Takemitsu, *Confronting Silence*, p. 119.

31 In the BBC film 'Thirteen Steps around Tōru Takemitsu', dir. Barrie Gavin (1986).

32 Cf. Hiroyuki Iwaki, *Sakkyokuka Takemitsu Tōru to Ningen Mayuzumi Toshirō* [The Composer Tōru Takemitsu and the Human Being Toshirō Mayuzumi], Okayama: Sakuyō Gakuen, 1999, p. 21.

33 Takemitsu, *Confronting Silence*, p. 45.

34 Funayama, *Takemitsu Tōru*, p. 167.

35 Fontec FOCD3202.

36 Akiyama, *Nihon no Sakkyokukatachi*, p. 255.

37 Ohtake, *Creative Sources*, p. 7.

38 Akiyama, *Nihon no Sakkyokukatachi*, p. 255.

39 Timothy Koozin, 'Octatonicism in Recent Solo Piano Works of Tōru Takemitsu', *Perspectives of New Music* 29/1 (1991), p. 125.

40 See Miyamoto, *Klang im Osten*, pp. 62–6.

41 Though disowned by Takemitsu for reasons described above, the work was finally readmitted to the canon of the composer's acknowledged works in a revised form in 1989. It is upon this revised score that the following observations have been based.

42 By Takashi Harada (Victor VICC-124).

43 Ryūtaro Iwata, *Kafe Takemitsu: Watashi no Takemitsu Ongaku* [Café Takemitsu: My Takemitsu Music], Tōkyō: Kaimei Sha, 1992, pp. 53–4.

44 See Allen Forte, *The Structure of Atonal Music*, Yale University Press, 1973, p. 180.

45 Koozin, 'The Solo Piano Works', p. 294.

3 Experimental workshop: the years of *Jikken Kōbō*

1 Shūzo Takiguchi, in the *Geijutsu Shinchō*, August 1955 number; quoted by Akiyama in Takemitsu, *Oto, Chinmoku*, p. 215.

2 The composers Jōji Yuasa, Kazuo Fukushima (1930–) and Keijiro Satō (1929–) did not join the group until later.

3 Kasaba, 'Notes sur la réception', p. 95.

4 An English translation can be found in Ohtake, *Creative Sources*, p. 78.

5 Pierre Schaeffer, *A la recherche d'une musique concrète*, Paris: Seuil, 1952, p. 32.

6 Kuniharu Akiyama, sleeve notes for LP recording of work, VX-21.

7 Heuwell Tircuit (trans. Atsushi Miura), 'Tōru Takemitsu ... The Inspired Tenderness', *Ongaku Geijutsu* 21/1 (1963), p. 16.

8 Hourglass-shaped drum in two sizes, the smaller (*ko-tsuzumi*) rested on the shoulder, the larger (*ō-tsuzumi*) on the knee.

9 Traditional Japanese theatrical genre, performed by male actors in masks, and accompanied by a small vocal and instrumental ensemble.

10 Lute-like instrument, used (as here) to accompany narrations from the epic *Heike Monogatari*, the story of the Heike clan.

11 However, in conversation with the author, the composer's widow insisted that she had abandoned her acting career by this time, and that Takemitsu's engagement in this kind of work was unconnected with her influence.

12 'Face of Another', dir. Hiroshi Teshigahara, 1966.

13 Cf. Peter Grilli, 'Takemitsu and the Movies', *Takemitsu Society Newsletter* 1/3 (Summer 1998), p. 8. Takemitsu's usage here is not entirely metaphorical; like several of his friends, he possessed an actual 'liberty passport', made and given to him by Shūzo Takiguchi.

14 Grilli, 'Takemitsu and the Movies', p. 6.

15 'Bad Boys', dir. Susumu Hani.

16 'The Ceremony', dir. Nagisa Ōshima, 1971.

4 The *Requiem* and its reception

1 The composer's programme note, in *Shinfonī* (Bulletin of the Tōkyō Symphony Orchestra), 2/28 (June 1957), p. 13.

2 Takashi Tachibana, 'Takemitsu Tōru: Ongaku Sōzō e no Tabi' [Tōru Takemitsu: the Journey Towards Musical Creation], *Bungakukai* (November 1993), p. 231.

3 Cf. for example Ozawa and Takemitsu, *Ongaku*, p. 146.

4 Tachibana, 'Takemitsu Tōru', p. 232.

5 Kuniharu Akiyama, in *Saishin Meikyoku Kaisetsu Zenshū*, Tōkyō: Ongaku no Tomo Sha, 1980, vol. 7, p. 459.

6 Narazaki, *Takemitsu Tōru*, p. 88.

7 'Tōkyō Trials', dir. Masaki Kobayashi, 1983.

8 'Black Rain', dir. Shōhei Imamura, 1989.

9 Akiyama, biographical notes in Takemitsu, *Oto, Chinmoku*, p. 216. Akiyama, however, incorrectly gives the date of this incidental music as 1954, which was the year in which Anouilh's play was produced under its original title (*Arudēru, mata wa Seijo*), with music by another composer.

10 Poirier, *Tōru Takemitsu*, p. 38.

11 Kenjiro Miyamoto is of another opinion, however, and argues for a thoroughgoing motivic relationship between the opening idea and all subsequent themes in the work. See *Klang im Osten*, pp. 96–116.

12 Interestingly, the work's dedicatee Hayasaka was also interested in the absence of clear beginnings and endings, although in his case he related this concept to the traditional Japanese picture-scroll or *emaki*.

13 Takemitsu, *Oto, Chinmoku*, p. 25.

14 Composer's programme note in *Shinfonī*, 2/28 (June 1957), p. 13.

15 Ozawa and Takemitsu, *Ongaku*, p. 146.

16 *Ibid.*

17 Tōru Takemitsu, *Ki no Kagami, Sōgen no Kagami* [Mirror of Tree, Mirror of Grass], Tōkyō: Shinchō Sha, 1975, p. 29; quoted in Ohtake, *Creative Sources*, p. 81.

18 Poirier, *Tōru Takemitsu*, p. 38.

19 Chung-Haing Lee, 'Japanese Elements in the Piano Works of Tōru Takemitsu', DMA Thesis, University of North Texas (1991), p. 36.

20 Sleeve notes for Victor SJX-1002; quoted in Narazaki, *Takemitsu Tōru*, p. 94.

21 The original version of *Masque* comprised two movements only, *Continu* and *Incidental*. A third movement, *Incidental II*, was added in 1960.

22 The reference here is apparently to Messiaen's *Technique de mon langage musical*; cf. English edition, Paris: Leduc, 1944, p. 51.

23 Narazaki, *Takemitsu Tōru*, p. 88.

24 Koozin, 'The Solo Piano Works', p. 86.

25 Funayama, *Takemitsu Tōru*, p. 90.

26 The pitches of twelve-note sets in all examples have been numbered 1–12, not 0–11.

27 Koozin, 'The Solo Piano Works', p. 80.

28 Cf. Tōru Takemitsu (trans. Sumi Adachi with Roger Reynolds), 'Mirrors', *Perspectives of New Music* 30/1 (1992), pp. 59, 77 n.43.

29 Luciana Galliano, 'Takemitsu Tōru: il primo periodo creativo (1950–70)', *Nuova rivista musicale italiana* 33/4 (1999), p. 515.

30 Koozin, 'The Solo Piano Works', p. 93.

31 Ohtake, *Creative Sources*, p. 80.

32 Donald Richie, 'Tōkyō no Stravinsky', *Ongaku Geijutsu*, Sept. 1959; quoted by Akiyama in Takemitsu, *Oto, Chinmoku*, p. 218.

33 Ozawa and Takemitsu, *Ongaku*, p. 146.

34 'I.S. in enjoying himself more than V.[era], partly, I think, because of his Japanese height. Standard-size installations fit him exactly. Whereas my head is a foot above the mirror when I shave, and my knees press against the wall of the W.C., these utilities are comfortably tailored to I.S.' Robert Craft, in Igor Stravinsky and Robert Craft, *Dialogues and a Diary*, London: Faber, 1968, p. 192.

35 Takemitsu, 'Afterword', p. 207.

36 First performed in 1966 at the San Francisco 'Musica Viva', with Aaron Copland conducting.

5 Projections on to a Western mirror

1 Takemitsu, *Ki no Kagami, Sōgen no Kagami.*

2 Ohtake, *Creative Sources*, p. 25.

3 Takemitsu, 'Mirrors', p. 47.

4 Poirier, *Tōru Takemitsu*, p. 26.

5 To quote Takemitsu's own words from the preface, this refers to 'the instrument tuned a minor third higher than the ordinary guitar: to make it a terz-guitar. It is already transposed'.

6 Miyamoto, *Klang im Osten*, p. 129.

7 Koozin, 'The Solo Piano Works', p. 64.

8 *Ibid.*, p. 67.

9 Miyamoto, *Klang im Osten*, p. 167.

10 George Russell, *The Lydian Chromatic Concept of Tonal Organisation for Improvisation*, New York: Concept Publishing, 1959, p. 4.

11 'Tōru Takemitsu Pop Songs', recorded by Seri Ishikawa (female vocalist), Denon COCY-78624.

12 Masafumi Ogawa asserts the presence of a second, unacknowledged quotation in *Wind Horse*, observing that 'the opening melody is apparently adopted from Tibetan folksongs'. See 'Tōru Takemitsu's Compositional Techniques and his Identity as Japanese in Western Art Music: an Analysis of *Kaze no Uma* ("Wind Horse")', *Research Bulletin of the Faculty of Education, Oita University* 13/1 (1991), p. 115.

13 '21-year-old Father/Our Happiness Alone', dir. Noboru Nakamura.

14 'Longing/Once a Rainy Day', dir. Hideo Onchi.

15 'The Ruined Map/The Man Without a Map', dir. Hiroshi Teshigahara, 1968.

16 This, at least, is my best guess as to the identity of the 'Furansowa E. Koroa' mentioned in Kunihara Akiyama's liner notes for the CD recording of the music (JVC VICG5128).

17 Dir. Hiroshi Teshigahara, 1989.

18 'Mouth-organ' consisting of seventeen bamboo pipes, used to sound five- or six-note chords.

19 Barrel-shaped drum with two heads, placed horizontally in front of the performer on a stand and played with two sticks.

20 Ogawa, 'Tōru Takemitsu's Compositional Techniques', p. 114.

21 Quoted in Akiyama, *Saishin Meikyoku*, vol. 13, p. 455.

22 *Ibid.*

23 'Suna no Onna', dir. Hiroshi Teshigahara, 1964.

24 Dana Richard Wilson, 'The Role of Texture in Selected Works of Tōru Takemitsu', Ph.D. Dissertation, Eastman School of Music (1982), p. 152.

25 As Miyamoto notes (*Klang im Osten*, p. 185), the date 'March 1961' in the published score is erroneous.

6 'Cage shock' and after

1 Takemitsu, *Confronting Silence*, p. 137.

2 *Ibid.*

3 Ohtake, *Creative Sources*, p. 75.

4 'The Pitfall/Cheap, Sweet and a Kid', dir. Hiroshi Teshigahara.

5 'The Assassin', dir. Masahiro Shinoda.

6 'Yotsuya Ghost Story', dir. Shiro Toyoda.

7 Miyamoto, *Klang im Osten*, p. 167.

8 Takemitsu, 'Mirrors', p. 55.

9 Tōru Takemitsu, 'Watashi no Hōhō – Myūjikku Konkurēto ni tsuite' [My Method – Concerning *musique concrète*], *Bijutsu Hihyō* 1 (1956), p. 70.

10 Ohtake, *Creative Sources*, p. 7.

11 Takemitsu, 'Afterword', p. 208. This kind of 'layering' is also, of course, a standard procedure in the building up of textures in the electronic music studio.

12 Robin Julian Heifetz, 'Post-World War II Japanese Composition', DMA Thesis, University of Illinois (1978), p. 60.

13 Koozin, 'Octatonicism', p. 126.

14 Koozin, 'The Solo Piano Works', p. 294.

15 In the film 'Tōru Takemitsu: Music for the Movies', dir. Charlotte Zwerin, 1994.

16 Wilson, 'The Role of Texture', p. 90.

17 Takemitsu, *Confronting Silence*, p. 120.

18 Cf. for example Takemitsu, *Confronting Silence*, p. 66; Taniyama, 'The Development of Tōru Takemitsu's Musical Philosophy', p. 80; Funayama, *Takemitsu Tōru*, p. 175; Shinji Saitō and Maki Takemitsu, *Takemitsu Tōru no Sekai* [The World of Tōru Takemitsu], Tōkyō: Shūei Sha, 1997, p. 176; Ohtake, *Creative Sources*, p. 90; Miyamato, *Klang im Osten*, p. 195.

19 Funayama, *Takemitsu Tōru*, p. 173.

20 Takemitsu, *Confronting Silence*, p. 95.

21 *Ibid.*, p. 114.

22 *Ibid.*

23 Ohtake, *Creative Sources*, p. 91.

24 Akiyama, *Nihon no Sakkyokukatachi*, p. 262.

25 Poirier, *Tōru Takemitsu*, p. 80.

26 Takemitsu, *Confronting Silence*, p. 120.

27 Funayama, *Takemitsu Tōru*, p. 103.

28 Ohtake, *Creative Sources*, p. 94.

29 RCA SB 6814.

30 Narazaki, *Takemitsu Tōru*, p. 86.

31 Akiyama, *Saishin Meikyoku*, vol. 7, p. 470.

7 Projections on to an Eastern mirror

1 Takemitsu, 'Contemporary Music in Japan', p. 199.

2 Traditional Japanese puppet theatre.

3 Takemitsu, 'Mirrors', p. 55.

4 Miyamoto, *Klang im Osten*, p. 128.

5 A specific variety of *biwa* (lute-like traditional instrument), which appeared in the *Meiji* era in the northern province of Kyūshū formerly known as Chikuzen (present-day Fukuoka).

6 'Hara-kiri', dir. Masaki Kobayashi, 1962.

7 Transverse bamboo flute used in the *kabuki* drama.

8 Transverse bamboo flute used in *gagaku* music.

9 'Mouth-organ' comprising a windchest and seventeen bamboo pipes; used in *gagaku* music.

10 Once again, however, the situation was to prove different in his incidental music, where traditional Japanese instruments continued to be used for anecdotal purposes right up to his music for *Sharaku* (dir. Masahiro Shinoda, 1995).

11 Miyamoto, *Klang im Osten*, p. 55.

12 Wilson, 'The Role of Texture', p. 35.

13 Takemitsu, *Confronting Silence*, p. 63.

14 Takemitsu, *Oto, Chinmoku*, pp. 185–95.

15 Harich-Schneider, *A History of Japanese Music*, p. 419.

16 Takemitsu, *Confronting Silence*, p. 63.

17 Akiyama, *Saishin Meikyoku*, vol. 10, pp. 407–11.

18 Polydor POCG-3357.

19 Ohtake, *Creative Sources*, p. 58.

20 Edward Smaldone, 'Japanese and Western Confluences in Large-Scale Pitch Organization of Tōru Takemitsu's *November Steps* and *Autumn*', *Perspectives of New Music* 27/2 (1989), p. 223.

21 Tōru Takemitsu (trans. Mimi Yiengpruksawan), 'Sound in the East, Sound in the West: the Way to *November Steps*', *Ear* 5/8 (1990), p. 21.

22 Poirier, *Tōru Takemitsu*, p. 24.

23 Wilson, 'The Role of Texture', p. 139.

24 *Ibid.*, p. 365.

25 Smaldone, 'Japanese and Western Confluences', p. 218.

26 *Ibid.*, p. 221.

27 Roger Dettmer, sleeve notes for original recording of work (RCA SB 6814).

28 *Ibid.*

29 Wilson, 'The Role of Texture', p. 183.

30 Takemitsu, 'Contemporary Music in Japan', p. 210.

31 Poirier, *Tōru Takemitsu*, p. 65.

32 *Ibid.*, p. 224.

33 'Double Suicide', dir. Masahiro Shinoda, 1969.

34 Koozin, 'Octatonicism', p. 126.

8 Modernist apogee: the early 1970s

1 'Taiyō no Karyudo', dir. Hideo Onchi, 1970.

2 Quoted in Wilson, 'The Role of Texture', pp. 44–5.

3 Funayama, *Takemitsu Tōru*, p. 117.

4 Cf. Carlos Salzedo, *Modern Study of the Harp*, New York: Schirmer, 1921, 1948, p. 11: 'Æolian rustling: The hands, pressing the strings, are drawn slowly across them, fingers close together in the horizontal position'.

5 Takemitsu, *Confronting Silence*, p. 117.

6 Ohtake, *Creative Sources*, p. 59.

7 Poirier, *Tōru Takemitsu*, p. 70.

8 David Osmond-Smith, *Berio*, Oxford University Press, 1991, p. 120.

9 Ting-Lien Wu, 'An Analysis of Tōru Takemitsu's *Bryce* (1976), with an Emphasis on the Role of Articulation', Ph.D. diss., University of California at Los Angeles (1987), p. 14.

10 Large, flat drum with two heads, suspended in a circular frame and mounted on a stand.

11 Funayama, *Takemitsu Tōru*, p. 110.

12 Sleeve notes for original recording, Q4 EMD 5508.

13 Wilson, 'The Role of Texture', p. 142.

14 *Your eyes, your hands, your breasts …*
    You are twins in yourself.
    From *Tezukuri Kotozawa* ('Handmade Proverbs') by Shūzo Takiguchi.
    Takemitsu was to set the same text for six male voices in his 1987 work of the same title.

15 Preface to score.

16 Takemitsu, 'Afterword', p. 208.

17 Takemitsu, 'Mirrors', p. 79 n.54.

18 Oliver Knussen, obituary for Takemitsu in *The Independent*, 22 February 1996.

19 See chapter 10, Ex. 91 (p. 178).

20 Timothy Koozin, 'Spiritual-temporal Imagery in the Music of Olivier Messiaen and Tōru Takemitsu', *Contemporary Music Review* 7 (1993), p. 193.

21 Allen Hughes, 'Concert: Takemitsu, Tashi and Ozawa', *New York Times*, 25 March 1977. I am grateful for Ms Rie Suzuki of the Peabody Institute for drawing my attention to this review, which she quotes in her paper 'Sound in the East', read at the Takemitsu Society Symposium in London, July 1999.

9 Descent into the pentagonal garden

1 Poirier, *Tōru Takemitsu*, pp. 67–8.

2 Smaller transverse bamboo flute, used in *gagaku*.

3 Kuniharu Akiyama, liner notes for CD recording of work (VICC-23015), p. 12.

4 *Ibid.*, p. 13.

5 *Ibid.*, p. 11.

6 Cf. Takemitsu, 'Afterword', p. 210.

7 Akiyama, liner notes to the CD VICC–23015, p. 11.

8 Shigeo Kishibe, *The Traditional Music of Japan*, Tōkyō: Ongaku no Tomo Sha, 1984, p. 27.

9 Takemitsu, *Confronting Silence*, p. 117.

10 *Ibid.*, p. 121.

11 See Steven Nuss, 'Looking Forward, Looking Back: Influences of the Tōgaku Tradition on the Music of Tōru Takemitsu'. To my knowledge, Nuss's paper has not appeared in print, but it can be accessed online at: http://www.hamilton.edu/academic/Music/erichards/nuss.htm.

12 Tōru Takemitsu, CD notes for *In an Autumn Garden* (VICC-23015), p. 2.

13 Wilson, 'The Role of Texture', p. 207.

14 *Ibid.*, p. 6.

15 Akimichi Takeda, 'Manazashi no Ongaku: Saikin no Takemitsu-Sakuhin o Meguru Shōyō' [Music of Observation: A Look at Some Recent Takemitsu Scores], *Ongaku Geijutsu* 52/12 (Dec. 1994), p. 19.

16 Takemitsu, 'Afterword', p. 209.

17 Takemitsu, *Confronting Silence*, p. 103.

18 *Ibid.*, p. 119.

19 Tōru Takemitsu, *Yume to Kazu*, Tōkyō: Libroport, 1987, p. 14. Translation by Taniyama, 'The Development of Tōru Takemitsu's Musical Philosophy', p. 87.

20 These two terms are probably more familiar to Western readers in the form of their original Chinese equivalents, *yang* and *yin*.

21 Jeong Woo Jin, 'Comparative Analysis of Takemitsu's Recent Works *Rain Tree* and *Rain Spell*', Ph.D. diss., University of California at Los Angeles (1987), p. 36.

22 Takemitsu, 'Afterword', p. 208.

23 Poirier, *Tōru Takemitsu*, p. 86.

24 Takemitsu's own explanations can be found in the original Japanese in his *Yume to Kazu*, pp. 14–16. An English translation appears in Takemitsu, *Confronting Silence*, pp. 97–126; there is also a summary in English in Ohtake, *Creative Sources*, pp. 29–33.

25 Akiyama, *Saishin Meikyoku*, vol. 7, p. 471.

26 Poirier, *Tōru Takemitsu*, pp. 84–5.

27 Takemitsu, 'Afterword', p. 208.

28 Takemitsu, liner notes for CD recording of work, BIS CD-829.

29 Takemitsu, *Confronting Silence*, p. 105.

10 Towards the sea of tonality: the works of the 1980s

1 Poirier, *Tōru Takemitsu*, pp. 90–1.

2 *Ibid.*

3 Composer's own punctuation.

4 Takemitsu, preface to score of *Rain Coming*.

5 Sawabe, 'Alpträume und Träume', p. 52.

6 Takemitsu, *Confronting Silence*, p. 112.

7 Dotted barlines have not been included in the numbering of the bars in this and other examples.

8 Koozin, 'Octatonicism', p. 136.

9   Takemitsu, *Confronting Silence*, p. 112.
10 Takemitsu, preface to score of *Rain Coming*.
11 Takemitsu, *Oto, Chinmoku*, p. 206. Quoted in Ohtake, *Creative Sources*, p. 27.
12 Koozin, 'The Solo Piano Works', p. 269.
13 Takemitsu, *Confronting Silence*, p. 140.
14 From Ōe's novel *Atama no ii, Ame no Ki*, quoted in preface to score.
15 Takemitsu, *Confronting Silence*, p. 106.
16 Takemitsu, sleeve notes for DC 282 3; quoted in Ohtake, *Creative Sources*, pp. 38–9.
17 See: Tōru Takemitsu, *Tōi Yobigoe no Kanata e* [Beyond the Far Calls], Tōkyō: Shinchō Sha, 1992, pp. 77–8.
18 Takemitsu, programme note for *Far calls. Coming, far!* quoted from programme booklet for performance by the Tōkyō Metropolitan Symphony Orchestra at the Barbican Centre, London, 12 April 1988.
19 Funayama, *Takemitsu Tōru*, p. 41.
20 Takemitsu, programme note for *Far calls. Coming, far!*
21 Poirier, *Tōru Takemitsu*, p. 93.
22 Takemitsu, programme note for *Far calls. Coming, far!*
23 Takemitsu, *Confronting Silence*, p. 112.
24 Quoted by Akiyama in Takemitsu, *Ongaku o Yobimasu Mono*, p. 175.
25 Ohtake, *Creative Sources*, p. 26.
26 *Ibid.*
27 Poirier, *Tōru Takemitsu*, p. 71.
28 Narazaki, *Takemitsu Tōru*, p. 134.
29 *Ibid.*, p. 94.
30 Sleeve notes for FOCD3255; quoted by Ohtake in *Creative Sources*, p. 49.
31 Programme notes for CD recording of the work, Philips 426 667-2PSL.

11 Beyond the far calls: the final years

1   Tōru Takemitsu, *Sairento Gāden – Tai-in Hōkoku* [Silent Garden – Report on Discharge from Hospital] and *Kyarotin no Saiten* [Carotin Festival], Tōkyō: Shinchō Sha, 1999. A selection of Takemitsu's illustrations can also be found in Saitō and Takemitsu (eds.), *Takemitsu Tōru no Sekai*, pp. 22–5.
2   Tōru Takemitsu and Kenzaburo Ōe, *Opera o Tsukuru* [Making an Opera], Tōkyō: Iwanami Shoten, 1990.
3   For further speculation on Takemitsu's incomplete operatic project, see Funayama, *Takemitsu Tōru*, pp. 253–7.
4   Sukeyasu Shiba, interview with Susumu Shōno in 'The Role of Listening in Gagaku', *Contemporary Music Review* 1 (1987), p. 23.
5   Takemitsu, *Ki no Kagami*, p. 30. English version quoted from Takemitsu, 'Mirrors', p. 63.
6   See Tōru Takemitsu, *Toki no Entei* [Time's Gardener], Tōkyō: Shinchō Sha, 1996, p. 124.

7 Quoted in Saitō and Takemitsu (eds.), *Takemitsu Tōru no Sekai*, p. 28.

8 Oliver Knussen, CD liner notes for DGG 453 495–2, p. 4.

9 In *Dream/Window* (John Junkerman, 1992).

10 *Ibid.*, p. 5.

11 Tōru Takemitsu, CD liner notes for Denon COCO-78944.

12 *Ibid.*

13 This same theme had also been used in 1986 by Toshio Hosokawa, in his *Seeds of Contemplation* for *shōmyō* chanting and *gagaku* ensemble.

14 Takemitsu, 'Afterword', p. 207.

15 The two words are identical in the original Japanese titles.

16 Wilson, 'The Role of Texture', p. 256.

17 Cf. Takemitsu, *Oto, Chinmoku*, p. 22.

12 Swimming in the ocean that has no West or East

1 Saitō and Takemitsu, *Takemitsu Tōru no Sekai*, p. 148.

2 Tōru Takemitsu, 'A Mirror and an Egg', *Soundings* 12 (1984–5), p. 4.

3 Takemitsu, *Confronting Silence*, p. 91.

4 Ogawa, 'Tōru Takemitsu's Compositional Techniques', p. 109.

5 Poirier, *Tōru Takemitsu*, p. 91.

6 Koozin, 'The Solo Piano Works', p. 295.

7 Koozin, 'Tōru Takemitsu and the Unity of Opposites', *College Music Symposium* 30/1 (1990), p. 34.

8 Quoted in Frederic Lieberman, 'Contemporary Japanese Composition: its Relationship to Concepts of Traditional Oriental Musics', M.A. thesis, University of Hawaii (1965), p. 143.

9 Koozin, 'The Solo Piano Works', p. 549.

10 Takemitsu, 'Afterword,' p. 212.

11 Koozin, 'Tōru Takemitsu and the Unity of Opposites', p. 34.

12 *Ibid.*

13 Miyamoto, *Klang im Osten*, pp. 154–5.

14 *Ibid.*, p. 150.

15 *Ibid.*

16 *Ibid.*

17 Takemitsu, 'My Perception of Time in Traditional Japanese Music', *Contemporary Music Review* 1 (1987), p. 9.

18 Takemitsu, 'Mirrors', p. 46.

19 Takemitsu, 'My Perception of Time', p. 9.

20 Takemitsu, *Ki no Kagami*, p. 148; quoted in Miyamoto, *Klang im Osten*, p. 131.

21 Takemitsu, *Ki no Kagami*, p. 20; quoted in Miyamato, *Klang im Osten*, p. 132.

22 Takemitsu, *Confronting Silence*, p. 65.

23 Koozin, 'The Solo Piano Works', p. 282.

24 Takemitsu, 'Mirrors', p. 42.

25 *Ibid.*

26 Takemitsu, 'My Perception of Time', p. 9.

27 Takemitsu, 'Sound in the East, Sound in the West', p. 21.

28 *Ibid.*, p. 23.

29 Ohtake, *Creative Sources*, p. 25.

30 Takemitsu, *Confronting Silence*, p. 110.

31 *Ibid.*, p. 144.

32 Akira Tamba, *Musiques traditionelles du Japon*, accompagné d'un compact-disque, Cité de la Musique-Actes Sud, 1995, p. 39; quoted in Poirier, *Tōru Takemitsu*, p. 57.

33 Takemitsu, 'Mirrors', p. 41.

34 Ogawa, 'Tōru Takemitsu's Compositional Techniques', p. 112.

35 Takemitsu, *Confronting Silence*, p. 80.

36 *Ibid.*, p. 4.

37 John Allison, 'Craft Going Nowhere', *The Times*, 6 October 1998, p. 34.

38 Takemitsu, *Confronting Silence*, p. 14.

39 *Ibid.*, p. 80.

40 Paul Driver, 'Empty Spirits', *The Sunday Times*, 25 October 1998, p. 22.

41 Roger Reynolds and Tōru Takemitsu, 'Roger Reynolds and Tōru Takemitsu: a Conversation', *Musical Quarterly* 80/1 (Spring 1996), p. 70.

42 *Ibid.*, p. 69.

43 *Ibid.*

44 *Ibid.*, p. 70.

45 Driver, 'Empty Spirits', p. 22.

46 Robert Sherlaw-Johnson, *Messiaen*, London: Dent, 1975, p. 40. Messiaen himself, indeed, described his own aims as the fashioning of a 'theological rainbow' (*Technique de mon langage musical*, Paris: Leduc, 1944, p. 21).

47 Roland Barthes (trans. Richard Howard), *Empire of Signs*, London: Jonathan Cape, 1983, p. 78.

48 Takemitsu, *Confronting Silence*, p. 13.

49 *Ibid.*, p. 86.

50 *Ibid.*

51 Bernard Rands, 'I sing only for myself …', *Musical Times* 128/1735 (Sept. 1987), p. 477.

52 Takemitsu, 'A Mirror and an Egg', p. 3.

53 Wu, 'An Analysis of Tōru Takemitsu's *Bryce*'.

54 Jin, 'Comparative Analysis'.

55 Wu, 'An Analysis of Tōru Takemitsu's *Bryce*', p. 45.

56 *Ibid.*, p. 44.

57 Jin, 'Comparative Analysis', p. 5.

58 Takemitsu, *Yume to Kazu*, p. 21; translation from Taniyama, 'The Development of Tōru Takemitsu's Musical Philosophy', p. 90.

59 Takemitsu, *Yume to Kazu*, p. 6; translation from Taniyama, 'The Development of Tōru Takemitsu's Musical Philosophy', p. 78.

60 Takemitsu, *Confronting Silence*, p. 51. Miyamoto interprets this statement rather differently, as meaning that such a sound is 'already too complex and complete in itself to represent a dialectic totality by being understood in a functional sense with reference to other tones' (*Klang im Osten*, p. 151).

61 Takemitsu, *Confronting Silence*, pp. 65–6.

Takemitsu's works

The following summary of Takemitsu's vast compositional output makes no claims to be exhaustive, especially since it represents the conflation of several, often conflicting, sources. Of these the most important have been: Schott's catalogue of the composer's works (Tōkyō: Schott Japan, 1998); Kuniharu Akiyama's list of works in *Takemitsu Tōru no Sekai*, pp. 252–66; Yōko Narazaki's worklist in the *Ongaku Geijutsu* (May 1996), pp. 60–73; Akiyama's biographical notes in the endpages of various volumes of Takemitsu's writings; plus odd hints found by chance in assorted literature on the composer. Above all, however, I have leaned most heavily on Mitsuko Ono's scrupulously thorough listing in Chōki and Higuchi (eds.), *Takemitsu Tōru: Oto no Kawa no Yukue*, pp. 398–444, which appeared as this work was nearing completion. Ms Ono's researches into Takemitsu's compositional activity are by far the most thorough of any undertaken to date, and I am supremely indebted both to her example and for the personal help she has given me in the following compilation.

(* = unpublished work)

1 Orchestral works

*Joie de Vivre, ballet score in collaboration with Hiroyoshi Suzuki (1951)
*A Trip on the Galactic Railway, ballet score (1953)
Requiem for String Orchestra (1957)
*Solitude Sonore (1958)
Music of Tree (1961)
The Dorian Horizon for seventeen strings (1966)
Green (1967)
Winter (1971)
Marginalia (1976)
A Flock Descends into the Pentagonal Garden (1977)
Dreamtime (1981)
A Way a Lone II for string orchestra (version of *A Way a Lone* for string quartet) (1981)
Star-Isle (1982)
Rain Coming for chamber orchestra (1982)
*Lacrima for String Orchestra, arrangement of music from film *Yogen* (1983)
Dream/Window (1985)
*At Evening (arrangement of Hitoshi Komuro) (1987)
Twill by Twilight – In Memory of Morton Feldman (1988)

Tree Line for chamber orchestra (1988)
Visions (1990)
   I Mystère
   II Les yeux clos
How slow the Wind (1991)
Archipelago S. for twenty-one players (1993)
Spirit Garden (1994)
Three Film Scores – transcriptions for string orchestra of music from films (1994)
   I Music of Training and Rest from *Jose Torres*
   II Funeral Music from *Black Rain*
   III Waltz from *Face of Another*
Nami no Bon (arrangement of music originally written for TV, 1996)
Alone on the Pacific, suite for orchestra (arrangement of music originally written
for film *Taiheiyō Hitoribocchi* in collaboration with Yasushi Akutagawa, 1996)
Two Cine Pastrali: concert suite for orchestra on music from films (1996)
   1. Orin (from *Orin/Banished*)
   2. Kaoru (from *Izu Dancer*)
Dodes'ka-Den (arrangement of music originally written for film *Dodes'ka-Den*,
1996)
Death and Resurrection – from *Black Rain* – for string orchestra (arrangement of
music originally written for film *Kuroi Ame*, 1996)

2. Works for soloists and orchestra

Scene for cello and string orchestra (1959)
Arc Part I for piano and orchestra (1963–66/76)
   I Pile (1963)
   II Solitude (1966)
   III Your love and the crossing (1963)
Arc Part II for piano and orchestra (1964–66/76)
   I Textures (1964)
   II Reflection (1966)
   III Coda . . . Shall begin from the end (1966)
November Steps for *biwa*, *shakuhachi* and orchestra (1967)
Asterism for piano and orchestra (1967)
Crossing for guitar, harp, piano/celesta, vibraphone, female voices and two
orchestras (1969)
Eucalypts I for flute, oboe, harp and string orchestra (1970)
Cassiopeia for percussion solo and orchestra (1971)
Autumn for *biwa*, *shakuhachi* and orchestra (1973)
Gitimalya, 'bouquet of songs' for marimba solo and orchestra (1974)
Quatrain for clarinet, violin, cello, piano and orchestra (1975)
Far calls. Coming, far! for violin and orchestra (1980)

Toward the Sea II for alto flute, harp and string orchestra (version of *Toward the Sea* for alto flute and guitar) (1981)

To the Edge of Dream for guitar and orchestra (1983)

Orion and Pleiades for cello and orchestra (1984)

Vers, l'arc-en-ciel, Palma for guitar, *oboe d'amore* and orchestra (1984)

riverrun for piano and orchestra (1984)

Gémeaux for oboe, trombone, two orchestras and two conductors (1971–86)
    I Strophe
    II Genesis
    III Traces
    IV Antistrophe

I Hear the Water Dreaming for flute and orchestra (1987)

Nostalghia – In Memory of Andrei Tarkovsky – for violin and string orchestra (1987)

A String Around Autumn for viola and orchestra (1989)

From me flows what you call Time for five percussionists and orchestra (1990)

Fantasma/Cantos for clarinet and orchestra (1991)

Quotation of Dream – Say sea, take me! – for two pianos and orchestra (1991)

Ceremonial – An Autumn Ode – for orchestra with *shō* (1992)

Fantasma/Cantos II for trombone and orchestra (1994)

Spectral Canticle for violin, guitar and orchestra (1995)

*****Comme la sculpture de Miró** for flute, harp and orchestra (commissioned by BBC; unfinished at composer's death)

3. Works for chamber ensemble

*****Chamber Concerto** for thirteen winds (1955)

Le Son Calligraphié I–III for four violins, two violas and two cellos (1958–60)

Landscape for string quartet (1960)

Ring for flute, terz guitar and lute (1961)

Sacrifice for alto flute, lute and vibraphone (1962)

Corona II for string(s), graphic work in collaboration with Kōhei Sugiura (1962)

Arc for Strings, graphic work (1963)

Valeria for violin, cello, guitar, electric organ and two piccolos (1965)

Stanza I for guitar, piano/celesta, harp, vibraphone and female voice (Text: Ludwig Wittgenstein, 1969)

Eucalypts II for flute, oboe and harp (1971)

In an Autumn Garden for *gagaku* orchestra (fourth part of complete version *In an Autumn Garden*, 1973)

Garden Rain for brass ensemble (1974)

Bryce for flute, two harps and two percussionists (1976)

Waves for clarinet, horn, two trombones and bass drum (1976)

Quatrain II for clarinet, violin, cello and piano (1977)

Waterways for clarinet, violin, cello, piano, two harps and two vibraphones (1978)

In an Autumn Garden, complete version for *gagaku* orchestra (1979)

    I Strophe

    II Echo I

    III Melisma

    IV In an Autumn Garden

    V Echo II

    VI Antistrophe

A Way a Lone for string quartet (1981)

Rain Spell for flute, clarinet, harp, piano and vibraphone (1982)

Entre-temps for oboe and string quartet (1986)

Signals from Heaven – two antiphonal fanfares for two brass groups

   Day Signal – Signals from Heaven I (1987)

   Night Signal – Signals from Heaven II (1987)

And then I knew 'twas Wind for flute, viola and harp (1992)

Between Tides for violin, cello and piano (1993)

Herbstlied for clarinet and string quartet, transcription of a solo piano work by Peter Ilyich Tchaikovsky (1993)

4. Piano works

*Kakehi *(Conduit)* (1948)

Romance (1949)

*2 Pieces (1949)

*Lento in Due Movimenti (1950) (see also *Litany*, 1989)

Uninterrupted Rest (1952–59)

*At the Circus (1952)

*Awaremitamae *(Miserere)* (1960)

*Ai shite *(Love Me)* (1960)

Piano Distance (1961)

Corona for pianist(s), graphic score (in collaboration with Kōhei Sugiura, 1962)

Crossing, graphic work for piano(s) (in collaboration with Kōhei Sugiura, 1962)

For Away (1973)

Les yeux clos (1979)

Little Piano Pieces for Children (1979)

    I Breeze

    II Cloud

Rain Tree Sketch (1982)

Les yeux clos II (1988)

Litany – In Memory of Michael Vyner (recomposition of *Lento in Due Movimenti*, 1950/89)

*Golden Slumbers (arrangement of Lennon and McCartney) (1992)

Rain Tree Sketch II – In Memoriam Olivier Messiaen (1992)

5. Other instrumental works

Distance de Fée for violin and piano (1951, rev. 1989)
*Solitude Sonore for solo flute (1957)
Masque I & II for two flutes (1959)
   1. Continu
   2. Incidental I
Masque III (= Incidental II) for two flutes (1960)
Bad Boy for two guitars (based on film music for *Furyō Shōnen*, 1961/93)
Eclipse for *biwa* and *shakuhachi* (1966)
Hika for violin and piano (1966)
Munari by Munari for percussion solo (1969–72)
Cross Talk for two bandoneons and tape (1968)
Seasons, graphic work for four percussionists, or one percussionist and tape (1970)
Voice for solo flautist (1971)
Stanza II for harp and tape (1971)
Distance for oboe with or without *shō* (1972)
Voyage for three *biwa* (1973)
Folios for solo guitar (1974)
Le Fils des Etoiles – Prélude du 1er Acte 'La Vocation' – for flute and harp (transcription of a solo piano work by Erik Satie, 1975)
Twelve Songs for Guitar, transcriptions of:
   Londonderry Air (Irish trad.); *Over the Rainbow* (Harold Arlen); *Summertime* (George Gershwin); *A Song of Early Spring* (Akira Nakada); *Amours Perdues* (Joseph Kosma); *What a Friend* (Charles C. Converse); *Secret Love* (Sammy Fain); *Here, There and Everywhere, Michelle, Hey Jude* and *Yesterday* (John Lennon and Paul McCartney); *The International* (Paul Degeyter) (1977)
Toward the Sea for alto flute and guitar (1981)
   I The Night
   II Moby Dick
   III Cape Cod
Rain Tree for three percussion players (or three keyboard players) (1981)
*Cross Hatch for marimba and vibraphone (or two keyboard players) (1982)
The Last Waltz (arrangement of Les Reed/Barry Mason) for guitar (1983)
Rocking Mirror Daybreak for violin duo (1983)
From far beyond Chrysanthemums and November Fog for violin and piano (1983)
Orion for cello and piano (1984)
Rain Dreaming for harpsichord (1986)
All in Twilight, four pieces for guitar (1987)
Itinerant – In Memory of Isamu Noguchi – for solo flute (1989)
Toward the Sea III for alto flute and harp (version of *Toward the Sea* for alto flute and guitar) (1989)

Equinox for guitar (1993)
*Autumn Leaves, arr. of Joseph Kosma for guitar (1993)
Paths – In Memoriam Witold Lutosławski for trumpet (1994)
A Bird came down the Walk for viola accompanied by piano (1994)
In the Woods, three pieces for guitar (1995)
  1. Wainscot Pond – after a painting by Cornelia Foss
  2. Rosedale
  3. Muir Woods
Air for flute (1995)

6. Vocal works

Tableau Noir for reciter and chamber orchestra (text: Kuniharu Akiyama, 1958)
*'Town Song' for Bihorochō, Hokkaidō (1953)
*Be Sleep Baby!, song to celebrate birth of Shuntarō Tanikawa's son (1960)
Wind Horse for mixed chorus (text: Kuniharu Akiyama, 1961–66)
   I Vocalise I
  II Spell of Fingers
 III Vocalise II
  IV Vocalise III
   V Legend of the Dining Table
Coral Island for soprano and orchestra (text: Makoto Ōoka, 1962)
*School Song for Yokkaichi High School (text: Shuntarō Tanikawa, 1963)
Uta *(Songs)* for mixed chorus (1979–92)
   Will Tomorrow, I Wonder, be Cloudy or Clear (text: Tōru Takemitsu; *In a Small Room* (text: Akira Kawaji); *Small Sky* (text: Tōru Takemitsu); *The Game of Love* (text: Shuntarō Tanikawa); *A Song of ○'s [Circles] and △'s [Triangles]* (text: Tōru Takemitsu); *Unseen Child* (text: Shuntarō Tanikawa); *Sakura (Cherry Blossom),* Japanese trad.; *Sayonara* (text: Kuniharu Akiyama); *To the Island* (text: Mann Izawa); *All That the Man Left Behind When He Died* (text: Shuntarō Tanikawa); *Wings* (text: Tōru Takemitsu); *I Just Sing* (text: Shuntarō Tanikawa)
Grass for male chorus (text: Shuntarō Tanikawa, trans. into English by W. S. Merwin, 1982)
*Kumegawa-Higashi Primary School Song (text: Shuntarō Tanikawa, 1983)
Handmade Proverbs – Four Pop Songs for six male voices (text: Shūzo Takiguchi, trans. into English by Kenneth Lyons, 1987)
My Way of Life – In Memory of Michael Vyner for baritone, mixed chorus and orchestra (text: Ryūichi Tamura, trans. into English by Yasunari Takahashi, 1990)
*Akiba-Gakuen School Song (text: Makoto Ōoka, 1991)
Family Tree – Musical Verses for Young People for narrator and orchestra (text: Shuntarō Tanikawa, 1992)
Songs – piano/vocal arrangements by Takemitsu (**) and Henning Brauel (2000):
   Sayonara; In a Small Room; I Just Sing (**); The Game of Love; A Song of ○'s [Circles] and △'s [Triangles]; Small Sky; La Neige (text: Shin-ichi Segi); *Take Off for the Clouds* (text: Shuntarō Tanikawa); *Unseen Child; A Marvellous Kid* (text:

Fumio Nagata); *In the Month of March* (text: Shuntarō Tanikawa); *All That the Man Left Behind When He Died; Waltz (from* Face of Another, text: Tatsuji Iwabuchi); *The Encounter* (text: Ichirō Araki); *Glowing Autumn (**)* (text: Hiroyuki Itsuki); *Wings; To the Island; Will Tomorrow, I Wonder, Be Cloudy or Clear?; Potsunen* (All Alone) (text: Shuntarō Tanikawa); *Yesterday's Spot* (text: Shuntarō Tanikawa)

7. Works for electronic tape, theatre pieces, etc.

(a) Tape pieces

*Kine Karigurafi (accompaniment to animated images, 1955)
Relief Statique (1955)
*Eurydice (1956)
*Vocalism A. I (1956)
*Trees, Sky and Birds (1956)
*Clap Vocalism (1956)
Sky, Horse and Death (1958)
*Dialogue (1958)
*Quiet Design (1960)
Water Music (1960)
*Requiem for the Unknown Soldier (1960)
*I Left My Heart in San Francisco (1964)
Kwaidan (based on composer's music for film of that name, 1964)
*YEARS OF EAR 'What is Music?' collaboration between: Tōru Takemitsu, Shuntarō Tanikawa, Makoto Ōoka, Akimichi Takeda and Takashi Funayama (1970)
Toward (1970)
A Minneapolis Garden, environmental music (1986)
The Sea is Still, environmental music (1986)

(b) Other

Blue Aurora for Toshi Ichiyanagi, 'event musical' (1964)
*Time Perspective, theatre piece (in collaboration with Toshi Ichiyanagi and Yoshiaki Higashino, 1964)
*Seven Hills Event, theatre piece (1966)
Wavelength for two percussionists, two dancers and video installation (1984 –)

8. Music for stage productions (all *)

(a) For Bungakuza theatre

Summer and Smoke by Tennessee Williams (1954); *The Death of K* by Shuntarō Tanikawa (1956); *L'Avare* by Molière (1957); *Kokuseiya* by Yashirō Seiichi (1958); *Look Back in Anger* by John Osborne (1959); *Orpheus Descending* by Tennessee

Williams (1961); *Black Tragedy* by Yashirō Seiichi (1962); *White Night* by Shūji Terayama (1962)

(b) For Shiki theatre

La Sauvage by Jean Anouilh (1955); *Amphitorion 38* by Jean Giraudoux (1955); *Ai no Jōken* ('Love's Stipulation', version of *Eurydice)* by Jean Anouilh (1956); *Semushi no Seijo* (version of *Ardèle, ou la Marguérite*) by Jean Anouilh (1956); *La Guerre de Troie n'aura pas lieu* by Jean Giraudoux (1957); *Le Corsaire* by Marcel Achard (1959); *La Reine morte* by Henri de Montherlant (1959); *The Wolf must Live, the Pig must Die* by Shintarō Ishihara (1960); *The Play is Finished* by Shuntarō Tanikawa (1960); *The Brothers Karamazov* by Fyodor Dostoyevsky (1966); *Poseidon Mask Festival* by Kuninari Tsuji (1974); *Cyrano de Bergerac* by Edmond Rostand (1975)

(c) Other

Romantic Suite – Nutcracker for Children, children's ballet, arrangement of Tchaikovsky in collaboration with Jun Date (1954); *Eve of the Future*, ballet music for magnetic tape, collaboration with Toshirō Mayuzumi (1955); *Ichinoya Story* by Shintarō Ishihara (1964); *Love Wears Tinted Glasses* by Abe Kōbō (1973); *Festival of the Meridian*, Yasue Yamamoto Company (1979); *Wings*, by Arthur L. Kopit (1982)

9. Music for radio and television (all *)

(a) Radio

Four Seasons of Sound (NHK, 1955); *Illusions of the Sea,* radio drama by Kuniharu Akiyama (NHK, 1955); *Honō* (Flame), radio drama by Yasushi Inoue (Shin Nihon Hōsō, 1955); *Death of a Man,* radio drama by Shuntarō Tanikawa (NHK, 1957); *Blind Panic* (Asahi Hōsō, 1960); *Records of a Long, Black Shadow* (TBS, 1962); *Gan Kingu* (TBS, 1962); *Beyond Love and Hate* (Mainichi Hōsō, 1967); *Chronicles of Toku Market* (Asahi Hōsō, 1968); *Alice in the Subway,* stereo drama (NHK, 1976); *Heartlessness* (NHK, 1978); *Ganjin* (Asahi Hōsō, 1980); *Why did the S.S. Tōya sink?* (Tōkyō Hōsō, 1980); *To You, Far Away* (NHK, 1980); *Natives of the Port* (TBS, 1980); *Sadness without Form* (NHK, 1983); *Shanghai – Road of Illusions* (TBS, 1983)

(b) Television

Dream Star (Asahi TV, 1958); *Word Place*, theme music (NHK, 1960); *Japanese Crest Patterns* (NHK, 1961); *Who are you?* (NHK, 1961); *Woman Blowing a Mukkuri* (NHK, 1961); *Annals of the Present – 'Ruins'* (NHK, 1962); *Festival*

(Hokkaidō Hōsō, 1962); *Eyewitness* (TBS, 1964); *The Tale of Genji* (Mainichi Hōsō, 1965); *Yoshitsune Minamoto* (NHK, 1966); *You* (Tōkyō Hōsō, 1966); Various background pieces for NHK, 1967/8; *Sword*, theme music (CAL/Nippon TV, 1967); *A Woman of the Genroku Period* (Mainichi Hōsō, 1968); *A Villain* (Asahi Hōsō, 1969); *The Emperor's Era* (Asahi Hōsō, 1971); *One More Injury* (NHK, 1971); *In Motion, musical work for sounds and images* (in collaboration with Kōhei Sugiura, NHK, 1972); *Illusion of Woman* (NHK, 1972); *My Love* (TBS, 1973); *Bequest to the Future* (NHK, 1974); *Winter Rainbow* (NET, 1976); *Tales of a Distant Field* (NHK, 1977); *The Legend of Takimori Saigō* (TBS, 1977); *Ohan* (TV Asahi, 1977); *The Louvre Art Gallery* (Fuji Television, 1979); *The Rōshi from Akō* (TV Asahi, 1979); *Blood Relative* (NHK, 1979); *Diary of Yumechiyo* (NHK, 1981; second series 1983); *The Silk Road*, video production (Victor Video, 1981; music composed in collaboration with Masaru Tanaka); *Shimin Daigaku* ('Citizens' University') theme music (NHK, 1982); *Giovanni's Milky Way* (NHK, 1983); *Unable to Speak* (NHK, 1983); *Maa, eewaina!* (Well, that will do!) (NHK, 1983); *Nami no Bon* (Wave Festival) (NTV, 1983); *New Diary of Yumechiyo* (NHK, 1984); *Warning of the 21ˢᵗ Century* (NHK, 1984); *I came to Meet Myself*, video production (Tōhō, 1985); *Music for the Matsushita Pavilion at the Tsukuba Exposition* (Tōhō, 1985); *The Love of Osan* (NHK, 1985); *Tanizaki* (NHK, 1985); *The World of Zen* (NHK, 1986); *This Morning's Autumn* (NHK, 1987); *Santōbi* (NHK, 1989); *Apparitions – Picture Scroll of the Tale of Genji* (NHK, 1993)

(c) TV commercials

Xerox 9200 (1976); *Hitachi TV* (1977); *IBM* (1979); *Tōshiba Colour TV*; *Ōzeki, The Network – Seibu Special* (1979); *Suntory Reserve* (1982); *US Cotton* (1989)

10. Film scores (all *)

Hokusai (scenario by Shūzo Takiguchi, 1952) (Unused)
Sarariman Mejiro Sanpei *(Salaryman Sanpei Mejiro)* (Hiroshigi Chiba, 1955) in collaboration with Yasushi Akutagawa
Ginrin *(Silver Ring)*, promotional film for bicycle industry (Toshio Matsuki, 1955) in collaboration with Hideyoshi Suzuki
Kurutta Kajitsu *(Crazed Fruit/Juvenile Passions)* (Kō Nakahira, 1956) in collaboration with Masaru Sato
Shu to Midori *(Red and Green/Midnight Visitor)* (Noboru Nakamura, 1956)
Tsuyu no Atosaki *(The Rainy Season)* (Noboru Nakamura, 1956)
Doshaburi *(Cloudburst)* (Noboru Nakamura, 1957)
Kaoyaku *(The Country Boss)* (Noboru Nakamura, 1958)
Kamitsukareta Kaoyaku *(Bitten Leader)* (Noboru Nakamura, 1958)
Haru o Matsu Hitobito *(Waiting for Spring)* (Noboru Nakamura, 1959)
Itazura *(Joking/Love Letters)* (Noboru Nakamura, 1959)
Kiken Ryokō *(Dangerous Trip/Vagabond Lovers)* (Noboru Nakamura, 1959)

Jose Torres (Hiroshi Teshigahara, 1959)

Ashita e no Seisō *(Fully Dressed for Tomorrow)* (Noboru Nakamura, 1959)

Nami no Tō *(Tower of Waves)* (Noboru Nakamura, 1960)

Kawaita Mizuumi *(Dry Lake/Youth in Fury)* (Masahiro Shinoda, 1960)

Yoru ga Kuru *(Evening is coming)* (Shintarō Ishikawa, 1960)

X (Tōru Takemitsu, Shuntarō Tanikawa, 1960)

Too Blue (Ishio Shirasaka and Yoshie Imai, 1960)

Mozu *(The Shrikes)* (Minoru Shibuya, 1961)

Hannyo *(Hannyo/Woman of Tōkyō)* (Noboru Nakamura, 1961)

Furyō Shōnen *(Bad Boys)* (Susumu Hani, 1961)

Ningen Dōbutsuen *(Human Zoo)*, animated cartoon (Yōji Kuri, 1961)

Mitasareta Seikatsu *(A Full Life)* (Susumu Hani, 1962)

Karami-Ai *(The Inheritance)* (Masaki Kobayashi, 1962)

Otoshiana *(The Pitfall/Cheap, Sweet and a Kid)* (Hiroshi Teshigahara, 1962)

Namida o Shishi no Tategami ni *(Tears in the Lion's Mane)* (Masahiro Shinoda, 1962)

Seppuku *(Harakiri)* (Masaki Kobayashi, 1962)

Ratai *(The Naked Body)* (Masashige Narisawa, 1962) in collaboration with Jōji Yuasa

Koto *(Twin Sisters of Kyōto)* (Noboru Nakamura, 1963)

Kanojo to Kare *(She and He)* (Susumu Hani, 1963)

Taiheiyō Hitoribocchi *(Alone on the Pacific)* (Kon Ichikawa, 1963) in collaboration with Yasushi Akutagawa

Subarashii Akujo *(A Marvellous Kid)* (Hideo Onchi, 1963)

Shiro to Kuro *(White and Black)* (Hiromichi Horikawa, 1963)

Love, animated cartoon (Yōji Kuri, 1963)

Suna no Onna *(Woman in the Dunes)* (Hiroshi Teshigahara, 1964)

Kawaita Hana *(Pale Flower)* (Masahiro Shinoda, 1964)

Te o Tsunagu Kora *(Children Hand in Hand)* (Susumu Hani, 1964)

Nijū-issai no Chichi *(21-year-old Father/Our Happiness Alone)* (Noboru Nakamura, 1964)

Ansatsu *(The Assassin)* (Masahiro Shinoda, 1964)

Nihon Dasshutsu *(Nippon Escape)* (Yoshishige Yoshida, 1964) in collaboration with Masao Yagi

Nyotai *(The Female Body)* (Hideo Onchi, 1964)

Jidōsha Dorobō *(The Car Thief)* (Yoshinori Wada, 1964)

Shiroi Asa *(The White Dawn)* (Hiroshi Teshigahara, 1964)

Kaidan *(Kwaidan)* (Masaki Kobayashi, 1964)

Utsukushisa to Kanashimi to *(With Beauty and Sorrow)* (Masahiro Shinoda, 1965)

Saigo no Shinpan *(Last Judgement)* (Hiromichi Horikawa, 1965)

Buwana Toshi no Uta *(Bwana Toshi)* (Susumu Hani, 1965)

Ibun Sarutobi Sasuke *(Extraordinary Sasuke Sarutobi/Samurai Spy)* (Masahiro Shinoda, 1965)

Kemono-michi *(Beast Alley)* (Eizo Sugawa, 1965)

Yotsuya Kaidan *(Yotsuya Ghost Story/Illusion Island)* (Shiro Toyoda, 1965)

Ki no Kawa *(The Kii River)* (Noboru Nakamura, 1966)

Shokei no Shima *(Punishment Island)* (Masahiro Shinoda, 1966)

Tanin no Kao *(Face of Another)* (Hiroshi Teshigahara, 1966)

Akogare *(Longing/Once a Rainy Day)* (Hideo Onchi, 1966)

Denshi Gijutsu de Mirai o Hiraku *(Opening up the Future with Electronic Art)* (Tsumura Hideya, 1966)

Monokurōmu no Gaka – Ibu Kurain *(Yves Klein – Painter in Monochrome)* (Shinkichi Noda, 1966)

Izu no Odoriko *(Izu Dancer)* (Hideo Onchi, 1967)

Akanegumo *(Clouds at Sunset)* (Masahiro Shinoda, 1967)

Jōi-uchi *(Rebellion)* (Masaki Kobayashi, 1967)

Midaregumo *(Billowing Clouds/Two in the Shadow)* (Mikio Naruse, 1967)

Meguriai *(The Encounter)* (Hideo Onchi, 1968)

Moetsukita Chizu *(The Ruined Map/The Man without a Map)* (Hiroshi Teshigahara, 1968)

Nihon no Seishun *(Hymn to a Tired Man)* (Masaki Kobayashi, 1968)

Kyō (Kon Ichikawa, 1968)

Hokkaidō Monogatari *(Tales of Hokkaido)* (Fuminao Sugihara, 1968)

Shinjū Ten no Amishima *(Double Suicide)* (Masahiro Shinoda, 1969)

Dankon *(The Bullet Wounded)* (Shiro Moritani, 1969)

Taiyō no Karyūdo *(The Sun's Hunter)* (Hideo Onchi, 1970)

Tōkyō Sensō Sengo Hiwa *(The Man who left his Will on Film/He Died after the War)* (Nagisa Ōshima, 1970)

Dodes'ka-Den (Akira Kurosawa, 1970)

Yomigaeru Daichi *(The Earth is Born Again)* (Noboru Nakamura, 1971)

Gishiki *(The Ceremony)* (Nagisa Ōshima, 1971)

Inochi Bō ni Furō *(Inn of Evil)* (Masaki Kobayashi, 1971)

Chinmoku *(Silence)* (Masahiro Shinoda, 1971)

Summer Soldiers (Hiroshi Teshigahara, 1972)

Natsu no Imōto *(Dear Summer Sister)* (Nagisa Ōshima, 1972)

Kaseki no Mori *(The Forest of Fossils)* (Masahiro Shinoda, 1973)

Seigen-Ki *(Time within Memory)* (Tōichirō Narushima, 1973)

Himiko (Masahiro Shinoda, 1974)

Shiawase *(Happiness)* (Hideo Onchi, 1974)

Kaseki *(Kaseki/The Fossil)* (Masaki Kobayashi, 1974)

Sakura no Mori no Mankai no Shita *(Under the Blossoming Cherry Tree)* (Masahiro Shinoda, 1975)

Nihontō – Miyairi Yukihira no Waza *(Japanese Swords – Craftsmanship of Miyairi)* (Tokio Yamauchi, 1975)

Sabita Honō *(Incandescent Flame)* (Masahisa Sadanaga, 1977)

Hanare Goze Orin *(Orin/Banished)* (Masahiro Shinoda, 1977)

Ai no Bōrei *(Empire of Passion)* (Nagisa Ōshima, 1978)

Moeru Aki *(Glowing Autumn)* (Masaki Kobayashi, 1978)

Kataku *(House of Blaze)* (Kihachirō Kawamoto, 1979)

Meido no Hiyaku *(Messenger from Hades)* (Marty Gross, 1979)

Tenpyō no Iraka (*Roof Tile of Tenpyō*) (Kei Kumai, 1980)

Ki = Breathing (Toshio Matsumoto, 1980)

Minamata no Zu *(Map of Minamata)* (Noriaki Tsuchimoto, 1981)

Rennyo to sono Haha *(Rennyo, the Priest, and his Mother)* (Kihachirō Kawamoto, 1981)

Yogen *(Prophecy)* (Susumu Hani, 1982)

Tōkyō Saiban *(Tōkyō Trial/Tōkyō Verdict)* (Masaki Kobayashi, 1983)

Antonio Gaudi (Hiroshi Teshigahara, 1984)

Ran (Akira Kurosawa, 1985)

Shokutaku no Nai Ie *(The Empty House/House without a Table)* (Masaki Kobayashi, 1985)

Himatsuri *(Fire Festival)* (Mitsuo Yanagimachi, 1985)

A. K. (documentary film about Akira Kurosawa) (Chris Marker, 1985)

Yari no Gonza *(Gonza a Spear Man)* (Masahiro Shinoda, 1986)

Hiroshima to iu Na no Shōnen *(A Boy Named Hiroshima)* (Yoshiya Sugata, 1987)

Arashi ga Oka *(Onimaru)* (Yoshishige Yoshida, 1988)

Kuroi Ame *(Black Rain)* (Shōhei Imamura, 1989)

Rikyū (Hiroshi Teshigahara, 1989)

Gō-hime *(Basara, the Princess Goh)* (Hiroshi Teshigahara, 1991)

Inland Sea (Lucille Carras/Donald Richie, 1991)

Dream Window (John Junkerman, 1992)

Rising Sun (Philip Kaufman, 1993)

Sharaku (Masahiro Shinoda, 1995)

Select bibliography

1 Japan: culture and history (general)

Barthes, Roland, *Empire of Signs*, trans. Richard Howard, London: Jonathan Cape, 1983

Sansom, G. B., *Japan: a Short Cultural History*, Rutland, Vermont: Tuttle, 1979
    The Western World and Japan, London: Cresset, 1950

Smith, Bradley, *Japan: a History in Art*, Tōkyō: Gemini Smith, 1979

Toynbee, Arnold J., *Civilization on Trial*, Oxford University Press, 1948
    The World and the West, Oxford University Press, 1953

2 Japan: traditional music

Harich-Schneider, Eta, *A History of Japanese Music*, Oxford University Press, 1973

Shigeo, Kishibe, *The Traditional Music of Japan*, Tōkyō: Ongaku no Tomo Sha, 1984

Shōno, Susumu, 'The Role of Listening in *Gagaku*', *Contemporary Music Review* 1 (1987), 19–43

3 Japan: reception of Western music

Dahlhaus, Carl (trans. Mary Whittall), *Between Romanticism and Modernism: Four Studies in the Music of the Later Nineteenth Century*, Berkeley, California: University of California Press, 1980

Dan, Ikuma, *Nihonjin to Seiyō-Ongaku: Ibunka to no Shukkai* [The Japanese and Western Music: Encounters with an Alien Culture], Tōkyō: Nippon Hōsō Shuppan Kyōkai, 1997

Eberl, Monika, 'Durst nach Mozart: über Geschichte und Gegenwart der europäischen Musik in Japan', *Musica* 37/4 (1983), 317–21

Galliano, Luciana, 'I compositori giapponesi del primo Novecento e l'apprendimento della musica Europea', *Rivista italiana di musicologia* 29/1 (1994), 183–208
    Yōgaku: Percorsi della musica giapponese nel Novecento, Venice: Cafoscarina, 1998

Kasaba, Eiko, 'Notes sur la réception de la musique de Messiaen en Japon', *Revue internationale de musique française* 30 (Nov. 1989), 93–9
    'Reflections on the Reception of Claude Debussy's Music in Japan', in *Tradition and its Future in Music* (Report of SIMS 1990 Ōsaka), Ōsaka: Mita Press, 1991, 503–8

Komiya, Toyotaka (ed.), trans. & adapted by Edward D. Seidensticker and
    Donald Keene, *Japanese Music and Drama in the Meiji Era*, Tōkyō: Obun Sha,
    1956
Yoshida, Hidekazu, 'Über die Musikentwicklung Japans in den letzen 100 Jahren',
    in *Aspekte der neuen Musik (Professor Hans Heinz Stuckenschmidt zum 65.
    Geburtstag)*, Kassel: Bärenreiter, 1968, 97–111
Yoshida, Takatoshi, 'How Western Music came to Japan', *Tempo* 40 (Summer
    1956), 16–17

4 Twentieth-century music (Western)

Forte, Allen, *The Structure of Atonal Music*, Yale University Press, 1973
Messiaen, Olivier, *The Technique of my Musical Language*, Paris: Leduc, 1944
Osmond-Smith, David, *Berio*, Oxford University Press, 1991
Sherlaw Johnson, Robert, *Messiaen*, London: Dent, 1975
Stravinsky, Igor and Craft, Robert, *Dialogues and a Diary*, London: Faber,
    1968

5 Twentieth-century music (Japanese)

Akiyama, Kuniharu, *Nihon no Sakkyokukatachi* [Japanese Composers], Tōkyō:
    Ongaku no Tomo Sha, 1978–79
Aoki, Yōko, *A Catalogue of Printed Music by Japanese Composers*, Kunitachi
    College of Music Library, 1991 (Bibliography and Index Series, no. 12)
Fukui, Masa Kitagawa, 'Japanese Piano Music, 1940–1973: a Meeting of Eastern
    and Western Traditions', DMA thesis, University of Maryland (1981)
Heifetz, Robin Julian, 'Post-World War II Japanese Composition', DMA thesis,
    University of Illinois at Urbana-Champaign (1978)
Herd, Judith Ann, 'The Neonationalist Movement: Origins of Japanese
    Contemporary Music', *Perspectives of New Music* 27/2 (Summer 1989),
    118–59
Hori, Tadashi (ed.), *Nihon no Sakkyoku Nijū Seiki* [Japanese Composition in the
    Twentieth Century], Tōkyō: Ongaku no Tomo Sha, 1999
Japanese Composers and their Works since 1868, Tōkyō: Japan UNESCO NGO
    Council, 1972
Malm, William P., 'Layers of Modern Music and Japan', *Asian Music* 4/2 (1973),
    3–6
Matsushita, Hitoshi, *A Checklist of Published Instrumental Music by Japanese
    Composers*, Tōkyō: Academia Music, 1989
Narazaki, Yōko, *Nihon no Kangengaku Sakuhin-hyō 1912–1992* [Orchestral Works
    by Japanese Composers, 1912–1992], Tōkyō: Japan Symphony Foundation,
    1994
Nihon no Sakkyoku 1959/Masterpieces of Contemporary Japanese Music 1959,
    Tōkyō: Ongaku no Tomo Sha, 1959

Nobutoki, Yūko, *A Checklist of Published Instrumental Music by Japanese Composers*, Kunitachi College of Music Library, 1990 (Bibliography and Index Series, no. 9)

Ogawa, Takashi, *Nihon no Kōkyōgakudan* [Japanese Symphony Orchestras], Tōkyō: Kawai-Gakufu, 1972

Reynolds, Roger, 'A Jostled Silence: Contemporary Japanese Musical Thought (Part One)' (introduction), *Perspectives of New Music* 30/1(1992), 22–35

Shibata, Minao, 'Music and Technology in Japan', in *Music and Technology*, Stockholm: UNESCO, 1971, 173–80

Takeda, Akimichi, 'Contemporary Music and Traditional Japanese Musical Instruments', in *International Conference on Japanese Studies: Report*, Tōkyō: Japan P.E.N. Club, 1974, 177–83

Tann, Hilary, 'Tradition and Renewal in the Music of Japan' (introduction), *Perspectives of New Music* 27/2 (Summer 1989), 45–7

Ueno, Akira, 'Zwischen den Ufern: Die Beziehung zwischen Tradition und zeitgenössischer Musik in Japan', *MusikTexte* 59 (June 1995), 44–8

6 Writings by Takemitsu (Japanese)

Takemitsu Tōru Chosakushū [Tōru Takemitsu: Collected Writings], Tōkyō: Shinchō Sha, 2000 (5 vols.)

Genganku no tame no Rekuiemu [Requiem for Strings – Programme Note], *Shinfonī* 2/28 (June 1957), 13

Hitotsu no Oto ni Sekai o Kiku [Hearing the World in One Sound], Tōkyō: Shōbun Sha, 1975

 (with Mario Ambrosius) *Kamera no mae no Monorogu – Haniya Yutaka, Inokuma Gen-ichirō, Takemitsu Tōru* [Monologues before the Camera – Yutaka Haniya, Gen-ichirō Inokuma, Tōru Takemitsu], Tōkyō: Shūei Sha, 2000

Ki no Kagami, Sōgen no Kagami [Mirror of Tree, Mirror of Field], Tōkyō: Shinchō Sha, 1975

Kojiki Kagyō, Kara Jurō Taidanshū [Collection of Conversations with Kagyō Kojiki and Jurō Kara], Tōkyō: Fuyuki Sha, 1979

Kotsugetsu – aruiwa 'a honey moon' [Bone Moon, or a Honeymoon], private publication, 1973

 (with Seiji Ozawa) *Ongaku* ('Music': Conversations with Seiji Ozawa), Tōkyō: Shinchō Sha, 1981

Ongaku no Niwa: Takemitsu Tōru Taidanshū [Music Garden: Collection of Conversations with Tōru Takemitsu], Tōkyō: Shinchō Sha, 1981

Ongaku no Techō [Music Notebook], Tōkyō: Seido Sha, 1981

Ongaku no Yohaku kara [From the Space Left in Music], Tōkyō: Shinchō Sha, 1980

Ongaku o Yobimasu Mono [Awakening of Music], Tōkyō: Shinchō Sha, 1985

 (with Kenzaburō Ōe) *Opera o Tsukuru* [Making an Opera], Tōkyō: Iwanami Shoten, 1984

Oto, Chinmoku to Hakariaeru hodo ni [Sound: Confronting the Silence], Tōkyō: Shinchō Sha, 1971

   (with Junzō Kawada) *Oto, Kotoba, Ningen* [Sound, Word, Humanity], Tōkyō: Iwanami Shoten, 1990

Sairento Gāden – Tai-in Hōkoku [Silent Garden – Report on Discharge from Hospital] and *Kyarotin no Saiten* [Carotin Festival], Tōkyō: Shinchō Sha, 1999

   (with Shigehiko Hasumi) *Shinema no Kairaku* [Pleasure of Cinema], Tōkyō: Libro Port, 1986

Subete no Inshu kara Nogareru tame ni [For Escaping from all Conventionalism: Conversations with John Cage, Keith Jarrett, R. Murray Schafer, Iannis Xenakis, Isang Yun, *et al.*], Tōkyō: Ongaku no Tomo Sha, 1987

Takemitsu Tōru ← *1930 …* ∞, private publication, 1964

Takemitsu Tōru Taidanshū – Sōzō no Shūhen [Collection of Conversations with Tōru Takemitsu – Circle of Creativity], Tōkyō: Geijutsugendai Sha, 1976

Tōi Yobigoe no Kanata e [Beyond the Far Calls], Tōkyō: Shinchō Sha, 1992

Toki no Entei [Time's Gardener], Tōkyō: Shinchō Sha, 1996

Yume no Inyo [Quotation of Dream], Tōkyō: Iwanami Shoten, 1984

Yume to Kazu [Dream and Number], Tōkyō: Libroport, 1987

'Watashi no Hōhō – Myūjikku Konkurēto ni tsuite' [My Method – Concerning *musique concrète*], *Bijutsu Hihyō* 1 (1956) 70–3

7 Writings by Takemitsu (translations)

(with Tania Cronin and Hilary Tann) 'Afterword', *Perspectives of New Music* 27/2 (Summer 1989), 206–14

Confronting Silence: Selected Writings, trans. and ed. Yoshiko Kakudo and Glenn Glasow, Berkeley, California: Fallen Leaf Press, 1995

'Contemporary Music in Japan', *Perspectives of New Music* 27/2 (Summer 1989), 198–204

'Kein dunkler Schatten', in Heister, Hanns-Werner, and Sparrer, Walter-Wolfgang (eds.), *Der Komponist Isang Yun*, Munich: Text und Kritik, 1987, 28

'Klang im Osten, Klang im Westen: Der Weg zu *November Steps*', *MusikTexte* 59 (June 1995), 53–9

'A Mirror and an Egg', *Soundings* 12 (1984–85), 3–6

'La Musique de John Cage', trans. Annie Meygret, *Revue d'esthétique* 13–15 (1987–88), 461–4

'Mirrors' (trans. Sumi Adachi with Roger Reynolds), *Perspectives of New Music* 30/1 (1992), 36–83

'My Perception of Time in Traditional Japanese Music', *Contemporary Music Review* 1 (1987) 9–13

'One Sound', *Contemporary Music Review* 8/2 (1994), 3–4

'Sound in the East, Sound in the West: the Way to *November Steps*', trans. Mimi Yiengpruksawan, *Ear* 5/8 (1990), 19–25

8 Writings about Takemitsu (Japanese)

(In the interests of brevity, only periodical articles directly cited in the text have been listed)

Akiyama, Kuniharu, articles on works by Takemitsu in *Saishin Meikyoku Kaisetsu Zenshū*, Tōkyō: Ongaku no Tomo Sha, 1980: vol. 7, pp. 458–72 (*Requiem for Strings, Arc* for piano and orchestra, *Asterism, A Flock Descends into the Pentagonal Garden*); vol. 10, pp. 404–10 (*November Steps*); vol. 3, pp. 454–6 (*The Dorian Horizon*)

Chōki, Seiji and Higuchi, Ryūichi (eds.), *Takemitsu Tōru: Oto no Kawa no Yukue* [Tōru Takemitsu – Traces of the Stream of Sound], Tōkyō: Heibonsha, 2000

Funayama, Takashi, *Takemitsu Tōru: Hibiki no Umi e* [Tōru Takemitsu: Towards the Sea of Sound], Tōkyō: Ongaku no Tomo Sha, 1998

Iwaki, Hiroyuki, *Sakkyokuka Takemitsu Tōru to Ningen Mayuzumi Toshirō* [The Composer Tōru Takemitsu and the Human Being Toshirō Mayuzumi], Okayama: Sakuyō Gakuen, 1999

Iwata, Ryūtaro: *Kafe Takemitsu: Watashi no Takemitsu Ongaku* [Café Takemitsu: My Takemitsu Music], Tōkyō: Kaimei Sha, 1992

Konuma, Jun-ichi, *Takemitsu Tōru – Oto, Kotoba, Imēji* [Tōru Takemitsu – Sound, Word, Image], Tōkyō: Seido Sha, 1999

Narazaki, Yōko, *Takemitsu Tōru to Miyoshi Akira no Sakkyoku-Yoshiki: Muchōsei to Ongun-Sakahō o Megutte* [The Compositional Styles of Tōru Takemitsu and Akira Miyoshi: their Use of Atonality and Tone-cluster Methods], Tōkyō: Ongaku no Tomo Sha, 1994

Takemitsu Tōru Sakuhin-hyō [Table of Works by Tōru Takemitsu], *Ongaku Geijutsu* 54/5 (May 1996), 60–73

Ono, Mitsuko, *Takemitsu Tōru no Ongaku to Mizu no An-yu* [Tōru Takemitsu's Music and the Metaphor of Water], M.A. Thesis, Kunitachi College of Music (1995)

'Takemitsu Tōru no Sōzō no Minamoto o Saguru: "Oto no Kawa" to *Marginalia* o Megutte' [The Source of Creation of Tōru Takemitsu: the 'Stream of Sound' and *Marginalia*], *Kunitachi College of Music Journal* 31 (1996), 57–67

'Takemitsu Tōru no Gagaku *Shūteiga Ichigu* e no Ikkōsatsu: Geijutsu ni okeru Fueki to Ryūkō' [Takemitsu's *In an Autumn Garden, Complete Version* for *Gagaku*: Constancy and Fashion in the Arts], in *Ongaku Kenkyū: Daigakuin Kenkyū Nenpō Dai 9-shū* [Music Research: Annual Report of Postgraduate School Research no. 9], Kunitachi College of Music, 1997, 80–98

Saitō, Shinji and Takemitsu, Maki (eds.), *Takemitsu Tōru no Sekai* [The World of Tōru Takemitsu], Tōkyō: Shūei Sha, 1997

Shiraishi, Miyuki, 'Umi kara, Futatabi Ame tonari: Takemitsu Sakuhin – Shuhō no Hensen o Todoru' [From the Sea comes Rain Once Again: Tracking the Changes of Technique in Takemitsu's Work], *Ongaku Geijutsu* 54/5 (May 1996), 48–52

Tachibana, Takashi, 'Takemitsu Tōru: Ongaku Sōzō e no Tabi' [Tōru Takemitsu:
the Journey towards Musical Creation], transcripts of thirty hours of
interviews with the composer, appearing in the magazine *Bungakukai*
between 1992 and 1997

Takeda, Akimichi, 'Manazashi no Ongaku: Saikin no Takemitsu-Sakuhin o
Meguru Shōyō' [Music of Observation: a Look at Recent Works of
Takemitsu], *Ongaku Geijutsu* 52/2 (Dec. 1994), 18–23

Tircuit, Heuwell, 'Takemitsu Tōru', *Ongaku Geijutsu* 21/1 (1963), 11–17

Tōyama, Kazuyuki, *Henkyō no Oto: Sutoravinsuki to Takemitsu Tōru* [Sounds
from the Frontier: Stravinsky and Tōru Takemitsu], Tōkyō: Ongaku no
Tomo Sha, 1996

9 Writings about Takemitsu (other than in Japanese)

Akiyama, Kuniharu, 'Cosmic Eye of Tōru Takemitsu', in *Takemitsu Tōru-ten: Me
to Mimi tame ni* [Tōru Takemitsu: For Eyes and Ears], catalogue of exhibition
held at Bunpodo Gallery, 19 November 1993–20 December 1993, Tōkyō:
Bunpodo Gallery, 1993, 6–7

Burt, Peter, 'The Music of Tōru Takemitsu: Influences, Confluences and Status',
Ph.D. diss., University of Durham (1998)

Feliciano, Francisco F., *Four Asian Contemporary Composers: the Influence of
Tradition in their Works*, Quezon City: New Day Publishers, 1983

Galliano, Luciana, 'Takemitsu Tōru: Il primo periodo creativo (1950–1970)',
Nuova rivista musicale italiana 33/4 (1999), 506–33

Gibson, James Robert, 'Tōru Takemitsu: a Survey of his Music with an Analysis of
Three Works', DMA thesis, Cornell University (1979)

Jin, Jeong Woo, 'Comparative Analysis of Takemitsu's Recent Works *Rain Tree* and
Rain Spell', Ph.D. diss., University of California at Los Angeles (1987)

Koozin, Timothy, 'Octatonicism in Recent Solo Piano Works of Tōru Takemitsu',
Perspectives of New Music 29/1 (1991), 124–40

   'The Solo Piano Works of Tōru Takemitsu: a Linear/Set-theoretical Analysis',
Ph.D. diss., University of Cincinnati (1988)

   'Spiritual-temporal Imagery in the Music of Olivier Messiaen and Tōru
Takemitsu', *Contemporary Music Review* 7 (1993) 185–202

   'Tōru Takemitsu and the Unity of Opposites', *College Music Symposium* 30/1
(Spring 1990), 34–44

Laade, Wolfgang, 'Tōru Takemitsus *November Steps,* Shakuhachi-Musik und Zen',
Indo-Asia 12/1 (Feb. 1970), 84–6

Lee, Chung-Haing, 'Japanese Elements in the Piano Works of Tōru Takemitsu',
DMA Thesis, University of North Texas (1991)

Miyamoto, Kenjiro, *Klang im Osten, Klang im Westen: Der Komponist Tōru
Takemitsu und die Rezeption europäischer Musik in Japan*, Saarbrücken: Pfau,
1996

Ogawa, Masafumi, 'Tōru Takemitsu's Compositional Techniques and his Identity as Japanese in Western Art Music: an Analysis of *Kaze no Uma* ("Wind Horse")', *Research Bulletin of the Faculty of Education, Oita University*, 13/1 (1991), 109–27

Ōoka, Makoto, 'Not as a Composer Who "Make People Listen" [*sic*]', in Kuniharu Akiyama, *Takemitsu Tōru-ten: Me to Mimi tame ni*, 11

Ohtake, Noriko, *Creative Sources for the Music of Tōru Takemitsu*, Aldershot: Scolar Press, 1993

Palmer, Anthony J., 'To Fuse or Not to Fuse: Directions of Two Japanese Composers, Miki and Takemitsu', in *Tradition and its Future in Music (Report of SIMS 1990, Ōsaka)*, Ōsaka: Mita Press, 1991, 421–5

Poirier, Alain, *Tōru Takemitsu*, Paris: TUM/Michel de Maule, 1996

Rands, Bernard, 'I sing only for myself . . .', *Musical Times* 128/1735 (Sept. 1987), 477–8

Reynolds, Roger, 'Japan', *Musical Quarterly* 53/4 (1967), 563–71
   'Rarely Sudden, Never Abrupt', *Musical Times* 128/1735 (Sept. 1987), 480–3
   'Roger Reynolds and Tōru Takemitsu: a Conversation', *Musical Quarterly* 80/1 (Spring 1996), 61–76

Sawabe, Yukiko, 'Alpträume und Träume: Der japanische Komponist Tōru Takemitsu', *MusikTexte* 59 (June 1995), 49–52

Smaldone, Edward, 'Japanese and Western Confluences in Large-Scale Pitch Organization of Tōru Takemitsu's *November Steps* and *Autumn*', *Perspectives of New Music* 27/2 (1989), 216–31

Tanikawa, Shuntarō, 'The White Wall of Everyday Life', in Kuniharu Akiyama, *Takemitsu Tōru-ten: Me to Mimi tame ni*, 13

Taniyama, Sawako, 'The Development of Tōru Takemitsu's Musical Philosophy', *Kōbe Joshi Tanki Daigaku Ronkō* 37 (Oct. 1991), 71–95

Toop, David, 'half japanese', *Wire* 176 (Oct. 1998), 26–30

Usami, Keiji, 'Adjacent to Sound', in Kuniharu Akiyama, *Takemitsu Tōru-ten: Me to Mimi tame ni*, 9

Wilson, Dana Richard, 'The Role of Texture in Selected Works of Tōru Takemitsu', Ph.D. diss., Eastman School of Music (1982)

Wu, Ting-Lien, 'An Analysis of Tōru Takemitsu's *Bryce* (1976), with an Emphasis on the Role of Articulation', Ph.D. diss., University of California at Los Angeles (1987)

Index

9 780521 026956